The Healing Art of Pet Parenthood

Nadine M. Ros...

The Healing Art of Pet Parenthood

Published by Wheatmark®
610 East Delano Street, Suite 104, Tucson, Arizona 85705 U.S.A.
www.wheatmark.com

ISBN: 978-1-60494-040-4
LCCN: 2008920592

Front cover photo: Jennea Bono, www.jennea.com

Buttons Rosin (her one white paw)
Chapter sketch of Buttons sleeping, by Nadine M. Rosin

rev201001

"The greatness of a nation can be judged
by the way its animals are treated."

—Mahatma Gandhi

To dear friend Anne
& her kitties

Wishing you VIBRANT health
and
precious moments.

Love —
Nadine &
Button

Lovingly dedicated...

to **Shannon Ward** who always saw the best in me and who continues to buoy me with her thoughtful love and the memory of her amazing mettle. Take care of my girl, Ms. Shannon.

Also

to **Dan Fogelberg** whose wondrous songs began weaving themselves throughout the tapestry of my life back in 1973, when my college roommate gave me a copy of her former high school sweetheart's recently released, debut album (before she married the architect).

You both left your bodies far too soon for us.
May your spirits soar—joyful and free.

With Deepest Appreciation...

To my Grandma Sonia. Because of you, I recognize love. Thank you for keeping me always enveloped in yours.

To Mitch Alperin. Thank you for catapulting me onto the spiritual part of my journey. My love for you is forever.

To my beloved teachers: Sri Eknath Easwaran, Rev. Deborah L. Johnson, Dr. Ernest Holmes, Laz Ross, Hugh Prather, Eckhart Tolle, Byron Katie, and **Abraham-Hicks** for helping me to know who I really am.

To Shana Ross for teaching me how to look at ordinary things in extraordinary ways.

To Janine d'Haven for inestimable kindness, insight, and wisdom.

To Dr. Gary A. Love, DC for years of selflessness and care that lives up to the name. Your karma bank is surely overfull.

To Dennis Graf, Cindy Hiller, and **Mi Lady Matilda Silverbell** for loving me through the worst of it... for providing safe passage.

To Scott and Tracy Ott for your unbridled generosity, continuous loyalty, and constant, "leg-up" support.

To Michael C. Flowers for your amazing thoughtfulness. It would take pages and pages to list all the ways, big and small, that you've been there for me.

To Ron and Chrystal Nielson. Thank you, my cherished friends, for dolphins and rainbows... which, you must admit, is about as New Age as it gets (grin).

To Tana Butler for your unflinching example of a life lived with poetry, passion, and juice.

To Brooke Monfort for coming to the rescue when no one else knew how.

To Pamela Hanson for your gentle heart, side-splitting laughter, and for always acknowledging the milestones.

To Betty Kovács and Kimberly Saavedra for fearless trailblazing, inconspicuous baton passing, and steadfast encouragement.

To Gayle Meadows for forging the path so eloquently.

To Darlene Buck for demonstrating the transformational power of the story.

To Wynne Rife: violin teacher extraordinaire. Thank you for your angelic presence in my life, for giving me back the music and its healing embrace.

To Judith Parker, DVM for the unwavering compassion, understanding, and respect that you brought to partnering with us on the final leg of our physical journey together.

To Bob Dinga and Diana Rose for giving me the missing link—even though it took me twelve years to realize it. Thank you, Sweet Ones, for the ultimate down-line.

To the California pet parent moms: Dolores Sudduth, Patty Fox, and **Patti O'Brien** for insisting the manuscript become a book—for such enthusiastic tail wagging!

To Jan Bonwell: hell on wheels with a table saw and my favorite mother of the bride. Thank you for your willingness to play full out and for eagerly carrying me forward.

To my computer guru, Steve Lee. Thank you for your calming presence… for so delightfully and willingly keeping me functional and connected.

To Stepheny Keith. Clearly, I thank you for all the terrific video production, editing and archiving. But most of all, I thank you for always having seen into the depths of me, for liking what you saw, and for reflecting it back with such clarity and kindness. It makes you stand out from the flock.

To Acacia Betancourt for your sensitive and imaginative perspective… for being the open channel through which such incredible well-being and freedom has flowed into my life.

To Liz The Knitting Angel Barlow for patterns, prayers, and perusal patience.

To Yvonne Divita: social media mentor, marketing rock star, and Carmie's mom. Thank you for showing me the way—even in the midst of your own grief.

To Colleen DiBiase, Maude Adjarian, Carolyn Niethammer, Ford Burkhart, and **Bob McMahon.** Thank you for being indispensable midwives of the text.

To Hallie Loewy for cheerleading, **Andrew Clark** for balancing, **Breland Atkinson** for pampering, **Peggy Morrison** for networking,

David Vore for hours of printing and smiling, and the crew at **Choate's Post Office** for never giving up hope.

To **Patrick Grimes** for flattering angles and affordable dentistry.

To the charming **Tony Hatch,** also **Linda Thompson, Richard Marx, Tom Springfield, Nathan Osher**/Wixen Music Publishing, Inc., to the affable **Robert H. Sommer:** publisher, and the fabulous **Erika Navarrete**/Alfred publishing company. Thank you all for being shining gems of heart and goodwill in the business world.

To the folks at **Wheatmark Publishing,** especially **Sam Henri, Grael Norton,** and **Lori Sellstrom,** who contributed greatly with their time, patience, and belief in the project as well as my ability to carry it through.

And of course, **to Rachel.**

Thank you for the most precious gift in the entire universe...

Preface

When my "adopted daughter," an eleven-year cancer survivor on all natural remedies, died in my arms the week before her nineteenth birthday, some people treated me as if I had just lost an easily replaceable houseplant. Why? Because her stalwart, humorous, and loving spirit, which inspired and impelled my own emotional healing, happened to reside in a canine body.

In my search for comfort and camaraderie throughout the grieving process, I found no pet-loss books that fully addressed the depth of my pain or the spiritual companionship and telepathic communication that my dog, Buttons and I shared. What I did find was a poll conducted by Purina concluding that forty-seven million people in the U.S. consider their pets to be their children or family members. It was reassuring to know I was not alone in my experience.

Buttons was much more than a beloved pet for two decades. She was the soul who helped me open and heal my heart, which for much of my adult life, and most of my childhood, had been bolted shut and shattered.

In writing this, one of my intentions is to help pet parents realize that we may be unconsciously contributing to the skyrocketing increase of cancer in our pets by unknowingly creating highly toxic environments in our homes. The more informed we are as consumers, the better our chances are of well-being becoming the bottom line, rather than lining the pockets of manufacturers.

I've also done my best to lovingly and truthfully embrace all aspects the unique grief of losing a four-legged family member entails, in the hopes that my story will provide comfort, camaraderie, and validation for other pet parents experiencing the devastating loss of a beloved animal. And hopefully in the telling, I am able to shine some light on the often closeted and belittled bond many people have with their animals so as to help remove the words, "It's just a dog/cat" from the lips of non pet parents everywhere.

Of course, as with any memoir, the writing process has led me to a place of clarity and compassion about my own patterns and blind spots as well. One of my favorite Oprah quotes is: "You have taken your pain and turned it into power. You have taken your pain and used it to empower someone else." My greatest hope is to accomplish that here.

This then, is a narrative about healing cancer naturally, holistic pet care, hope and hopelessness, and spiritual connection after death. It is the odyssey of two resilient beings as they travel a rocky road into vibrant health and joy. It is my story, but it is only one version of a story shared by at least forty-seven million other pet parents.

—Nadine M. Rosin/Tucson, AZ

PART I

Before the Storm

"There's a **New World** somewhere they call the **Promised Land**,
and I'll be there someday if you will hold my hand.
I still need you there beside me, no matter what I do,
for I know I'll never find another you.
There is always someone for each of us they say,
and you'll be my someone forever and a day.
I could search the whole world over, until my life is through,
but I know I'll never find another you.
It's a long, long journey, so stay by my side.
When I walk through the **storm** you'll be my guide, be my guide.
If they gave me a fortune my pleasure would be small, I could lose it all
tomorrow and never mind at all, but if I should lose your love,
dear, I don't know what I'd do, for I know
I'll never find another you."

—Tom Springfield

My cousin Rachel and I were relaxing in the courtyard of my Chicago apartment building, enjoying the first spring-like day of the year, when she suddenly turned to me and said, "You're going to be twenty-nine next month, you've got no kids, no husband, and no prospects. How 'bout I get you a dog for your birthday?"

It sounded like a great idea. Little did I know how dramatically that one simple suggestion was about to change me and my life, forever.

I'd recently ended my five-year long relationship with Ben—having finally done enough therapy and self-growth seminars to feel I deserved more than to go through life with a well-read, witty alcoholic. But behind the capable persona and smiling face I presented convincingly to others, inside I secretly harbored an ocean's worth of unrelenting terror. I couldn't possibly bring myself to risk another relationship with a man just yet, but a dog? Ah. I could definitely love a dog.

It was 1984. While Ronald Reagan was ordering U.S. Marines out of Beirut, the rest of us were singing along to, "Rock Me, Amadeus" on the radio. I was living alone in the cozy garden apartment of an old, well-kept brownstone on North Sheridan Road, two blocks from The Lake. (Chicagoans never refer to it as Lake Michigan, but rather, just The Lake—upper case.) I knew that even though I could exercise a dog at the beach eight or nine months out of the year, it was only fair that it be a smaller breed to fit the apartment size.

In those days I was working full time as a waitress, or as the management titled us, server, at the elegant, Lawry's The Prime Rib Restaurant. Lawry's is the same company that makes the seasoned salt, salad dressings, and marinades, and yes, I've seen Michael Jordan dining there. Because my hours were long and varied, the plan was to find a Cockapoo: a Cocker Spaniel and Poodle crossbreed. Their reputation as a small to medium, even-tempered dog appealed to me. I had had one friend who swore his Cockapoo always mirrored his moods and schedule by being either full of energy or mellow at precisely the same time he was.

I'd made one past attempt at bringing home a different breed from the local shelter, but it had ended disastrously with my shamefully returning the dog after a few days. In addition to pooping on my bed and destroying a pair of expensive leather boots, the full-grown, supposedly housebroken Basset Hound and I seemed unable to establish any kind of an emotional connection. So Rachel and I decided to forgo political correctness and instead, headed down to New Lenox, Illinois, to the only Cockapoo breeder listed in the Yellow Pages: Waggin' Tails.

We arrived after an hour's drive through the city and out into the country. Most of the way there I'd been stressing about the choice I was about to have to make. Deep down I worried how I'd really know which dog would be a good match for me. I was glad my cousin would be there to help; the drive was too far to make another mistake.

We parked in the gravel lot adjacent to the sprawling, white ranch house. A cheerful woman named Judy, who looked to be about my age, walked across the well-kept yard to greet us. She then led us towards a spacious, two-car garage used only for the puppies. I was impressed as she opened the door and we stepped into the temperature controlled, immaculately clean room. Next to us along the wall to our immediate right was one long wire cage. Further in, at the center of the space, were many square, wire cages filled with rambunctious, furry balls of squeaky pups. As Judy lifted the top of the long cage next to us, she explained that the two, eight-week-old, almost all black puppies inside were brother and sister. They were the only pups of the litter of two and they were not pure Cockapoos. Instead of being round and cute in their puppiness, they were more pointy and slightly feral looking. Judy went on to tell us that somehow a Terrier had gotten onto her property and that this pair was the unplanned, though still adorable result.

The brother sat at one end of the cage directly in front of where we stood. At the opposite end, about four feet away, the sister lay alert and all curled up. As I reached in to pet the male pup, I was startled, when the female, who had been watching me closely, suddenly shot up and made three amazingly athletic leaps to bridge the gap between us. She then immediately and determinedly burrowed her entire front end up the sleeve of my winter parka.

Like the first time hearing some beautiful song with lyrics that seem perfectly written and personal, an unexpected surge of familiarity and tenderness raced through my body. It threatened to pierce the numbness at my core and was at the same time, both alarming and seductive. Judy looked just as surprised as I felt. She told us that this was highly unusual behavior for that female who'd only exhibited extremely shy and submissive behavior since the day she'd been born. I smiled, flattered to think that the cute little puppy was singling me out. And so at her insistence, I petted her instead of her brother, until Rachel suggested that we spend some time looking at the other dogs—the pure Cockapoos.

As we walked the few feet over to the cages in the center of the room, the little black female began to cry and whine quite loudly. Again, her behavior shocked and amused Judy who said that that was the first sound she'd ever heard from the pup. As I sat on the concrete floor playing with the Cockapoo puppies while the serenade continued, I became aware of the subtle scent of magic in the air. Every time I glanced up from whichever pup I was playing with, the black one in the cage was staring at me intensely as she cried.

We'd been there less than ten minutes when I surrendered to the inevitable, knowing there was no mistake and that the decision had already been made. I had spent my entire life second-guessing and doubting myself, but in that moment, I was completely sure. I was the one who had been chosen. The black, female, Cockapoo Terrier mix was my dog, or more accurately, I was her person. That's all there was to it. Period. Settled.

In retrospect, I wish I had taken her brother too, thus preventing their separation. But at that point, I wasn't operating from the place of confidence, unconditional love, and wisdom that she would spend the next nineteen years teaching me about. So after some paperwork, money exchange, and feeding instructions, Rachel and I walked back to the car with my new treasure and twenty-ninth birthday gift quietly and secure- ly snuggled up with a small blanket in an open box.

Our conclusion was that she looked like a little black rat. A cute rat, mind you, but a rat, nonetheless. For the first ten miles or so that's what my cousin and I called her, Rat-Dog. For the next twenty miles, we toyed with different names: two I remember were Mojo and Gandhi (she had a small white spot resembling a *bindhi* on her forehead), but none of them felt just right.

We then decided to stop at a park we'd passed on the way down and let my new nameless canine stretch her little legs and have some water. We watched her scramble clumsily along the ground. Her left front paw, the only white one, was instantly dubbed her Michael Jackson paw. Her ears, all black, were expressive and pointy. We could already tell that a huge amount of her personality resided in her tail, which was bushy like a fox's and curled like a question mark over her backside when she was happy or excited. Her legs seemed too long and spindly for her tiny body and not strong enough to support her yet. If I hadn't seen her make those leaps across the length of the cage an hour before, I never would have believed it possible. In that one surprising moment it had felt like some force, some power, some freckle of fate had taken over and made itself known. This little puppy, who would later end up saving my life in more ways than one, had tunneled herself up my sleeve while at the same time burrowing her way completely into the depths of my tortured soul and lonely heart. Maybe she looked like a little black rat... but, by God, she was <u>my</u> little black rat!

She slept most of the rest of the way home. When we walked into the apartment and put the box down near the radiator, she woke up so I put a wind-up alarm clock in the box with her, hoping the sound would comfort her. She just looked at me like I was nuts, a look I would see again more times than I could count over the next two decades.

I was impatient to name her, but still, nothing we came up with seemed to fit. Rachel suggested I just wait and see how the pup acted over the next few days, and in a sense, let her earn her name. And so I made sure my nameless puppy was settled in her box before leaving to give my cousin a ride home.

North Sheridan Road sported a fair to heavy amount of traffic most all the time and did that day as we headed towards my parked car. Rachel, who was walking a few feet in front of me as we crossed the busy street, suddenly pointed to the sky and shouted, "Buttons!"

I thought for a moment. "Yes!" I yelled back, "That's it! Buttons! It's perfect! She's as cute as a button! My little love button!"

By this time we were at my car where Rachel stopped, turned and peered at me, her face scrunched up with a look of total confusion. "What the hell are you talking about?"

"The name you just came up with... Buttons, I love it."

She then looked at me with the same "you are nuts" expression I had just seen a few moments earlier on the pup's face. "Mountains," she said as she turned and pointed once again to the sky, "I said those clouds look like mountains."

For the second time that day it was as if I'd received a perceivable nudge from the universe. I felt once again as if I never really had a choice, or that the choice had already been made and was simply being revealed to me. It certainly wasn't the most clever or creative name for a dog, but I somehow knew that my job was to just go along with things as they were presented, which is exactly what I did. My girl's name was Buttons, and that's all there was to it. Period. Settled.

Like any well-loved canine, during the next few years Buttons earned many other names as well. Kooker-nut and Poopy Loop were born of the times I'd come home to find her sprawled on the couch, lying on her back, legs asunder, exhausted after another hard day of gathering and balling up every throw rug and pillow in the apartment. I dubbed her Shtoonkhead in response to her eccentric and un-doglike ways: refusing to be petted for any length of time, and avoiding interaction with most people past the initial curious sniff.

Buttons also became quite a well-traveled pooch, weathering several cross-country road trips in the U.S. and Mexico plus one first-and-last cargo flight on a major airline. All this landed her the title of Super Doop-er Trouper Pooper (it's my understanding that a canine must sniff and pee—the doggy mantra—in a minimum of ten states before qualifying for that one). Then there were the "holiday" names used only during the specific months they represented: Poopy Valentine, Birthday Butts, Fun-ny Bunny, Pumpkin Face, Turkey Girl, and Sweet Angel. There were also the Buttons derivatives: Butts, Butski, Butonés (with alternating French or Italian accents), Butskerooski and ButtonsLove (all one word—can be either noun or verb).

In the end there were over two-dozen names I was able to list hav-ing used consistently, yet it was probably the look in my eye that she answered to the most. She spent the majority of my otherwise childless childbearing years with me. As those years passed, she came to know me as her adoring, devoted Mom who ended up loving her more completely than I had ever loved anyone. And I grew to know her too: not just as a cute dog or family pet, and not as an animal I anthropomorphized, but as the multi-feeling, joyful soul she was with her own particular wants and needs, moods and quirks and distinct ways of communicating.

For nearly two decades she was the delight of my life, partner-in-crime, adopted daughter, teacher, and dearest friend. She was the reason why I never gave up, the life preserver I clung to when the inner tides of fear, isolation, and confusion, and the outer circumstances that those states of being attracted threatened to drown me for good. The mind knows the difference between human and animal. The heart knows no such difference and I loved her with all of mine.

Buttons grew lean and strong and resembled a small black coyote. Her fur was so soft it almost felt like touching nothing. Full grown, her back stood sixteen inches off the ground, her head and neck adding an additional five inches of height, though most of that height was due to her long, thin legs. The rest of her looked like a fox especially her bushy, black tail and those ever-expressive ears that pointed straight up nearly all the time.

As the months passed, her intricate personality continued revealing itself. She was extremely independent, never wanting to be the center of attention while still maintaining awareness and interest in all her surroundings. Indoors her demeanor was similar to that of a feline or perhaps a devout Buddhist monk. She seemed a very old soul gracing me with her evolved energy and wisdom while at the same time really enjoying being in a dog's body. She was so autonomous she spent most of her time while in the apartment either in the corner watching or under the couch (meditating?).

Her posture wasn't at all aggressive, but vacillated instead between confident and timid. She was never yappy or annoying, hyper or lethargic, never a lapdog, a licker or a jumper, though she'd come close and let me pet her for a moment after an especially tasty treat or fun outing. In that way, her hesitant and wary behavior more closely resembled that of a wolf than of a domesticated canine: I had to earn every bit of her love, trust, and attention. Truthfully, I had much more respect for her because of that than I would have had she automatically showered me with canine affection. Ours was a working relationship—not just a given.

She had her routines. When it was time to go outside, she'd come running through the rooms so fast it was comical. More than once, other people witnessing that bounding, racehorse-like mad dash were compelled to start humming the theme to the Lone Ranger. Then, right before reaching the door, she'd wipe-out because she couldn't stop herself soon enough. Even a piece of carpeting there wasn't adequate to ensure her smooth braking. After a flurry of indistinguishable paws, legs, and tail, she'd right herself to a standing position on all fours just before springing onto her back legs and hopping with impatience until I opened her way to freedom. She did it every time. Every time it made me laugh. She did the same exact thing when she heard her food bowl being filled.

Her exuberance for life was contagious. Her somewhat odd behavior was totally endearing. I noticed that some of the burning sadness, which I had carried with me all of my life, was beginning to fade. I could barely look at her without smiling.

Butski loved sleeping with me on the waterbed and would curl up behind my knees every evening—one of her rare, affectionate behaviors. But she was never a wimp about it. In fact, there was one week when I had picked up several extra shifts at work and was only home to feed her, walk her, shower and sleep. She didn't like that at all. How did I know? Well, she put up with the schedule for seven days. On the seventh night I came home, exhausted after another double shift, walked her, fed her and then quickly showered and got ready for bed. I couldn't wait to get off my feet and crawl in; the sheets were calling my name. I threw back the comforter and as I poured myself into bed, I startled, recoiling from the wetness as I realized the waterbed had sprung a leak. Moaning and grumbling, I stripped off all the bedding and then went to dig around in the kitchen drawer and find the patch kit. I also brought back some towels, wiped the mattress dry and in order to find the precise location of the leak, began gently applying pressure to see where the water would reappear. Usually that part takes a few moments. But not that night.

For ten minutes I kept pressing and feeling and pressing some more and still no sign of water or a pinhole. Then, through the haze of my fatigue, the truth began to dawn on me and one close whiff of the bedding confirmed it. I turned and looked at Buttons who stood a few feet away staring at me. I didn't say anything, but just kept looking at her. For the first time I can remember, she didn't look away, but held my gaze. She was "pissed off" at me and she let me know in no uncertain terms, no game-playing, just plain, straightforward communication.

That event would be the first of many, which would go on to form the foundation of our life-altering connection. I had no idea how life-saving our rapport would become for both of us. At that point, I only knew to never again work two doubles in a row, and our bond only continued to deepen.

Our first vacation together was also the first time Buttons rescued me from a physically threatening situation. The same trip included the only cargo flight Buttons ever took. It was 1987. Buttons was three years old and we were still living in Chicago, but my cousin, Rachel and her husband had moved to Tucson the year before.

In preparation for our Tucson visit, I began an extensive telephone investigation to find out every detail about flying there with Buttons in the cabin with me. The thought of her in cargo was unacceptable as far as I was concerned. Many calls and long stretches of being on hold later, I was told that one particular airline would indeed let us fly together in-cabin as long as she was sedated and in a specifically sized carrier designed to fit on the floor by my feet. I wrote down the dimensions and after double-checking all the information with a supervisor, made arrangements with the vet for sedatives, purchased both Buttons' and my nonrefundable tickets, and found and bought the carrier.

It was basically a heavy plastic box. Its cage-like metal top had a carrying handle and small trap-door-like piece in the center that slid open or closed. Buttons could fit sitting comfortably inside, especially if she was drowsy from doggy-downers. If she wanted to stick her head out and look around, all I had to do was slide open the little trap door. I measured the entire thing just to make absolutely sure I had the FAA required, legally correct size. It was perfect.

Now because I know that communication between humans can often be a messy thing, a few days later I called the airline once again, asked for a different supervisor and confirmed the requirements for a third time. I was told that, yes indeed, as long as the dog was sedated and the carrier met those particular dimensions, we were set to go.

The day of departure, I waited until an hour before leaving for the airport to give Buttons the sedative. I wasn't crazy about introducing a drug into her system. Although I had self-medicated my way through much of my teenage years with recreational drugs, for most of my adult life I've been a non-medicated, alternative, natural health care advocate. I wanted to keep her system pure.

We got to O'Hare, Buttons' eyes rolling a bit in circles, mine full of excitement and anticipation. At the counter, I handed our tickets to the agent waiting to help us. As she shuffled through the paperwork, she calmly glanced down at Buttons in the carrier on the floor next to me and said, "Oh, your dog can't go in the cabin with you, it will have to fly in cargo."

Just as calmly, I ignored her use of the "it" pronoun, and stated, "Oh, no, I spoke with several of your supervisors and was assured that as long as I had the FAA specified carrier, which I do, there would be no problem."

"Well," she replied, "That is the right carrier, but the requirements state that your dog must be able to stand up and turn around in it and I can see that your dog only fits in it sitting down."

I couldn't believe my ears. What about all my research? I had a nonrefundable ticket. What in the world was this girl trying to tell me? Buttons' legs were too long? How dare she refute all my responsibly gathered information! I asked to speak with her supervisor and waited, not bothering to take another breath until he appeared.

By then I'm sure I was the one who looked like they needed sedation. He gently explained that obviously no one I had talked to in any of my phone calls to confirm the facts I had been given had remembered to give me <u>this</u> fact.

"I'm sorry, Ms. Rosin. You can either forfeit your tickets or purchase a larger carrier so your dog can fly in the cargo compartment. Would you like to see one of the larger carriers?"

Absolutely furious, I glanced down at Butts and her woozy, innocent face. Feeling helpless, I agreed to inspect a larger carrier which they hurriedly brought out from the back. It was new and clean, but there was no time to spruce it up with padding or anything. I asked about temperature control in cargo. The supervisor assured me that it was comfortable enough temperature-wise that anyone could fly in it. I asked if I could purchase the extra, extra large carrier and fly in it with Buttons, even offering to do it for my original ticket price. I really wasn't kidding—I've never been a big fan of peanuts, even the ones drenched in sugar and salt, and I really would have been much happier sitting in a big box for a few hours next to my sweet pooch, than squished between two strangers with their unfamiliar ways and smells. But the FAA says no humans in cargo.

As my hands and voice shook with anger, I asked what would happen to the carrier at our destination. I was assured repeatedly that a skycap would be waiting with Buttons at a special counter right by the baggage claim in the Tucson airport. The supervisor insisted that I would just have to show I.D. and claim check to be given the carrier. This was traumatic. I had no idea how un-traumatic it was compared to events that awaited us just a few years down the road.

Opening my suitcase, I pulled out a sweatshirt to cover the bottom of the cargo carrier. I checked my luggage and the smaller FAA regulation in-cabin carrier and paid for the new carrier. Buttons, who was now on her leash, was half-asleep at my feet. I scooped her up in my arms and went to sit on the floor next to the new carrier at the side of the ticket counter.

Holding her was a treat. The ever-independent Buttons Dog was not one for cuddling or lap sitting. Her life seemed to be too full of anticipation and fun to waste time with that stuff. After all, she might miss something really exciting.

Gently, I stroked her head while softly singing a version of a song my grandma used to sing to me, *"You are my Buttons, my baby, Buttons. You make me happy all of the day. You'll always know just how much I love you. So please don't take my Buttons away."*

Ignoring the rapid heartbeat in my chest and the burning acid in my stomach, I focused instead on comforting my girl who hadn't noticed much of anything since the sedative had kicked in. Then looking up I saw a nun about to walk past us on her way to the ladies room and reaching out I tugged the hem of her skirt. With the conviction of the most fervid believer, I asked her to please bless my girl who would have to ride in the cargo compartment of the plane. She was gracious enough to say a prayer over the carrier. I'm not Catholic, but I felt a bit calmer afterwards. Any port in a storm, I guessed.

The skycap showed up and I shoved a twenty-dollar bill at him. Initially, he refused it saying it was his job to transport the animals to the planes. Briefly I shared the story of how unexpected a situation this was, and insisted he take the money while pleading with him to make sure she didn't get knocked around or handled roughly. He finally took the bill I'd been waving in front of him and gave me a reassuring look as I helplessly surrendered my adopted daughter to his care.

I love to fly. But not that flight. On top of everything else, there was a lot of turbulence. I had brought some knitting and every time we hit more turbulence, I'd drop another stitch and order another alcoholic beverage. Finally it got so rough, I couldn't stand it. I grabbed my purse, pulled out a photo of Buttons and called the flight attendant over. "Excuse me, would you happen to know if the pilot has any children?"

"Yes, he does, three."

"Great. Would you be willing to deliver a message to him for me?"

As she nodded yes, I shoved the photo into her hand. "This is my only child. Please tell him she is in the cargo compartment of this plane and to please try and take it a little easier with the bouncing around."

She smiled broadly, turned and headed for the cockpit. A few minutes later she returned with the pilot's assurance that he'd do his best to accommodate us and that he thought Buttons was very cute. She handed me back my photo.

I was miserable. But I was used to that—I'd had a long history of being miserable. This wasn't about my discomfort. This was about the possibility of Buttons' discomfort. This wasn't about taking care of my needs, it was about taking care of hers, and that's what made all the difference when it came to my taking action. I'd been forced to part with my baby, and now I had no idea how she was or what was happening to her. And then, a moment later, I noticed the plane climbing to a slightly higher elevation and calmer sky. Rather than worrying about what the crew might think of me, I had let my concern for Buttons motivate my actions and lead the way. In that moment, she had taught me that love was more powerful than worry—powerful enough to change even the cruising altitude of a 747. The remainder of the flight was turbulent-free, both in my mind and in the air.

As soon as the plane came to a stop (okay, a bit before it stopped completely) I was up and heading down the aisle, walking as fast as possible as I passed through the doorway into the airport. My cousin and I spotted each other immediately.

"Where's Buttons?" was the first and last thing out of her mouth before I grabbed her hand and burst into a full run. I may have given her a slight whiplash though I'm hoping she's forgotten that part by now.

"Come on! They made her ride in cargo!" was my only greeting.

After weeks of hearing me boast about my patient and thorough investigative/research skills in finding a way to fly Buttons in-cabin, this was the last thing Rachel expected. We were the first ones from my flight to reach the deserted baggage area. Did we find the promised skycap vigilantly guarding my precious cargo? Heck, no.

What we <u>did</u> see was the moving conveyor belt empty of everything save one recently purchased dog carrier going round and round, no one in sight, with Buttons' heart-wrenching cries heard over the Muzak. I ran to the carrier, yanked it onto the floor and swung open the door to find Buttons cowering in the far corner. Reaching in, I snapped her collar around her neck and led her outside to find a patch of earth as quickly as possible. Together in the warm, dry night air, I watched as the look in her eyes mellowed and relaxed. While Buttons happily peed her first time in the desert, I stood, finally able to breathe a sigh of relief over the whole ordeal.

So there we were, Ms. Buttons and her mom: two Chicago girls on vacation in Arizona. This was one of Buttons' first times free from the confines of the city. Of course, at home I made sure she spent as much time as possible at the beach, the park, and on the grass while I was working in the garden behind our apartment building, but all this wide-open, undeveloped land? This was the big leagues, baby!

Our first full day there, my cousin took us hiking at Catalina State Park—hundreds of acres of wild desert located just north of Tucson at the base of the Santa Catalina Mountains. Just being in the parking lot was like being in another world, it was so natural and rugged. Brown boulders loomed and spiky cactus threatened under a glaringly bright and blazing sun. Rachel assured me that we would be taking the easy three-mile loop hike for amateurs. So, loaded up with lunch, water, and doggy bowl, we headed away from the car and civilization.

A few hundred yards later, we came upon a flowing wash. I knew that during monsoon season, July through August, the washes could turn from empty, dried up wasteland-looking pathways to raging rivers in minutes. It was July, and there had been enough rain during the last week to keep the wash semi-full and flowing in places. The trail across it consisted of smooth rocks turned stepping-stones if one was relatively balanced and somewhat brave. I carefully mounted the first stone and looked down to check the depth of the clear running water. It seemed shallow enough for Buttons to navigate. I turned around and tugged gently on her leash, telling her to come—that it was okay. She looked at me with nervous apprehension, her ears pointed straight up and trembling slightly. I tried again, "Come on, Poop, you can do it—and the cold water will feel good!"

In a flash, Buttons left her city upbringing in the dust and me up to my ankles in water. I had slipped from the rock when she took off across the wash, dragging behind her the leash she had pulled right out of my grip. As I stood moaning in my soaked shoes and socks, Buttons stood at the opposite bank watching us and, I swear, grinning. She certainly looked invigorated, perhaps as much from seeing me standing there in the water than from the water itself.

It was apparent to me then that Buttons' had spent only a moment indulging her fear and trepidation before totally surrendering to her instinct and joy. Clearly, that letting go led her to a more independent, powerful, and happy place. And yet I'd have to witness her surrender many more times before I'd be brave enough to follow her example and live my own life with such abandon and trust. Instead, I was always careful and busy trying to protect myself from the danger I knew was ready to strike. Unbeknownst to me, in just a few hours it would be Buttons' protection I'd need.

Our hike continued, and we fell into a comfortable rhythm. My cousin and I chatted while Buttons scurried up ahead, then either stopped to sniff and pee, or came running back towards us as if wondering why we were so slow. Soon we noticed that the long, bushy hair of Buttons' tail had begun to collect various leaves and twigs from her trail explorations. She either dragged them around or curled them up over her back depending on her tail's position. From then on, that underbrush-dragging phenomenon became my visual signal as to how much fun she was having. I admit, there was never any scientific testing, but it certainly seemed to me that the amount of joy she exuded was in direct proportion to the amount of flora her tail had accumulated per outing. And all the while, her nose was excitedly exploring every detail on the ground, which was after all, the canine version of the *New York Times*.

I was proud of my little trouper. This was a far cry from her comfy window seat at home, which she'd climb onto from the back of the couch and sit for hours, looking like a canine monarch as she granted passage to all who passed by along the sidewalk. This was also our first time breaking the leash law anywhere in the U.S. Park Service—it seemed more of a crime for me to restrict her joy. I was always willing to risk the rest. She'd never so much as growled at anyone ever.

Other hikers we met along the trail delighted in watching Buttons enjoying herself so much and usually they'd approach grinning, asking what kind of dog she was. It was then that I came up with the answer that became my standard reply to that question anywhere in Arizona,

"Why, she's not a dog... she's a rare Sonoran Black Fox!" People always got a kick out of that one.

I was also quite proud of her considerate and efficient ways. Perhaps this had something to do with her partly French heritage, but Ms. Buttons had impeccable manners. She never jumped on people, never sniffed them, other than the occasional foot or outstretched hand, and she always peed and pooped off to the side of any trail, never on the trail itself.

We came to a sign that read "Loop Trail—left, Romero Trail—right" and decided to leave the Loop behind for a bit and find a more secluded spot for lunch. Ten minutes later, we were climbing down the side of a rugged, secluded gorge where we wandered around until we found the perfect spot to spread out our picnic lunch on some big rocks in the prized shade of a small mesquite tree grove.

We'd just finished eating when we heard the first, deafeningly loud rumble. Looking up we saw that the sky had started to blacken from a menacing bank of clouds rolling into the canyon. We were too deep in the gorge to have noticed it until it was upon us. Throwing everything into our backpacks, we started back up the slope. We knew that being in the desert with no equipment, protection, or supplies and being caught in the middle of a monsoon was potentially dangerous as the storms and lightening could be exceptionally violent. We also knew we needed to get out of that gorge before it started to fill with water. It was then we realized we'd somehow lost the trail. No matter which way we turned, we ended up in denser desert. Both of us were wearing shorts and soon our legs were scratched and bleeding. Buttons kept walking close to our feet as we tried every which way to rediscover the trail, to no avail. By then, the thunder was almost constant and the lightning strikes far too close for comfort. Finally, in our growing desperation, my cousin came up with a wonderfully logical idea, though I wasn't convinced initially. "Maybe we should just let Buttons lead and follow her?"

I thought for a moment before responding. "She's only been out of the city once in her life and has never been in the desert before, do you really think we should?"

"Absolutely. We certainly have no idea where the trail is at this point... she's a dog. She can do it."

Far from confident that she could improve our plight, I looked down at Butts.

"Okay, Buttons... we'll follow you. We need to get back to the car. Go find the trail, Poop!"

Without hesitation Buttons ran off in a direction that Rachel and I were convinced was wrong, but, committed to our plan, we followed her anyway as she zigzagged further up the steep slope. With the rain beating down on us, Buttons suddenly stopped, and there we were, back on the trail. We let out a cheer and Butts took off again. We didn't stop until we reached the car twenty minutes later, drenched, tired, relieved, and me, in awe of my canine companion. My name wasn't Timmy and I hadn't fallen down a mine shaft, but I suddenly felt safe and trusting in a way I never had before. Was it possible? Could I actually let myself rely on this funny, furry being I had brought into my home and was building my life with? And Buttons not only seemed more confident in herself, she actually looked bigger to me. Or perhaps I was just beginning to assimilate some of Buttons' wisdom by seeing things more from a dog's perspective: beyond all outward appearance?

Like it or not, this relationship was leading me into myself in ways I dared not go before, even with the best reputed, most expensive Michigan Avenue therapists Chicago had to offer. Understanding my past with them was all well and good, but the damage I'd suffered had been to my heart, emotions, and sense of self, not to my mind or intellect. Relating to Buttons required more feeling than thinking, and I had the vague awareness that she was tutoring me in that otherwise foreign language. Our lessons continued for a while longer before I was presented with my first big test.

Buttons' new found strength as the seventeen-pound wild creature she was born to be surprised me once again on that trip. The following weekend we joined my cousin, her husband, Richard, and another couple on a two-day camping trip in the Chiricahua National Monument near the Arizona-New Mexico border.

We drove up the forested side of the lush mountain and stopped near the top at the campground before we headed into a more remote area. We all got out to stretch our legs and as I stood in the quiet, breathing in the richly scented loam and pine-laden air, I heard Richard chuckle. I walked over and saw him watching a small hole in the ground near his feet. Suddenly a chipmunk-looking critter, sometimes informally referred to as a desert rat, poked his head out, took a quick look around and then, just as quickly, disappeared back underground. Richard called out to Buttons who was happily sniffing and peeing about ten feet to our left. "Oh, don't," I pleaded, "She'll be terrified!"

I knew my dog. She was afraid of the oddest things. She would run to the opposite side of the room whenever I would take my guitar out of the case (I don't think it was how I played that scared her since she did stay within earshot). I thought of how we used to play a little game together while sitting on the bed eating popcorn. I'd toss a kernel up in the air and she'd move under it and catch it in her mouth and eat it. How cute is that? We had great fun doing this until the one time a kernel landed on her snout instead of in her mouth. She jumped off the bed as if she'd been shot by a

BB gun. From that day forward she was terrified of popcorn. I mean, if she even heard it popping in the kitchen, she'd run and hide. She refused to ever play that game again or eat popcorn in any manner at all.

She was always somewhat skittish and wary of people and definitely of other animals, but Richard ignored my pleas and called her over anyway.

"Look, I know her. She's just going to freak out and try to hide behind me," I warned him.

"We'll see," said Richard.

Buttons pranced over and stood between my feet as she began tentatively sniffing the hole. In the very next moment, the desert rat popped his head out and sent Buttons lurching backwards. "See?!" I shouted, as I bent to quell her fear.

But before I knew it, Buttons had regained her balance and pounced on that desert rat like a true hunter. In the next instant, she was standing there holding the desert rat in her teeth by its scruff and shaking her head back and forth for all she was worth. I was totally shocked! Richard laughed. And then I got scared. What if it somehow bit her? I mean, it had the word rat in its name! "BUTTONS, NO! Drop it NOW!" She let it go, and it scurried right back into its hole. It seemed scared, but uninjured. Buttons on the other hand, pranced away with her head held quite a bit higher than normal. Secretly, I was proud of my baby girl. I made a note to myself, however, to never again put limitations on her behavior or capabilities. Even though, I still had a lot to learn, and it hadn't yet dawned on me to also apply that valuable guideline to my own life.

Our flight back to Chicago from Arizona was much smoother than our flight out, and this time without surprises. My cousin and I had spent several days "remodeling" the cargo dog-carrier for the trip home. By the time we were finished, it was complete with a thick layer of foam padding covered by lusciously soft material on the inside. The outside was now plastered with homemade, vibrantly colored "Beloved Live Animal, Please Handle With Extreme Care" stickers. There was no turbulence, dropped stitches or alcoholic beverages on this leg of the journey, and an un-tranquilized Buttons seemed no worse for wear upon our return home.

Like the calm before the storm, our days and nights were full of fun and love, antics and routine. After our first few years together, people would comment that we resembled one another, though unfortunately, my legs were never as skinny as hers. I could always tell how she was feeling by watching her tail. The more tightly wrapped a question mark it was over her back, the more excited and exuberant she felt. Fully unfurled and straight up was a sure sign of bliss, often seen while eating. Pointed towards the floor was always a harbinger of bad news—alerting me to something along the lines of the occasional garbage can pillage. We were communicating well.

There were also her undeniably, straightforward expressions of emotion and opinion. She always caught on to people and situations so much faster than I did. Had I been any smarter, I would have started paying closer attention to her on all matters, especially those involving the heart and specifically, mine. One obvious example of this was the time I started dating a neighbor from the apartment upstairs. Now most people know that just those circumstances alone portend certain disaster. And like myself, most people choose to ignore that knowledge when the attraction is strong enough.

It was 1986, and in hindsight, the fact that it was the same year as the nuclear explosion at Chernobyl and the Challenger space shuttle disaster makes sense in an odd, cosmic-energy sort of way.

He was smart, funny, charming, silly, liked dogs and was a very talented performer, in this case, a magician. Things went well for a while, and we both enjoyed the convenience of living just a flight of stairs away from each other.

One day the neighbor/magician announced that he had finally landed a job performing on a cruise ship, was leaving in one week and would be gone for several months. I knew this was something he had been working towards since before we'd met. We had a dramatically wonderful farewell. I vowed to write often, he vowed to be so busy he'd have little time to write at all. Over the next few months, I did write and he did send a few post-cards. He said he was enjoying himself, but that the cramped living conditions and overall ship life were getting to him, and he was looking forward to coming home. I mistakenly translated that to mean he was looking forward to coming home to me. I also missed the fact that "enjoying himself" meant that he had become seriously involved with a woman he'd met on the ship, and that she was planning to move to Chicago to be with him.

So the day he returned to our apartment building, the front windows bedecked in my "welcome home" signs, I sat waiting anxiously in a state of ignorant bliss. The phone rang. He was back and invited me upstairs. Buttons and I were there in a flash. He answered the door, and gave me a bear of a hug, then led me down the hall, through the dining room and into the kitchen.

We stood there telling each other how good the other looked. Every question I asked about the ship and his travels and the people was pretty much dismissed or avoided as he insisted on knowing everything that had happened on the home front while he'd been gone. Something felt very odd to me. I had anticipated a possible awkward reentry stage, but this felt different, as though a very definite, solid distance had developed between us. I kept asking him if everything was okay. He kept insisting it was while his eyes looked everywhere but into mine. Things were starting to feel extremely uncomfortable, and then he darted his gaze towards the dining room and suddenly shouted, "Oh no!"

I swung around to see Buttons, her head turned sideways so she was staring directly at us as she stood poised in the middle of his expensive, imported, hand-woven Persian rug—taking a dump. It had been years since she'd relieved herself anywhere inside and only an hour or so since she'd been out. But I guess my girl just figured I needed a little clarity and that maybe I needed it spelled out for me when I was being fed a load of crap. It was another week before the magician and his carpet came clean. And though we still lived in the same building after that and occasionally passed each other in the lobby, there was never anything magical between us again.

His rejection stung. The more I tried to ignore my feelings and get over it, the less I seemed able to focus on anything other than how unworthy I felt. So I just tried to keep busy.

It was a cloudless, summer day. I had joined my landlady, Irene, to chat and pull weeds at the side of the building where rows of yellow daffodils and purple irises grew. As the empty sky glowed, an innocent coolness blew in off The Lake, taming the Midwestern heat. Buttons minded me well and stayed close, happily sniffing the flowers and walking around the spots where I'd weeded. After gathering up all the cleared-out greenery, the three of us walked a few steps along the sidewalk and then turned the corner into the deserted alleyway behind the building and headed for the back gate into the courtyard.

We entered the alleyway single-file: me in the lead, Irene bringing up the rear and Miss Buttons prancing along in the middle position. Suddenly, we were jolted by the sound of screeching tires. A car that had been speeding down our side street turned violently into the alley and headed for us from behind. At the sound, I swung around in time to see Irene lunge forward to grab Buttons even though we were all walking right next to the building itself. Irene's well-meaning action served only to scare Buttons who scurried away from her, directly into the path of the four-door Oldsmobile just a few feet away.

It all happened in the blink of an eye, and yet I can still see it unfolding in slow motion in my memory. The driver slammed on the brakes and the car jerked to a full stop. Buttons lay on her back, her back legs pinned under the front passenger wheel. Irene went to her instantly as I began pounding on the hood of the guys car screaming, "BACK-UP-GET IT OFF OF HER-BACK-UP!" As soon as he did and she was free, Buttons took off down the alleyway on her front legs, dragging her useless back legs behind her and leaving a trail of blood, skin, and fur. Tires squealed again as the guy backed out of the alley and tore off down the street.

The next few moments continued in that kind of blurry, slow-motion way that happens when your whole world stops and life as you know it is changed forever in an instant. I remember running after her and scooping her up as gingerly as I could. I remember Irene in the courtyard screaming for help. The next thing I knew, Irene was ushering me into the front seat of the nearest parked car, which happened to be her husband's, and since she didn't drive, tossing her keys to the one neighbor who'd heard our screams and come running. Yes, it was the magician. At that point, I didn't care if Houdini himself was driving, just so long as he got us to the emergency vet ASAP!

Buttons was conscious, her eyes bugged out and staring at me. I just held her as tenderly as I could while softly cooing, "Please don't die, Pooper... PLEASE don't die." I felt frozen with fear and totally helpless.

An agonizingly long ten minutes later, we arrived at the animal hospital. There they rushed us into an exam room where a vet and his two assistants immediately began asking questions and washing Buttons' wounds. They gave her a shot for the pain and one for infection. A seventeen-pound dog pinned under the wheel of a four-door Oldsmobile: the vet said it was an absolute miracle that her bones weren't crushed. I agreed.

He took X-rays to be sure there were no breaks anywhere. There weren't. Some of the outside and the entire inside of her back legs had all the fur and skin burned right off of them. They looked like those diagrams in a high school biology book that show the different muscle groups. That's mostly what we were looking at, the vet explained, some tissue and raw muscle. He then told me that her fur would never grow back, but if we were lucky, some of the skin would and we wouldn't have to do too many skin grafts.

This was all my fault. I had had her leash and collar right there around my waist, but never thought I'd need to put them on her just for the fifteen-foot walk to the courtyard. How could I have been so remiss? How could I be so irresponsible, such a bad mom?!? They slathered her legs with antibiotic salve and bandaged her from toes to tail. She seemed to be resting comfortably.

I didn't have my purse, and the magician didn't have his wallet. He handed me the keys so I could drive home for some money. I felt like a zombie. I was covered in black fur and red blood. When I got back to the vet, I paid the bill and they scheduled a follow-up appointment for two weeks later. We were sent home with more bandages and salve and I was told to change the dressing every three days. They gave me some oral antibiotics and told me to put them in liver sausage for her. We drove home. The magician helped me get Buttons into the apartment and settled onto a makeshift sickbed in the living room. She fell back asleep. The magician disappeared again, this time for good.

Still in shock, I just sat there watching her sleep. I had almost lost her. We weren't totally out of the woods yet, but I knew she would live and walk again. I felt blessed. Blessed! It had always sounded crazy to me when I'd hear someone say something like that. "Oh... he died in his sleep... we were blessed," or "she survived the accident with only scarring to her face, she was so blessed," and I'd think to myself, what the hell do they mean? He's dead! She's scarred! Blessed?

Yes, blessed. Now I understood. I knew what people were thankful for in those situations. There is always a blessing to see. No matter how horrible the circumstance, there is always something more awful that could have happened... a more tragic way it could have unfolded with potentially more suffering. Somewhere inherent in that fact is indeed a blessing, and the trick is finding a way to open one's heart to it. Looking there instead of at the pain and still being grateful, that was the blessing and perhaps the biggest challenge, after all.

I called Irene who was, of course, relieved to hear that all was "well." I called my Dad, the original alternative health care advocate of the family. For years, he'd treated our childhood maladies with oddball methods. In those days that included such things as chiropractic, Rolfing, Radionics, therapeutic massage, naturopathy, and color therapy to name a few. It would be another twenty years before most of those methods would be welcomed into the mainstream.

He suggested I use some of his energy plates to help with Buttons' healing process and a short time later, he dropped them off. They looked like oversized credit cards, made of aluminum, one gold and one purple. When you looked at them under a microscope, Dad explained, you could see that the aluminum had been poured in such a way as to create thousands of tiny pyramids on the surface. Those pyramid shapes, like vortexes, caused the energy or molecules around the plates to move in an upward spiral, which according to several ancient healing traditions, was optimum for healing regeneration. Sounded okay to me and at worst, harmless. They'd certainly have fewer side effects than I knew the antibiotics would have, or the nitrates in the liver sausage for that matter.

After checking on Butts again, I took a shower. I cried and scrubbed and eventually decided to focus on making Buttons well and comfortable instead of flogging myself to death with guilt. When she woke up, I carried her outside and held her up so she could pee. At bedtime, I carried her into the bedroom and laid her on the floor in a little nest I'd made out of some sweatshirts from the hamper, wanting her to feel comforted by having my smell near her. I placed the energy plates on the sweatshirt next to her, and she slept through the night. When I woke the next morning, she was still sound asleep. She had moved herself over and was lying with her chin resting on both energy plates. Interesting.

When she woke up a little later, I gave her the antibiotic in the liver sausage I had run out to buy earlier. It was encouraging to see her take it with such enthusiasm. Every three days, we went though the big change-the-dressing-production of unraveling her massive bandage, cleaning her wounds and redressing them. Looking back I see this was our "dress re-hearsal." Even the first time I took the bandage off, her legs looked better to me. Maybe we would be lucky and not need a lot of skin grafts. I certainly did not want to put her through that.

Every night she would move herself to be lying directly on the energy plates so I finally just taped them to the bandages themselves. By the end of that first week, she had ants in her pants, and it wasn't easy to keep her rested according to the vet's instructions. As stiff as her healing legs were, she kept trying to run to her bowl at mealtime and to the door when I got home from work.

At our two-week's vet appointment, the doctor put Butts on the ex-amining table and slowly unwrapped the bandaging covering both back legs and hips. His jaw dropped as the final layer revealed that in those two weeks, not only had all the skin grown back, but you could also see where new fur had begun to sprout. He looked at me incredulously and declared, "This is unbelievable! What in the world do you feed this dog?!"

At the time, I was feeding her one of the only "natural" dry dog foods on the market (the selection now is huge in comparison), but I knew that that had little to do with it. I stood there also knowing how futile it would prove, trying to explain aluminum plates and pyramid energy to this conservatively trained, Western medical person. Instead, I smiled and answered, "Just some kibble and a whole lot of love." There was no way I could have known at the time, the profound prophesy of that one statement.

Buttons continued to heal remarkably well. She never needed any skin grafts and within two years, all of the fur on her legs had grown back. I didn't know whether the energy plates had anything to do with it, but I knew that neither the vet nor any of his assistants, who had seen her condition when we first rushed into that room, had ever seen a recovery so impressive or complete. They could offer no explanation themselves.

A year later, my father introduced me to Mary Hardy, a renowned homeopath and author of books on pyramid energy. At our first consultation, using a dowsing-type method of energy diagnosis with a Polaroid photo and lock of hair belonging to the patient, Mary did her testing on Buttons' photo and fur. While holding them in one hand, Mary lightly rubbed the fingers of her other hand on a small metal plate that sat on the table in front of her. She explained that by noticing the degree of resistance as she rubbed, she would be led to which homeopathic remedies were needed, which would in turn, alert her to what the health problems were. Mary had never met Buttons, who was at home, and neither my father nor I had told her anything at all about the accident or Buttons' medical history. So, you can imagine my surprise when the first thing Mary said was, "Your dog has the beginnings of some arthritic degeneration in her hips and back legs. It seems she's had some kind of severe injury to that area. You should get her on some of these remedies as a preventative so it doesn't get any worse."

I sat there stunned at what I'd just heard. Of course I would take home any remedies Mary recommended. Slowly then, I opened my checkbook, picked up my pen, and thus began Buttons' lifelong journey and official induction into the Holistic Animal Hall of Fame.

It was a boring, gray afternoon in January of 1988 when I decided to have the ceiling of my apartment tested for asbestos. For several months, I had been cleaning white dust off my desk that had fallen from one of the acoustic tiles. I don't know what prompted me to call a testing company instead of just asking the landlady to replace it. But something did and by then, I was learning to follow those types of intuitive cues. If dowsing for remedies could reveal the information about Buttons' injuries to Mary, and energy plates could make skin and hair grow, then surely there was more going on around me than what my five senses could perceive.

The guys came out, took several samples of the tiles and said they'd call me in two to three business days with the results. When they called and told me the lab had confirmed that the tiles were almost pure asbestos, I was shocked. Their instructions were for me to move out of the apartment within ten days before they reported the situation to the building/health code authorities who would then evict me. They sent me their report, and I showed it to my landlady.

The timing couldn't have been worse. First, try finding an available apartment in Chicago in the dead of winter. They don't exist. Nobody's stupid enough to end a lease when the wind-chill is eighty below. Second, I discovered that my landlady and her husband were in the middle of negotiations to sell the building. The existence of a report stating that my entire ceiling needed to be replaced in accordance with the very expensive, environmentally correct method of asbestos removal was not something they wanted as part of their negotiations. I made many phone calls to the current owners, the city, and the prospective owners. Soon I realized that dealing with all the legalities of getting the responsible parties to do what was right would be a full time job. At that point, no one was even willing to take responsibility. So I focused instead on getting us out of there ASAP.

For more than ten years I had been living in the same apartment. It was small, but with two big storage sheds in the basement, I had accumulated a lot of stuff. And where would we live? The few places I could find that were available either didn't allow dogs or were totally out of my price range.

So I called an old friend who lived a few miles away. She was willing to let us stay with her and her daughter until we had another place to go. I knew it would have to be a temporary situation, but it would buy me some time. The plan was to continue working my great-paying job at Lawry's for a few more months while saving for a bigger move.

Both the asbestos and a desire for Buttons and I to be closer to the great outdoors are what inspired my decision to move to Tucson, Arizona, where my cousin, Rachel and her husband had relocated. Had they lived someplace like Denver or Seattle, I would have more happily moved there, preferring those climates to that of the desert. But Tucson was where they were, and over the next couple of months, they were willing to find us an apartment and make all the arrangements to save me the cost and hassle of another trip out. Arizona seemed the most logical destination.

Moving was a very unexpected, major change, but a bit exciting, too. It would feel good to finally get out of the apartment where my ex-boyfriend Ben—the well-read, witty alcoholic—and I had lived, not to mention, away from the magician and his girlfriend upstairs. The next two weeks I spent sorting, selling, and packing all my stuff. I was suddenly very grateful for my ground floor windows that had offered me little privacy in exchange for light over the last decade. Their store front-like exposure now made my unique midwinter moving sale signs quite successful.

After moving Buttons and our basic living necessities to my friend's, I returned to my now totally disheveled living room to resume packing. The shades were no longer covering the windows, which were now plastered with butcher paper moving sale signs and part of the reason why I was so startled when someone started pounding on one window. Jumping up, I ran over and put my face up to the inch-wide strip of exposed glass that bordered the sign. A bundled-up woman who looked to be about fifty, peered back at me and shouted desperately, "Where's the doggy?"

It turned out that this woman had made it part of her ritual every day on her way home from work, to say hello to Buttons who was always sitting on that windowsill. The woman explained that after a long ride on the El train and a five-block walk from the station, she always felt like she was almost home when she got to the black doggy sitting in the window. It had upset her to come by and not see Buttons there. She was afraid that something bad had happened to her or that we had moved before she'd had a chance to say goodbye to her pal.

When I explained about the asbestos, she understood why I wouldn't be bringing Butts back to that apartment again. She went on to tell me that the year before, she'd seen us outside, the doggy all bandaged up, and known that that's why her canine signpost hadn't been in the window for those few weeks.

I myself always loved coming home to see Buttons sitting there in that window. She'd always start barking and going nuts when she saw me before dashing off the sill, over the couch, and on to wipeout at the front door to greet me. The woman's story made me realize that there must have been hundreds of people who saw Butts as they passed on the sidewalk in front of that window every day, not to mention the ones who drove by and could see her from their cars. I really had no idea how many lives she'd touched or hearts she'd brightened just by sitting there like a sphinx on her windowsill perch, vigilantly watching, pointy ears a-twitching: my daughter's secret life… a life that was about to reveal its biggest secret yet.

We would be leaving the Chicago area soon, and there were a few places and people I wanted to connect with first. One of those places was Griswold Lake in northern Illinois. As a child growing up, I'd spent many weekend days there with my beloved grandma Sonia and grandpa Nicholas who owned a quarter-acre piece of land just a five-minute walk from the lake itself. Except for winters, when they'd stay in Florida until the Illinois snow melted, my grandparents visited their lot at Griswold Lake nearly every weekend, and on that land they had the most fantastic garden. The front third of the property from the dirt road back was soft, green grass with a picnic table on one side that my grandpa had built. He had let me pick out the color we'd paint it. I picked light gray (the other choice was dark green) and by the time we were finished, there was as much gray paint on me as there was on the wood.

The other side of the lot was lined with gorgeous clumps of intoxicatingly sweet-smelling pink and white peony bushes bordering white lattices covered with Grandma's Seven-Sisters climbing rose bushes. She loved those roses and explained to me that she'd planted them for the six sisters she'd left behind in Russia. At the age of fourteen, she had bravely stowed away in the engine room of a ship coming to America. I loved the stories she would tell me of her homeland and her family there as we dug in the garden. Until I reached the age of eleven or so, that consisted of her digging and me playing with the dirt. Usually, as she worked she would sing in her silky, rich voice, and she taught me a few of the songs in Russian. Our favorite one to sing together was "Polyushka, Polye," the rhythmic Russian Army song, which always made us work a little harder. I watched and learned as my grandmother cared for everything, including me, with great attention and tenderness.

Grandma had two gentle dimples when she smiled, and the kindest, saddest eyes I'd ever looked into. I loved sitting on her strong, sturdy lap and running my fingers across the velvety, softness of her face. Her touch was always nurturing—the skin on her hands calloused, weathered and worn. Every now and then, I'd get to stay overnight at her house in LaGrange Park. I'd sit and watch her, as she'd engage in her nightly ritual of absentmindedly rubbing Jergen's lotion from fingertips to elbows, while she sat concentrating on Jackie Gleason, Ed Sullivan, or Lawrence Welk. She smelled heavenly, my grandma, with the sweetest hint of cherries and almonds and love.

The back third of the Griswold Lake lot was lined with fruit trees and then there was the vegetable garden. Potatoes, green beans, broccoli, carrots, beets (for homemade borsch), onions, strawberries and watermelon were some of what I remember growing there. The entire rear of the garden was bordered by raspberry bushes. I remember when they were taller than I was and I could hide in them, eating merrily as I waited for Grandma to discover my "secret" hiding place.

My favorite thing about the lot was the baby pine tree growing smackdab in the middle of it. Grandpa had planted it the week I was born. Over the years I watched it grow, and it made me feel secure knowing it was there: that as long as it existed, there was proof that I existed too.

Often, when they would finish all their work in the garden, my grandparents would socialize with the other Russian immigrants from the local community who would gather in the late afternoon at Jerry's lot across the road from ours. Jerry had a really big lot with honey beehives in the very back. He also had the only water pump around unless you wanted to walk all the way down to the lake. It was a bright, shiny pump, etched with curlicue designs. Sometimes he'd let me work the pump handle, which was pretty hard for a little girl, but so rewarding once the water started coming out of the spout. After awhile, when they were finished talking Russian to each other, Grandma would walk me down to the lake, buy me an ice-cream cone at the little stand on the hill, and watch while I played in the water and on the sandy beach. I always had a glorious time. I loved everything about being there: the smells, the sounds, the tastes, the safety.

The year I turned thirteen was the year Grandma finally got her visa to return to the USSR to reunite with her long-lost siblings. Over the years she'd kept in touch through letters with her sisters and all the nieces and nephews she'd never met. We often packed up boxes of gifts to send, things like underwear and gloves, which she explained, were too expensive for our relatives to buy in Russia. I knew it had something to do with Communism and that that was also the reason why her family there couldn't go to church. Grandma had taken me a few times to St. George Orthodox Cathedral, the Russian church in Chicago where she was a member. Since my parents didn't practice any type of religion, I was unsure, unfamiliar, and clumsy with the spiritual aspects of what was going on there. Nonetheless, I always thought it a very magical, wondrous place with all its unexpected nooks and crannies, its colorful paintings, reliefs, and exotic-smelling, smoky incense.

It had taken my grandmother decades to get the governments of both countries to approve her return to the USSR for a visit. I was afraid she'd like it so much there, that she wouldn't come back. Even though I didn't see her that often—she lived in a town thirty-six miles away from ours—her presence in my life was vital. In sharp contrast to my parents, she was the only adult I felt safe with and loved by.

Like most little girls, I blindly worshiped my father, a handsome architect, who was seldom home and paid little attention to me even when he was. He had black, wavy hair and dark brown eyes that twinkled with his next, often sarcastic remark. He called it dry humor. My girlfriends all had crushes on him. They told me how lucky I was that he was my father, and I agreed with them. But any kind of genuine interaction with him was as rare as Christmas morning. I remember sitting silently for hours in the corner of the basement watching him as he sat working at his drafting table, hoping with all my heart that he would talk to me. He seldom did, though, unless it was to tease me about something or to tell me to go upstairs and leave him alone. I wanted to feel that he loved me, but was content instead, to know he didn't hate me.

Everyone in the family always talked about how intelligent and gifted my mother was. They had no idea how brutally she criticized them and her friends behind their backs. She had received a full scholarship to Redlands University which she began attending as a college freshman at the age of sixteen. There she also danced, modeled and acted. Her beauty was a puzzling combination of grace and sophistication blended with a high-strung, bird-like energy. Every hair was always exactly in place and outfits color-coordinated down to the shade of eye shadow she applied even if we were just going to the grocery store. But you could see in those eyes that she was never comfortable with how she looked. Her movements in public were always affected and overly dramatic as if for the stage or some camera that wasn't there. A leg was never crossed carelessly for example, while reading a magazine in the waiting room at the dentist's. Rather, she performed a slow, seemingly casual, elegant motion complete with the perfect tucking of her top foot just behind her bottom ankle—a classic pose just in case some Hollywood producer happened to be in our small town getting new caps.

She was well read, an accomplished pianist and gourmet cook who spoke both English and fluent Russian. My teachers loved her. The boys I sometimes befriended were more interested in her than in my girlfriends or me.

But I knew what lurked underneath her outwardly perfect composure, and unlike with my father, I walked on eggshells around her and tried my best to avoid her. Every morning I'd open my eyes and just lie quietly terrified in my bed, straining to hear even the slightest evidence that she was already awake in the other end of the house. The moment I'd hear the signal of her smoker's cough, my whole body would freeze, knowing her daily reign of emotional terrorism, which had been happening for as long as I could remember, was about to begin. Would this be the day she'd go too far and accidentally kill me? Behind the closed doors of our secluded home, I never knew when or what would make her explode. I could pick wild flowers for her in the woods on Monday, which she'd fawn over ceremoniously, praising my kind gesture while putting them in water and vase. The same wild flowers, picked from the exact same spot in the woods on Tuesday, would send her into a violent frenzy. She'd kick them from my hands and slap me hard while screaming at the top of her lungs, accusing me of murdering the flowers. What was right and what was wrong changed constantly. None of it made any sense. The only thing that stayed the same was that I knew I was never, ever safe.

On a typical day I'd be sitting silently in my bedroom playing with my dolls or doing homework when unexpectedly the door would come crashing open. There stood my mother, towering over me, her face contorted with rage. My body would tense helplessly as she grabbed me by the hair and threw me around the room and into walls, kicking me and screaming that I was a worthless piece of shit who'd ruined her life. She'd leave the room then, as quickly as she had appeared, only to return a few minutes later. This time, completely ignoring my shaken and battered state, she'd plop her head onto my lap, take my wrist and insist I gently stroke the side of her face while she cried and professed how sorry she was. It was terrifying and confusing. It was mind-numbing. It was severe Post Traumatic Stress Disorder in the making.

Sometimes her rages came in the middle of a meal when Dad wasn't home (she never abused me physically when he was in the house—another reason to adore him) and sometimes in department store dressing rooms. I remember countless times standing in front of mirrors watching as she'd pinch my upper arms and thighs until I could see the black and blue marks begin to appear, hissing that it was my fault that the clothes she'd picked out didn't fit me. Often, a well-meaning saleswoman would push aside a corner of the curtain and peak in, asking tentatively if everything was all right. I'd watch my mother's demeanor transform instantly then, as she'd smile sweetly to the lady and claim softly that everything was perfectly fine. To this day, I abhor shopping for clothes.

In her calmer, more rational moments, my mother explained to me that I was an unplanned child born eleven months after her wedding. She explained in detail how she and my father hadn't wanted to have their first child until four years after my birth.

I cannot go back far enough in my memory to recall a time when I wasn't afraid of everyone and everything except for my grandmother. But when we are little children, it's our parents who are gods to us, and the way they see us and the world is how we come to know the world and ourselves. It's not about intellect and knowing better, it's about what we learn as we are developing emotionally, and that's the part that's so difficult to override and unlearn as an adult. I was a good student and when my mom came after me screaming and hitting, I didn't run away from her: I curled up and took it, because according to her, I somehow caused it and deserved it. That was the way I subconsciously chose to survive in that crazy, dangerous environment—by believing I was the one who was horribly flawed: the crazy one, the too sensitive one, the black sheep, the mistake.

And so I shut down and ignored all my inner cues, entombing the most tender, inner workings of my heart. Music was the only vehicle by which I could ever enter that tomb—that deep secret place where I longed to be seen and loved. But I was too afraid and inexperienced to engage in any type of direct, interactive, authentic emotional intimacy. Instead, I settled for losing myself emotionally in writing music and poetry and be-friending a few others who did the same. I felt everything through music and lyrics—one step removed from the real thing.

To anyone who asked, including my father, my mother justified the constant black and blue marks I bore as the result of my own clumsiness. In retrospect, she may have been suffering from serious postpartum de-pression or perhaps some form of bipolar disorder. But as a vulnerable, impressionable child, all I knew was that, although in front of others she pretended to love me, the truth was my own mother hated me and I believed her unquestioningly when she insisted it was because I was so awful and unlovable.

Despite it all, I still recognized that it was safe to feel loved by my grandma. I knew how happy and excited she was about going back to where she'd been born, so I swallowed my fear that she'd like it more there and never come back to me. For weeks, according to my thirteen-year-old, hormonal and environmentally-influenced irrational logic, I'd acted coldly towards her—as if I didn't care at all that she was leaving. And then three days before her departure, she came to our house to say goodbye. My coolness continued right up until the moment she walked out of the house to leave. Running after her, I caught up to her in the carport, threw my arms around her and squeezed as tightly as I could. Surprised, she held me close for several minutes and told me it would be okay. When she finally went to disengage herself from me, I hung on for all I was worth and she chuckled lovingly when I refused to let go. That's when I started crying. Inside it felt as if some gigantic, speeding train of emptiness was roaring through me. After another minute, Grandma said she had to go as she pried my arms open and bent to kiss my cheek. She told me she loved me, promised to be back soon, and then got into her car and drove away.

Two days later Grandma was at Marshall Field's shopping for a few more last minute gifts to take on her trip when she fell to the floor, and died of a heart attack. She never made it back home to her beloved Russia. She never made it back home to me. She was only sixty-two.

My mom was dramatic with grief, her rages even more frequent than before. In order to protect myself, it was essential that I keep her as comforted and calm as possible. I did my best to feel nothing and to bury and ignore the almost physical pain in my own heart. Feeling horribly vulnerable, confused and alone, I started bingeing on all the sugar products I could get my hands on. Doing that was the one thing that made me feel better. When my Girl Scout troop held contests to see who could sell the most chocolate almond bars for our annual fundraiser, I always won by a landslide. I ate most of the bars myself, having paid for them with months of saved allowance. I'd hide in my closet and consume pounds of chocolate in one sitting. I became dependent on the magical way a whole box of cookies, an entire cake or bag of candy could numb my emotions, change my brain chemistry and keep the threatening, excruciating pain at bay. Like most addicts, I indulged my fix in secret. Soon, it wasn't much of a leap from there to sneaking into my parent's liquor cabinet or experimenting with the hard drugs being passed around school. I never considered myself addicted to recreational drugs since I rarely sought them out, but rather, just hung-out with friends who had them and shared them. I indulged often in pot, uppers, downers and hallucinogens, and was grateful for the numbness and diversion they provided, but sugar was still my greatest friend.

How could this awful thing be happening? How could Grandma die? How could I have been so mean to her the last few weeks? She was so good and kind and wonderful. Why wasn't Mom the one who died, I thought guiltily? It made no sense to me and without my grandmother's occasional presence, I was more powerless and terrified than ever. My insides went totally dead with that terror. Who in the world would love me now?

About a year after Grandma died, my grandfather sold the lot at Griswold Lake. He didn't have a driver's license, and now that Grandma was gone, had to rely on my mom to pick him up and take him out there. I overheard him saying that he didn't want to keep up the garden without my grandma and that the Russian people there had been more her friends than his. I didn't understand any of it. Suddenly, everything I loved was just gone.

Years later as an adult, I would often feel my grandma's presence—like she was right there in the room with me—but I usually brushed it off with my skeptical, logical thinking. The only thing I knew for sure was that I missed her and for decades, I kept that grief buried deep within me.

As I prepared to leave the Midwest for what might be forever, I knew I had to revisit Griswold Lake. I found it on the map, loaded Buttons in the car, and for the first time in twenty years, headed for Griswold Lake—this time to say good-bye.

Of course, I knew it would look different. But I hadn't expected it to look so different that I wouldn't recognize anything at all. I even doubted at first that I was at the right lake, but it's not like Griswold is a common name. There were no dirt roads anymore, only paved ones, and I realized that there could well be a house standing on what was once my grandparent's lot, preventing me from ever recognizing it. I drove around and around, searching for any kind of clue. From one vantage point, I could see the water and recognized the large metal swing set on the small rise above the sandy beach. This was the right lake, but where in the world was the road that went past Grandma's lot?

Feeling sad and disappointed after another hour of driving around, I reluctantly decided it was time to give up. Everything was totally changed and nothing I loved remained. Calculating my way back to the highway, I turned down the next empty side street to get myself there. All of a sudden, Buttons, who had been sitting quietly in the passenger seat, scared the dickens out of me when she began barking wildly and trying to climb on her window the way dogs do when they MUST GET OUT! The road was deserted, so I just stopped. She stopped. I looked around figuring there must be a squirrel or a rabbit or something she'd seen, but I saw nothing. Since she was no longer barking, I started to drive on. As soon as the car inched forward, she began the whole barking wildly, climbing the window thing again. BUTTONS: CANINE AMERICAN, was obviously seeing something so I made a U-turn, pulled off onto the driver's side of the road and parked.

We were in a rather undeveloped area with few houses and lots of overgrown, foot-tall grass, some gone-wild weeds and a few big trees. I turned off the engine and opened my door, but instead of running across my lap and out of the car, Buttons just sat there. Looking around, I saw and heard nothing that might have been the cause of her excitement.

"Ya wanna go out?" I asked her. She just sat there staring at me. Becoming frustrated, I closed the door and started the car again. As soon as the car began moving, she pounced onto my lap and began barking and jumping wildly on my window. Pulling over once more, I turned off the car and opened the door. "Well, what in the world do you want, Butts? What do you see, Pooper?"

She continued just sitting there on my lap so I picked her up and set her outside on the grass. We'd just stopped fifteen minutes ago so she could pee—how could she need to go again so soon? I got out of the car myself then, to wait for her and stretch my legs a bit before driving back to the city.

But Buttons didn't pee, she didn't chase anything, she just stood there. The moment I snapped on her leash, she began sniffing the ground and pulling me away from the car. When she stopped and burrowed her head far into the grass, I could see from her tightly wrapped tail that she'd found something really good to sniff, so I bent down to make sure it wasn't anything that could harm her. What I found, buried down deep within the tall grass, was a small pile of old, rotting boards... gray boards. The hair on my neck and arms stood up. I stood up. Turning around, I more closely examined the tree whose shade we'd been enjoying. It stood alone, well away from any other trees and it was the only one of its kind within sight—a big, towering, majestic pine tree. Partly shaken, partly stunned, I walked over and sat down with my back against its sturdy trunk. As Buttons continued sniffing out the area around us, I watched her closely. How could this be mere coincidence? I knew it wasn't. She'd made me stop the car at this exact spot. It was the only time in the hours we'd been at the lake that she'd barked and when I finally stopped and made her get out, there was nothing for her to chase and she didn't have to pee. And even if she had done either, it was still at this particular location. I mean, what were the chances?

I felt an eerie connection then, between the grandmother who'd loved me so much as a child and Miss Buttons who was here loving me now, as if she'd somehow been sent to me. Things suddenly felt quite a bit more orchestrated than just the arbitrary landing of some random freckle of fate.

I got up and began walking around again. This was definitely the lot. Obviously, whoever had purchased it from my grandfather never did anything with it, but just let it grow over. The only change I could see was that someone had cut down the fruit trees and just left the stumps, but there they all were in a row at the last third of the lot. I stood in the soft, afternoon sunlight taking deep breaths and remembering my grandmother's tender, nurturing love. I could feel it all around me. Inwardly, I stood face-to-face with the grief I had held inside of me all those years. Then, as I let myself feel how seriously I missed her, my grief began to thaw around the edges, and I could feel it burning the corners of my eyes as it slowly melted down my face.

Suddenly wanting to find my way to the water, I crossed the road with Butts by my side and entered more high overgrowth. A few yards in, over to my left, I saw something peeking through the high grass and reflecting the sun so I walked over to check it out. Mostly rusted and partly covered with moss, there in all its glory was Jerry's old water pump. As a wave of nostalgia washed through me, I glanced down at Butts who stood looking at me happily and playfully. I could only mirror her smile. We continued on towards the lake, Ms. Buttons leading the way. After much walking and remembering on my part and sniffing and peeing on hers, Buttons and I returned to the car and had a peaceful, reflective drive home.

That evening after dinner, I took my guitar out of its case and sat down on the couch. As if on cue, Buttons got up from where she'd been lying and took her position in the far corner of the living room as far away from me and the guitar as possible. After sounding out a few chords (I've always played by ear), I started strumming, and when I was sure I had figured out the entire chord progression, I began softly singing the Russian Army lyrics I hadn't sung in years,

"Polyushka, polye... Polyushka shirokoe polye..."

Buttons sprang up, dashed across the room towards me, jumped up on the couch and started climbing right on me and the guitar. She began licking my face so frantically, I couldn't move. Not only had Buttons never before jumped on me and licked my face, she had never once shown anything but abject fear when it came to the presence or sound of the guitar. Tears sprang from my eyes. I put the guitar down on the floor and hugged my dog (she let me hug her!). Somehow, I knew my grandma, who'd been physically gone for twenty years, had made sure this dog was here to love me.

The departure date of our big, cross-country move drew near. I'd worked my final week at Lawry's, and with reference letters in hand, said all my goodbyes. Everything I owned was either waiting in storage for the movers or jammed inside my car.

By the second week of April, 1988, I had already spent hours on the phone with my cousin making plans and hearing her describe my new apartment in Tucson: the rear half of a brick duplex with a huge fenced yard for Butts in a nice, quiet neighborhood in the central part of town. It even had a limited view of the mountains, my cousin excitedly told me. Before we left, I again contacted Mary Hardy, the homeopath, and got a month's worth of asbestos remedies for Buttons and myself. I found a bumper sticker I liked for the back of my car: "Auntie Em: hate you, hate Kansas, taking the dog. Dorothy." Seeing Buttons' smiling face and pointy ears looking through the hatchback window just above that bumper sticker was pretty hilarious and not just to me: often I caught people pointing and laughing in parking lots as I walked behind them. Having never before driven cross-country without another human prompted me to add one final touch: a cardboard sign in the rear window that read, "tucson or bust": the t's drawn like saguaro cacti.

We left on a cool, sunny, Chicago morning. I was well prepared with my AAA information including a list of various motel possibilities along my chosen route that were not only affordable, but also allowed dogs. As it turned out, Buttons couldn't sleep very well in a motel room—there were just far too many interesting, foreign smells. Often during the night, she would wake me from an exhausted sleep after I'd driven all day, by jumping off the bed to go check out everything just one more time. She was a very loud sniffer.

Like most every other dog on the planet, she loved riding in the car, but even Buttons got bored through Kansas and slept most of that leg. As we continued on through Colorado Springs I was filled with excitement and hope for things to come.

Our last night on the road, Buttons and I stayed with some friends of friends at their geodesic-domed retreat center in Sedona, Arizona. The thing I loved best about their place wasn't the special energy flow of the geodesic structure or the sacred energy vortexes of the surrounding area. It was the guest bathroom. Walking in, I saw to my left, the toilet, and next to that, in front of a set of French doors leading to an outside garden, an indoor garden. There were no pots, or built-in planter, but dirt and roses growing right there in the floor itself, a continuation, if you will, of the outside garden. I giggled, thrilled to discover a bathroom that could serve both Buttons' and my needs simultaneously! My host and hostess were not amused, however, when I shared this discovery with them, even though I assured them that all Buttons did while she was in there was sniff the roses.

There were a dozen other guests staying there also, including one man who was reputed to be an important shaman for several of the southwestern Native American tribes. Buttons and I attended his purification ceremony that evening. For an hour, everyone sat in a big circle and witnessed the wonderful sage-burning, drumming, and chanting. We sure weren't in Kansas anymore. At one point, the shaman came and stood in the circle in front of Buttons and me. For ten seconds or so he just stood there staring at the both of us with an odd, half-smiling expression on his face. I was getting uncomfortable as his staring continued when he suddenly broke into a beaming smile and said to me, "The love between the two of you just SIZZLES!" and then he danced away. It was a surprising, wonderful feeling to have my connection with Butts acknowledged like that. It was a relief to know I wasn't just making it up in my own mind and that he could sense the depth of love and kinship that Buttons and I shared.

The next morning the shaman approached me at the breakfast table to tell me that Buttons was a very special dog who had much to teach me. I smiled and thanked him, knowing that all dogs are special, but when he went on to say that she'd been sent to help me by my deceased grandmother, I just sat there with my mouth hanging open. Straight-faced, the shaman just nodded, and then left the room. It was 90° in the desert that day, but my skin was total goose flesh.

Anxious to arrive at my cousin's in Tucson, Buttons and I took our sizzling love and hit the road. Four hours later while approaching our exit ramp off I-10, I shed a few tears of relief as I rolled down my window and threw a thumbs-up outside in honor of our cross-country accomplishment. As the heady scent of mesquite surged through the car, Buttons stuck her smiling face out the window behind me. A moment later, two nearby truckers who must have seen our cardboard sign, joined in the celebration by blowing their big, loud air horns. Buttons immediately leapt to safety and hid somewhere amongst our things piled on the back seat.

Rachel was out the door to welcome us the moment she heard us pull into the driveway. For the first time in months, I felt a sense of relief as I climbed from the car, and we hugged each other warmly. We unloaded some of my stuff into her guestroom and then took Buttons and headed for the grocery store to pick up a few things. It seemed that tranquility and routine were just around the corner, but I couldn't have been more wrong.

When we returned to the house, we opened the front door, and Buttons dashed into the living room, scaring my cousin's two cats. As Rachel and I lugged the grocery bags into the kitchen, we heard a loud scuffle and afterwards I couldn't coax Buttons out from under the couch. She wouldn't even turn her head towards me. With all the changes and newness, I figured it best to just leave her be. When she wouldn't come out the next morning, I crawled in after her only to find that one of the cats had gotten her eye, which was now swollen shut and oozing. Oh, God! Why hadn't I checked the night before to make sure that she hadn't been hurt? Damn it! Once again, there wasn't time for guilt.

Luckily, one of my cousins' best friends was a veterinary ophthalmologist in Tucson and rushed to meet us at his office after our 6 a.m. call for help. Buttons' eyeball had been punctured and had the cat's claw gone even one thirty-second of an inch deeper, he told me, her eye could not have been saved. I believe he may have even used the word "miracle."

A generous "best-friend discount" later and armed with pharmaceutical drops and salve as well chamomile tea from the health food store, which I knew to use as natural eye drops, we returned to my cousin's. This time we made sure that the cats were partitioned off from Butts. Since she and my cousin's cats had been together on numerous occasions in Chicago with no trouble, we hadn't felt the need to take such precautions earlier. I just couldn't believe my girl was having to suffer more pain. Once again, my heart broke. Once again, I wished I had been paying closer attention to things from her perspective. And then as I gazed at her innocent, injured face, I felt myself release some of the guilt and instead, embrace the wisdom of the lesson that Buttons had offered up. In order to be more successful in any relationship I would need to be more aware of the other's viewpoint and experience.

Later the next day we went to take possession of the new apartment. It was as nice as I had imagined—the back half of a simple, brick duplex in a clean, quiet neighborhood. The living room was a comfortable size with a working wood-burning stove in one corner surrounded by lovely stonework. The bedrooms were bright, the kitchen and bathroom, big compared to my last apartment. I was extremely grateful to my cousin and her husband for their time and trouble in finding it. A week later the moving van arrived with most of my things: if a major moving company has ever moved you across country, I don't need to explain.

The drops, salve and chamomile had worked wonders on Buttons' eye and she was thoroughly enjoying her new, private back yard. There were no deep windowsills for her to sit on in our new location, but there was a front and a back screen door where she could sit and look out. Here there was no busy sidewalk for her to keep surveillance of, but there were plenty of birds to watch and a few neighbors to keep her entertained. She investigated everything closely as I spent the days unpacking and settling in. It was nice to be in a bigger apartment and have a yard—to be in a quiet neighborhood instead of on a busy city street. Life would be very different here I thought, and it would be very good.

I had plenty of money saved from my job at Lawry's so instead of job hunting right away, we spent a couple weeks scoping out the nearest parks for daily use. I bought a tent and some camping gear for our weekends. Two or three times a month we would discover another place in the mountains where we could pull off the road and walk in a little way to set up camp. I always felt safe camping without another human, miles away from organized campgrounds and in the middle of nowhere because Buttons was with me. I loved hiking for hours and seeing her complete enjoyment as she pranced and sniffed and peed along the trails.

Her favorite part of camping was mornings. The moment I'd open my eyes, she would jump up, bound towards the door of the tent and begin pushing her nose up against it. Then, it was always a race to see if I could get the door unzipped wide enough to accommodate her size before she would duck and bend and somehow squeeze herself through, nearly ripping the nylon in the process. I never had the heart to train her to do otherwise—that particular interaction always brought me such amusement.

Some mornings I'd wake up to her face hovering a few inches above mine as she stood there staring down at me like I was an idiot not to be up yet when the sun was already breaching the horizon and the birds were beginning to chirp. As soon as I had the door unzipped even a few inches, she'd plow her way through and run off to enjoy her world. I was certainly enjoying my world of being a single mom, even if the rest of the world might not understand.

When the time came to start working, I applied for a job at a metaphysical bookstore. I no longer wanted to subject myself to the frenzied, hectic, and stressful work environment of a restaurant, and figured a small bookstore would offer far gentler surroundings. I by no means considered myself a New Ager, though. Instead, I preferred the label of open-minded skeptic.

I was always willing to investigate different things and read about them, but never without some amount of initial reservation. If it didn't end up making sense to me or I hadn't had a personal experience with it that sounded off my "inner-knowing bells," then I wasn't interested.

I was very attracted, though, to the powerful simplicity of Native American spirituality because of its respect for the earth and the animals. I'd also always felt a strong affinity with Buddhism, its logical teachings so pure and untainted by political power-seeking, misinterpretation, or hypocrisy. Other than that, and excluding the natural health care and nontoxic, chemical-free lifestyle I was drawn to, I approached most things with an open, though initially wary mind.

Given my many years of service skills and my nearly lifelong exposure to alternative health care, it was only a matter of days before Rainbow Moods Bookstore hired me for a part-time position. It was calming, fun work, and the staff were wonderful. I got a 20-percent discount off everything in the store (candles, jewelry, music, incense, chimes, etc.) and could borrow any book as long as I brought it back totally clean, unharmed and unbent. I wasn't making much money, but I was reading extravagantly and enjoying it immensely.

The store was also an excellent resource for finding alternative health care practitioners in Tucson. As a follow up to the homeopathic remedies I'd gotten from Mary before leaving Chicago, I sought to locate someone locally who did similar work. I was able to find a woman, Dr. Lisa S. Newman ND, PhD, who did healing work with animals using remedies such as homeopathy and Bach Flowers, which influence the emotional body or energetic vibration that science has determined surrounds every living thing. I hired her for a consultation and was relieved when she declared Buttons clean from the asbestos. Dr. Newman recommended some remedies to clear the tissue from the medications I'd given Buttons for her eye. All in all we were settling in comfortably, though totally unaware of the life-changing events about to happen.

One afternoon as I was working at the register at Rainbow Moods, I glanced out the window and saw a thirty-something, handsome man get out of his car and enter the store. Immediately my heart rate climbed as if I'd just sprinted a three-minute mile. It wasn't that his presence was irresistibly dynamic and powerful. Instead, he radiated a deep and peaceful calm. He stood about five foot ten inches tall, had dark brown hair and a well-trimmed beard with a high forehead and somewhat chiseled features. I thought he bore a slight resemblance to Bruce Springsteen.

What was happening inside me as I watched him enter the store felt like some huge part of me, of my soul, a part that I had never even known existed before, had suddenly awakened and was now vibrantly alive. I felt totally anchored in the present moment and even though I knew I had never seen him before, I felt an overwhelming sense of familiarity. This wasn't a case of lust at first sight. I wasn't even attracted to him that way until later. No, this was some type of chemistry that reached well beyond hormones and pheromones. When he walked past the counter, smiled and said hello, I had to hold on to the shelf below so I wouldn't fall over. His low, resonant voice wrapped around me like a sweetly scented down comforter on a lonely winter night. I took some slow, deep breaths.

A few minutes later, he came back to the register and introduced himself. I couldn't really tell what color his eyes were since they'd change in the light: flecks of brown and gold and hazel creating a wonderland for me to get lost in as the rest of the world just faded away. We talked for nearly an hour, mostly casual, humorous banter, except for when I'd stop to help another customer. Then looking at his watch, he ended the conversation by telling me that he regretted needing to leave for an appointment.

I shocked myself then, by asking him for a hug. He smiled and opened his arms as he took a step closer. He smelled male and earthy and fresh, like pure, clean soap. It was an amazing hug full of electricity and attraction that left me with a sense of belonging, being home, and destiny that I had only felt one other time in my life—in an immaculately clean, two-car garage filled with squeaky pups in New Lenox, Illinois.

As soon as he left, I cornered the assistant manager and plied her with questions. She said that Connor was a musician, single, and very active in local metaphysical circles. She also told me that he had recorded a wonderful cassette tape which we sold in the store and that he came in regularly to check on sales and restock our supply as needed. She loaned me a copy to take home. The tape was magical: melodic, soothing and sensual.

The next day when Buttons and I got home from the park, there was a message on my answering machine from the assistant manager of the store. I wasn't scheduled to work again for three days, so I was hoping she needed me to cover someone else's shift. When I called her back, she seemed very excited to tell me that Connor had called the store earlier that day and asked for my home number. She had given it to him, having been pretty sure from our conversation the day before that I would approve. Yeah, Baby!

He didn't call that afternoon or evening. It was Friday. He didn't call the next morning. I knew I would make myself crazy, a prisoner of the phone, if I stayed home that weekend waiting. So instead, I packed our camping gear into the car and Buttons and I took off for the Chiricahua mountains three and a half hours away. Snuggled deep in the cool pines, we had another glorious camping weekend and the only thing out of the ordinary on that trip was that I sported a Sony Walkman for most of it. There was only one tape I had bothered to bring.

Butski and I arrived home late Sunday afternoon, rested and relaxed, to an empty answering machine. A few hours later my disappointment vanished when Connor called. We talked excitedly for about forty-five minutes, and then he invited me to meet him for lunch two days later. I hung up giddy and full of anticipation. I wasn't afraid. This time I knew—at long last I'd found authentic magic.

Wearing a sweet, yet sexy summer dress, and some just-picked jasmine in my hair, I drove to the restaurant nervous as a schoolgirl. But as soon as I sat down at the table across from Connor, looked into those dancing eyes and felt that deep, soothing, voice wrap around me again, I felt totally safe and fully content. He talked about his family and where he'd grown up, I talked about Buttons and Chicago. A few nights after that, he took me to a party given by some of his friends, and the next weekend we went to dinner.

As fate and convenience would have it, he lived only five blocks down the street from me. This was definitely advantageous and without being fraught with the potential dangers and risks of living in the same apartment building. By the end of the next month, we were together most of the time and by then lust had most definitely entered the equation. Something in my body recognized him, and I couldn't help but automatically lean into his every touch. A hand on the knee in the car, an arm around the waist in public; he touched me a lot. But it was never in a proprietary way. Rather, he seemed to be communicating something like, "Aren't I lucky? She's mine!" And then there were his kisses, each one a welcome home that left me bobbing defenselessly like a cork in the sea.

What was so different for me about how I felt about him compared to any other man I'd ever known, was that my emotional, spiritual, and mental lusting were just as strong as the physical. My soul soaked up his affection like the corner of a paper towel dipped into a spill, and left me feeling heavy with love.

For months I was walking on air. Buttons was obviously in love with him, too, for as rarely as it happened at all, she tended to go to him for affection as often as she came to me. Refusing to be excluded whenever Connor spent the night, she always fell asleep curled up on the bed between our feet or knees. She was our baby. Connor cared for both of us lovingly. He was attentive and kind, always making sure Buttons got lots of attention and several extra treats when he was around. Never a day went by that I didn't find a sweet or funny greeting card in my mailbox, a love note on the kitchen counter, or an endearing message on my answering machine from him. He became the one and only man I ever referred to as Buttons' "dad." We had discussed the fact that neither of us wanted to have human children, and so the circumstances fit us perfectly. Buttons filled all my maternal needs, and I could rest assured that I would not perpetuate my history of childhood abuse. I could now rejoice that I'd truly found the man of my dreams: smart, funny, handsome, thoughtful, deep, interesting, and one who didn't want kids. I looked forward to a healthy life of companionship, continued personal growth, and delving into the more artistic sides of myself. I loved my new, and for the first time ever, safe family.

The three of us indulged in frequent family outings, which included outdoor adventures all over Arizona and New Mexico. Soon the tent became our weekend home. When we couldn't get away long enough to go far, we drove up Mt. Lemmon. At 8,000-feet, it is Tucson's pine-laden, cool summer retreat and just an hour from front door to campground and hiking trails. Other trips we took were longer expeditions throughout Arizona and New Mexico.

Connor was a gentle, sensitive, and thoughtful man and in my mind, we balanced each other perfectly since I tended to be more boisterous and impulsive. When I thought I couldn't possibly adore him more, he proved me wrong by making our first Christmas together utterly enchanting. Not only had he gotten me several touching cards and included a beautifully written love letter in one, but he had remembered every little and big thing I had ever even mentioned wanting or needing over the last seven months, found it, bought it, wrapped it up and had it waiting for me under the tree. When I opened the final gift, a jumbo sized box of Buttons' favorite treats, I knew Connor was the first and only man I had ever wanted to marry.

December of 1988 was also the month I started an exciting, new job as a fill-in radio board operator. Someone I'd met at the bookstore had put me in touch with the program director of a local station. Cloud 95 played adult-contemporary music and was one of the top FM stations in town. When the DJs would need some time off or during the midnight to six a.m. shift that no one wanted to work, I was hired to sit at the controls and play cartridge tapes similar to eight-tracks. Among them were the ones the DJs had prerecorded for every scheduled commercial break of that particular shift, the ones introducing a certain song, and the ones talking about the song that had just finished playing. Once an hour, the DJs' tape would introduce me, and I'd go on live and read the weather. It was pretty fun sitting and juggling everything while listening to such artists as the Eagles, Phil Collins, and Billy Joel. When it ran smoothly, listeners had no clue that the DJ they were listening to not only wasn't even in the building, but was probably home fast asleep.

It wasn't long before I got permission from the program director and station manager to bring Buttons along on those overnight shifts. It was wonderful taking her with me when it was time to go to work, so much easier than leaving her behind wearing one of those pitifully sad, abandoned, and lonely looks that were practically unbearable to witness.

Even though I enjoyed my routine and coworkers at the radio station and was never bored there, my main focus and direction in life still centered on working to heal the severe emotional damage I had experienced as a child. Though hardly apparent to others, on a deeper level, I was still as afraid and untrusting of other people in social and work situations as I had been of my mother. Career and income were never as important to me as learning how to stop feeling powerless and unworthy. Intellectually I knew I was not the awful person my mother said I was, but emotionally, I couldn't help but react from that original place of terror and insecurity that she'd pounded and screamed into me when no one else was around. So I continued my extensive reading and participation in various therapies and workshops to build my sense of self-esteem. In both my romantic relationship with Connor and my work relationships at the radio station, I remained committed to the tedious job of unraveling my psychological and emotional knots while developing new beliefs that I was deserving and capable.

Eventually, I worked my way up to morning traffic reporter, noon news fill-in, morning DJ of the AM rock-and-roll station and public service director with my own half-hour interview show which aired on both stations every Sunday morning. It was much more fun than any other job I'd ever had though scary at times, since there's no going back once you've said something out over the air. But for the most part, I liked all the responsibility I'd been given and there was always something interesting happening.

I'll never forget standing in the newsroom one day when suddenly, the AP (Associated Press) machine began printing like crazy and sounding its alarm signaling "urgent story being transmitted." Several of us gathered around to read about the earthquake which at that moment was hitting the San Francisco Bay area while the third game of the World Series was being played at Candlestick Park. The tape went on to say that the epicenter of the quake was ten miles north of the town of Santa Cruz. I had no idea that a few years later, Buttons and I would be calling Santa Cruz our beloved home. I couldn't have imagined that one day I'd be listening to dear friends—people I had yet to know existed—telling me stories of what they were experiencing at that same exact moment, while I stood reading the tape on the AP machine, 800 miles away.

As in any relationship, the closer Connor and I grew and the more time we spent together, the more often we began having challenges and interactions that weren't so honeymoonish. We began experiencing the uncomfortable truth that being perfect for each other doesn't always translate into living happily or without conflict.

As I have heard Marianne Williamson, whose teachings are based on *A Course In Miracles*, say, "Love brings to the surface all that is unlike itself" and in my case that meant a lot of fear and insecurity. Connor had mostly female friends, and I was jealous and afraid when he would make plans to spend time alone with any of them. No matter how much he insisted I had nothing to worry about, I just couldn't surrender and trust him or them, at least not yet. *The Course* and many other sacred texts also say that love and fear cannot exist in the same place at the same time. I realized much later that those times when I was feeling afraid and insecure about myself and consequently, our relationship, Connor probably wasn't feeling very loved by me. He reacted to my insecurity by voicing impatience and frustration. The more impatient and frustrated he got, the more insecure and afraid I became and soon we found ourselves stuck and arguing in an angry emotional loop. Of course, being human, he also had his own issues of insecurity.

We went to a few counseling sessions together. Although our counselor was great at what he did, he was also Connor's longtime friend, which, it didn't take too long to figure out, made him a poor choice as our counselor. I broached the subject of exploring other options, feeling fully committed to finding a different therapist to work with, doing whatever it took to work through our issues and grow together into a place of oneness and trust. Connor responded by simply declaring that he wasn't willing to do any of it, at least not then, at least not with me. And then he announced that he was ending our relationship.

For some reason I may never know, his announcement came two days after his suggesting it was time we start discussing a wedding. Even though it hadn't been a completely formal proposal, I'd spent the next forty-eight hours in wedding daydream land, which made his sudden change of course all the more shocking, unexpected, and painful. He wasn't willing to discuss his decision or give me any kind of detailed explanation. He also wasn't willing to continue any communication after he left. He just left. Period. Settled. Gone.

You know how there are always those little red flags near the very beginning of an involvement with someone, but being so caught up in the bliss and endorphins, we choose to ignore them? Well, Connor had been married years before and had told me he'd totally cut off all communication with his ex soon after their divorce. I also recall him telling me how much he wanted to always have that "head-over-heels in love feeling" which is what he lost, I suppose, when other issues came bubbling to the surface. In just under a year, we had reached the stage in our relationship where some hard emotional work needed to be done, and it seemed to just bring everything to a halt for him. I hadn't really noticed any warning signs. The sex was still frequent, passionate, and spirited, the cards, notes, phone messages, and love letters still prolific.

The moment Connor started telling me that he was leaving the relationship, time went into that slow-motion-this-is-going-to-change-my-whole-world-forever mode again. Perhaps it has something to do with certain chemicals being released in the brain when it senses extreme pain pending, and it can only handle so much. I don't know.

What I do know is that for the next several months without any contact with Connor, as I continued to work and function "normally," I was feeling little else but dead and numb inside. For the first time in years, I began consuming massive amounts of sugar in the form of cake, candy, and cookies. Mechanically, I went through the motions of my life and taking care of Buttons. At work, I was an overachieving zombie. My closest coworker, who was privy to what was really happening, insisted I had missed my career calling as an award-winning actress. He expressed astonishment that outwardly, I appeared so calm and happy when inwardly I was consumed with such suffering. And then one afternoon as I was driving to the grocery store, without even thinking, I found myself pulling over to the side of the road. I turned off the engine and for the first time since Connor had left, I wept. For hours I sat in my car, sobbing until the sun went down. Unlike the sadness and loss I'd felt from the breakup of other romantic relationships, this pain was unbelievably excruciating. I felt gutted, devastated, like my life was really over.

For the next several months, I struggled. I vacillated between feeling the shock, disbelief, anger, sadness, self-pity, self-blame, and stuffing the feelings deep inside me. The longing I felt for his presence was at times unbearable. The cauldron, which had held all the grief from my childhood, was just not large enough to hold this grief, too. On Buttons' sixth birthday, I had some professional studio photographs taken of her and the two of us together. She still looked bright and happy, but I could see a definite difference in how I looked. There was no longer any smile or spark in my eyes. My spirit seemed gone.

Eventually, thanks to a lot of therapy, I would reach a point of resignation with the pain, enough to continue functioning in the world without having ill-timed sobbing breakdowns. It would be many more years before I would reach a place of acceptance and peace about my relationship with Connor. But for that first year, one of the things that my blinding emotions prevented me from seeing was how my pain was affecting

Buttons. I wasn't engaging with her outside of the basics and so the more I withdrew, the more she withdrew. I didn't pay attention to how we had drifted apart and were merely coexisting in the same apartment like some routinely functioning, elderly couple. I still took her to all the places she loved, and cared for her physical needs as devotedly as before, but now I was doing it all with a shattered heart. I was far too self-absorbed and broken to be sensitive to my condition's pronounced emotional influence on her. I couldn't see at the time how Buttons was absorbing my emotional pain and how it was manifesting itself in her own body. I once heard someone describe this effect on our animals as their becoming shunts for us. The UltraLingua English Dictionary defines shunt like this: *noun: a conductor having low resistance in parallel with another device to divert a fraction of the current.* Of course it's speaking in terms of electrical shunts, but if everything's made up of energy, especially thoughts and emotions, then this is an accurate description of what was happening: of what Buttons was doing for me.

I totally believe that not only did Buttons risk her life by intentionally taking on the role of being my shunt during that first year after the breakup, but that by doing so, she absolutely saved my life. Had I known then what she was doing, I would have told her not to do it. It's not that I was suicidal, although when the pain's that acute, the mind is certainly willing to consider anything to stop that pain. I'd entertained suicidal thoughts since my teens, but I had also vowed that I would never, in order to stop emotional pain, leave this life by my own hand. My goal was to die happy, and I was far from happy at that point. No, I would have told Buttons not to shunt for me because I loved her so much, because knowing she was in any kind of pain would be far worse for me than feeling my own pain. But I guess that's the thing about pure, positive, authentic love... she felt the same way about me. I was miserable inside my own skin and I would soon discover how my Buttons Girl had taken that on for me, literally, in every cell of her body.

PART II

The Storm

"Be not afraid, only believe."

– Mark 5:36

Right after the breakup, I threw myself into life at the radio station. I was working a lot, attending free concerts, hosting events and doing live remotes including one three-day, live broadcast from Disneyland. Being away from Butts for those few days was terribly hard for me. However, it was difficult to tell if she also had a hard time with the separation since she had taken to spending a lot of her time under the bed. The friend who'd stayed at my place to care for Buttons reported only seeing her come out from under the bed for meals and to go outside. But Buttons certainly seemed happy enough when she wasn't hiding, so I didn't make a big deal of it. In retrospect, I see that that form of her disconnecting from me was merely a reflection of my disconnecting from life in general.

I'd been to several therapists to deal with my grief about the breakup, but as much as I tried to work it out and then just get on with it, I no longer seemed able to muster any genuine enthusiasm for anything. I had always considered myself to be a relatively optimistic, warrior-like survivor, but now for the first time in my life, I felt a vague sense of hopelessness at my core. My own name, Nadine, means hope, but I had none. It had all left with Connor.

Eventually, I forced myself to follow the therapist's advice and start dating again. But no matter how much I tried to open myself emotionally, no man came even close to touching my soul with the feelings of safety, belonging, acceptance and partnership the way Connor had.

The only thing that seemed to bring me any real sense of aliveness was a good dose of ButtonsLove and that was most potent in the great outdoors. So I made a point of taking a lot of camping trips where there was no bed for Buttons to crawl under.

We drove to the Grand Canyon, and at the direction of a ranger at the already full facilities (not our regular fare), drove to a deserted field a few miles away. It was already dark and raining by the time we got there and set up camp, but we were rewarded and delighted to wake up the next morning in the middle of an enchanting, aromatic field of wild sage.

The following month Buttons and I hiked the flower-laden trails near Flagstaff at Humphrey's Peak, the highest point in Arizona. I still felt deeply moved watching her joyful antics along the trail, though I always flirted with the thought of how much better it would all feel if Connor, her dad, were there to share it with. I especially felt that way the day Buttons saved my life on Mt. Graham.

Mt. Graham, home of an international observatory with three giant telescopes, is four hours from Tucson, and Connor and I had often considered it as a destination, but had never made it there together. I must admit that when I went, I wasn't sure whether it was in tribute to our unfulfilled plans, or if I just hoped some kind of soul-mate magic might make it the same weekend he'd be there and destiny would put us both on the same trail at the same time. Delusion had come to visit the place where hope once lived.

It was a lovely long drive up the mountain, which offered Austrian-like vistas, huge, old growth pine, peaceful, flowered meadows and a midnight blue, serene fishing lake at the summit. But besides its elevation and telescopes, what Mt. Graham is most noted for is being the home of one of the world's endangered species, the red squirrel, a fact foremost in the heart and mind of
BUTTONS: HEAD OF SQUIRREL PATROL.

The hour-long drive up the mountain consisted of my oohing and aahing and Buttons jumping from window to window announcing our arrival with a piercing and enthusiastic bark at every hairpin turn. One glance from me would immediately quiet her, but the silence only lasted until the next squirrel was spotted. I eventually chose a place to pull off the road. The ground was dry with little undergrowth, and the pine trees as big as some redwoods I'd seen pictures of.

As I set up the tent, Buttons raced from tree to tree, pausing at every one to dance a little jig on her hind legs while watching in happy, game-playing frustration as the squirrels scurried up out of her reach. It was delightful to watch her fascination as the squirrels also flew from one treetop to the next. Buttons kept looking over at me, her eyes questioning as if I could somehow explain to her how in the world those creatures could do that. Chuckling to myself, I built a nice fire, and after we were both finished with dinner, we settled in for a peaceful night.

The next morning, we headed out for a leisurely hike. The sun dappled trail wound its way through deep forest and open meadows where several grazing deer eyed us curiously as we passed quietly by. Just watching Buttons prance along always brought a smile to my face regardless of how melancholic I might be feeling. Then all at once she stopped her prancing and just plopped her Buttons butt down right in the middle of the narrow trail blocking my way. We had only stopped a few minutes before for water so I couldn't understand why she was stop-ping now. She was nowhere near being tired and I had never seen her just stop like that. I tried encouraging her with words. "Come on, Butski ... let's go!" She continued sitting there like a stone statue. I put the inside of my ankle against her rear and tried to gently nudge her along. She wouldn't budge. "What is it, Poop?"

She turned her head and stared up at me, but remained frozen to her spot. I stood there quietly then and looked around, trying to determine what her message was. About five seconds later a big, old diamond-backed rattlesnake came slithering out of the brush three feet in front of where Buttons sat.

It's important here to note that I am one of those people who has an unexplainable, fierce aversion and fear of reptilian life, except for turtles, which are okay. That combined with the fact that a rattlesnake bite can actually kill you was more than I could take. I mean, I don't even like looking at pictures of animated snakes. In all fairness, though, I probably looked like a cartoon character myself at that point. I stood for another ten seconds, rigid with fear as I watched the thick rattler glide past, cross the trail and disappear into the brush on the other side. Then, at warp speed, I scooped Buttons up into my arms and took off down the trail heading back the way we had just come. The deer we'd passed so peacefully a little while before must have caught one look at me running like a maniac with Buttons bouncing in my arms and thanked Mother Nature that they themselves were not human.

In record time, I broke down camp and drove back to Tucson. That night I cooked Buttons an organic, grain-fed steak for dinner. How in the world could I ever repay her for saving my life yet again? I was about to find out.

I did my best to focus on the positive things: my brave doggy, my friends, my work. And then the radio station was sold. People were being laid off left and right. When the day came that the employee remaining with the least seniority was me, I marched up to the station manager's office and told him and the program director that if my turn was coming to just go ahead and fire me because the suspense was far too agonizing. We had all become good friends by then and when they responded with regretful expressions rather than denials, I realized by the surprise I felt that I hadn't really thought I'd be laid off, too. Great—just what I needed—another major, unpleasant, unexpected change. I went a little more numb inside. We sat, the three of us doleful, and reminisced.

I finished out the week and then applied for unemployment. None of the other stations in town were hiring. A few weeks later, I did some hard, outdoor work for a landscaper friend who needed some extra help. When that job was finished, I took a part-time job with the catering company of a locally owned restaurant, Café Terra Cotta, and worked one or two parties a week for them.

Buttons was still spending a lot of her time under the bed. I knew I had to keep myself as busy as possible, for any idle time always led me straight into reminiscence, deep mourning, and debilitating sadness about Connor. I decided a good distracting project would be to tackle the kitchen wallpaper. It had begun peeling, and rather than repair the outdated, orange and yellow flower/watering can design, I got my landlady's permission to replace it myself, and her promise to reimburse me for the supplies.

Once I had the newly purchased, swimming-pool-blue mottled paper straight and adhered, I realized I would also have to replace the framed poster I'd had on that wall. It was a 16" x 20" photograph of Sedona's Cathedral Rock at sunset. The vivid reds and oranges clashed uncomfortably with the new, pastel-colored paper. Figuring it would be less expensive and more fun to make something myself rather than purchase a new poster, I headed over to Michael's Arts and Crafts store with one of my kitchen placemats for the color scheme.

A helpful salesgirl sent me home an hour later with a canvas to fit the frame measurements plus an array of brushes and colorful paints. Since I'd never painted or taken an art class before, her suggestion was that the quick-drying, soap-and-water washable acrylic paints would be the most manageable for me.

At home, I covered my desk with newspaper and laid out the painting supplies. I had no idea what was the proper way to proceed so instead, I set aside my logical mind and just let the flow of creativity pour through me. It was a liberating, joyous, and deeply satisfying experience. Two hours later, I sat admiring the lively and vibrant abstract painting I'd created, which now adorned my newly papered kitchen wall. The very next day I was back at Michael's to purchase more supplies, and a week later, I had seven newly painted canvases to call my own.

Other hours were filled with studying Tai Chi and Qi Gong, and casually dating my friend, Joe, a self-taught Chinese herbalist and aromatherapist among other things, who taught me even more about natural living and alternative health care. I could tell right away that Buttons didn't like him, and though he was very sweet to her, she never warmed up to him. I learned a lot from him, which I'll always be grateful for, but in the end, I came to understand Buttons' trepidation. Once again, it was plain good judgment on her part. Many years later I discovered that Joe had been involved in some not-quite-above-board foreign business deals while I knew him.

But while he was in the picture, I started eating a diet of mostly vegan whole foods, drinking fresh, raw vegetable juice, and taking complex medicinal Chinese herbal elixirs. It was then that I also discovered and began drinking Essiac: a Cree Indian herbal formula used successfully for many years by a woman in Canada named René Cassie to heal cancer and other physical ailments. I had recently read her story in a magazine article written by Dr. Gary Glum, a chiropractor in California. The Essiac tea, Dr. Glum wrote, had a long history of being a simple, yet dramatically effective decoction to cleanse and balance one's entire system. The ingredients were hard to come by in those days, but I was able to order the individual herbs and was willing to go through the 12-hour process of making it at home.

My new nutritional lifestyle then led me to frequent a small health food store, Aqua Vita, which also produced and sold steam-distilled, ionized drinking water. The store was owned by Dr. Rich Anderson, the founder of Arise & Shine, a company specializing in nutritional supplements and intestinal cleansing products. The Arise & Shine offices, warehouse, and shipping department were also there on the property.

Together, Joe and I did several month-long intestinal cleanses using their products. I was in the store so often asking questions and buying water and cleanse supplies, that soon Dr. Anderson hired and trained me to man his international product help-line for others doing the cleanse. During my in-depth training, I learned fascinating information based on the century-old holistic medical theory that most all disease is the result of (or a symptom of) an overload of toxins that have accumulated in the intestines. In other words, the symptoms aren't the problem; they are pointers, indicators that there is, indeed, a problem. Neither is the disease the main issue. Rather, both disease and symptoms are the result of toxicity, non-alkaline pH, and imbalance in the body. That is what should be targeted and addressed through proper diet and a chemical-free, toxic-free lifestyle and environment.

With all the steps I was taking and positive physical changes I was making, I still wasn't feeling great emotionally, but I was feeling better, and Joe was an interesting and sexy, albeit temporary diversion.

It was a typical weekday afternoon in the autumn of 1992 that I sat in the living room talking with Joe while absent-mindedly petting an eight-year-old Buttons. She was making a rare appearance out from under the bed and was sitting on the floor next to my chair. Leaning forward, I shifted all of my attention towards her as I felt a small twig tangled in the long, soft fur at the base of her curly, bushy tail.

She had just come in from outside and had obviously had a good time if the tail-flora-collecting theory was still to be believed. I looked down and with both hands began parting the hair to better expose the twig for easy removal. When I reached the anticipated, innocent twig, I gasped. There was no twig. What there was, was a pinkish-red, horned and hideously ugly tumor the size of my little finger, growing out of her tail. I stared in disbelief as my heart stopped, or at least it felt that way as my mind took in what my eyes were seeing.

Letting go of her tail, I cradled her head in my hands and looked into her eyes. She was everything that was important in my life and I couldn't even force my mind to imagine losing her. Somehow I had survived losing Connor, but I knew I couldn't survive the loss of my little girl, too. I felt cold with shock. Like a robot, I rose from my chair, walked to the phone and dialed the vet's number. In a surprisingly controlled voice, I told the receptionist that this was an emergency, that I had found a tumor on Buttons' tail and that I needed to come in immediately and have it biopsied. She told me they'd be waiting.

When we got there, the vet took a good look at the tumor and concluded that it was probably nothing. He explained that at eight years old, Buttons was considered a senior dog and he felt that like older humans who sometimes have weird growths, that's probably what this was. He went on to say that these were most likely cells similar to fingernail cells that can grow kind of crazy in older dogs or people. He encouraged me not to spend the money on a biopsy since they were so expensive and this was most likely harmless. He just didn't think the lab work was necessary. His suggestion was to instead, lop off the tumor then and there and just leave it at that. I looked him in the eyes. I knew he was a kind man and a well-reputed vet.

In a voice that sounded too calm to be coming from me, I told him that I didn't care how much the biopsy cost, that this was my daughter and if she were human, there would be no question but to have the biopsy done. When he realized that there was no convincing me otherwise, he began explaining the procedure. He would shave the fur at the base of her tail around the tumor and then remove it at skin level and send it to the lab. He said it would take a week or two for the results and that he would call me as soon as he received them. He told me to go home and not to worry because he really thought there was nothing to worry about.

Buttons emerged from the surgical room looking normal except for the white bandage wrapped around her tail at the spot where the tumor had been. She let me hold her on my lap as I drove home. Neither of us ate much dinner that night.

For the next two days, I focused on her. I realized fully then, how much of our connection now seemed elusive. I loved her as much as ever and knew she loved me, but there was a definite, tangible, unbreached distance between us that I hadn't really noticed until I paid much closer attention. When Buttons was outside or napping, I worried. Everyone including Joe told me not to, that I should believe what the vet had told me and that it was going to be perfectly okay. I knew that wasn't true. I wasn't scared or freaked out that it might be cancer. I knew it was. I've never given birth, but I know from that experience what Mother's intuition is. I waited.

Two days later, Joe and I were in the kitchen chopping vegetables when the phone rang. It was the vet calling to tell me he'd already gotten the biopsy results—that the lab had rushed them to his office. When the next words came out of his mouth, "I'm so sorry to tell you this, Nadine..." time stopped and it seemed I was observing myself from across the room as my body lowered itself into a chair in slow motion. He went on to say that because of the seriousness of the results, the lab had tested the specimen twice and each time had reached the same conclusion: the cells were squamous cell carcinoma, a deadly, and in this case, insidious form of skin cancer. I asked him what he suggested I do. His answer was that since he had only taken the tumor at skin level for the biopsy rather than also surgically removing all the cells underneath the surface, I should bring her in the next morning to have the entire tail amputated and then start her on chemotherapy and radiation within forty-eight hours after that. He continued to explain that if we didn't follow that course of treatment within that time frame, the remaining cancer cells would travel to her kidneys and she'd be dead in six weeks. Again, he apologized. I thanked him for the information, told him I needed to sleep on it, and then I hung up. Dazedly, I rose from the chair, walked into the bedroom and sat down on the bed. Buttons was lying on the floor underneath. When Joe sat down next to me and put his arm around me, I felt myself stiffen. No, I wanted no comfort. I would not spend one moment feeling sorry for myself. My girl needed me. It was my turn to save her.

I lay awake all that night. If the cancer was in my body, I would absolutely forgo the surgery, chemotherapy and radiation. It wouldn't be my choice to cut, burn, and poison. My beliefs, based on all the years of reading I'd done and exposure to alternative methods I'd experienced since childhood, were that one needed to boost the immune system in the presence of disease and not destroy it. Western medicine's focus was on treating or suppressing the symptoms. A holistic approach called for focusing on the cause, clearing it, cleansing it, and then strengthening the body so it could do what an unburdened body does best: heal itself.

If it were in my body, I'd go to Mexico and cleanse and detoxify, meditate, visualize, and consume massive amounts of raw juice and fruits and vegetables at one of the alternative cancer clinics there. But it wasn't in my body. I tried to imagine Buttons without her tail. It would be like amputating her personality. I thought about what it might be like for her to go through radiation treatments and doses of chemotherapy. Horrendous. Demons wrestled violently in my mind. Who was I to force my beliefs on this innocent soul whose well-being I was responsible for? Who was I to risk her life for the sake of my preferences? How big a risk was it? The entire allopathic, Western perspective was screaming for me to follow the vet's advice. He was a trained professional, and I was a self-taught, quasi-hippie health nut.

The next morning as I lay there miserable and unrested, Buttons jumped up on the bed, and then popped back off and did her customary mad dash for the back door. Several hours later I left for my catering job, where I continued to think of little else but my girl and the cancer. By the end of the shift, I was just as confused and undecided as ever about how to proceed.

When I returned home that evening, Buttons was under the bed and Joe was waiting in the living room. After I checked on Buttons, Joe led me into the bathroom. To my delight, the entire room glowed with candlelight, as soft, relaxing music played on the boom box, and a steamy tub fragrant with his best imported German chamomile oil awaited me. I hugged him gratefully as he left the room to go start dinner.

After being in the tub for about fifteen minutes, my mind and body finally began to relax. Tears trailed slowly down my face. Safely enveloped in the warmth, soft light, tender melody, and gentle aroma, I felt carried away as I began pleading with Something, Anything, God, Spirit, WhatEVER, to, *"Tell me what to do... PLEASE, tell me what to do!"*

Of course, I didn't expect an answer. A few moments passed as I sat soaking, and then all at once my tears stopped and I was completely overtaken by a commanding stillness. Next I heard in my mind, not as a voice, but as a powerful, kindly, intrusive thought that was absolutely not of my own thinking, ***"What you need to heal Buttons is what the two of you already have the most of."*** There was a gentle pause. ***"Whatever you believe will work, will."***

I sat there in the bath water feeling not only utterly dumbfounded, but also completely present, unshattered, and confident. I <u>knew</u> how we would heal the cancer. Our love would <u>sizzle</u> it away!

I climbed out of the tub and dried myself off. Throwing on my robe, I raced to the kitchen phone, called information in L.A. and got the number for Dr. Gary Glum, the chiropractor who'd written the article I'd read about Essiac. A minute later, he was on the line telling me the dosage and schedule he would probably give to his dog under the same circumstances. I called Mary Hardy to cover the homeopathic angle. She told me to send her a recent Polaroid of Buttons and another fur sample and she'd put the new remedies in the mail as soon as she received everything and had tested it. I called Dr. Lisa S. Newman, the natural-care pet consultant I'd worked with a few years before, and scheduled an appointment for the next day.

That night when Buttons crawled under the bed to go to sleep, I lay down on the floor next to the bed and talked to her. I told her how everything was going to be okay, that she was going to feel much better very soon and that I wouldn't let anything painful happen to her. Then I started singing all the old love songs I used to sing to her before it got too hard for me to sing love songs at all.

The next morning I called the vet's office and told him my decision. He was adamant that it was a futile one, and proceeded to try and talk me out of it. I thanked him genuinely for all his help and concern, but reiterated that there would be no amputation, chemotherapy, or radiation. He then declared emphatically that Buttons would be dead within six weeks without his prescribed treatment because of all the cancer cells still under the surface of her skin where the tumor had been. When he was sure I understood the risk but was not changing my mind, he wished me luck and said good-bye.

A few hours later Dr. Newman arrived. She sat on the couch with Buttons at her feet and using a method similar to the one Mary Hardy the homeopath had used, dowsed over a box of remedies, pulling a different one out every few seconds. Her advice was to use the Bach Flower remedies to clear Buttons' emotional body (energy/vibration) of all her past traumas and suggested I take some, too. She then cited published documentation which explained that because it is not government-regulated, most commercial dog food is full of harmful chemicals, sugar, diseased animal parts (labeled as meat byproducts) and in extreme cases, the remains of euthanized animals. For the last year, I had been feeding Buttons a prescription dog food, which the vet had recommended. It was three months after starting that diet that I noticed Buttons having a difficult time peeing, and upon further investigation, a test had found crystals in her urine. Dr. Newman was of the opinion that they were likely from the food Buttons had been on and perhaps were a precursor to the cancer, so she recommended I home cook organic food for Buttons twice a day. She listed several cleansing and immune-boosting supplements, herbs, homeopathic cell salts, and vitamins I should give the Butts, some in megadoses like EsterC.® All of her recommendations were from her Holistic Animal Care Lifestyle™ which was a perfect fit with the holistic approach I knew to use of "clear/cleanse/build."

In addition to the things Dr. Newman advised, I chose also to give Buttons twice-daily doses of Essiac, aloe vera juice, Mary's homeopathic remedies, and some Chinese herbal elixirs. Most of these things were given for the purpose of cleansing Buttons' body of all the residual toxins her tissue and organs were storing. Others were to build and strengthen her body's immune system so it could resume its natural function of keeping her vibrantly healthy. That took care of "cleanse" and "build." The other base I needed to cover was "clear."

I stopped using scented laundry detergent, and had long ago given up dryer sheets, fabric softener and alcohol-based perfumes. Lemon juice and vinegar replaced the two chemical cleaners I was still using around the house. I already knew not to use chemical-based flea poisons, but was guilty of using them on occasion for convenience sake. Never again. When her vaccination notices came, I threw them away. I borrowed a gauss meter and measured the electromagnetic fields all around the apartment. The microwave was the first thing to go. Next, I moved Buttons' bowls away from the electrical outlet they had been sitting next to. I had already put Dad's energy plates under the bed where Buttons spent a lot of time and added a green light said to have a vibratory rate conducive to healing. We would cover every base we could think of. We had a program. We had our love. We had all the hope in the world.

Buttons sidled up to our new regime like it had been her idea to implement it and most of the time we partnered through the changes like a well-oiled machine. She loved her new diet, which consisted of cooked tofu and brown rice with grated veggies and what is now Azmira Sea Supreme. (I found out some years later from a holistic vet that most dogs are allergic to tofu and that it's better to cook free-range, organic ground turkey.) Butts didn't seem to mind the supplements I tried hiding in her food, though if I got a bit carried away with amounts, she'd just leave the entire meal untouched. That's how I learned just how much "medicine" she was willing to take in each meal.

With everything I had on the list to give her on a daily basis and some things several times a day, it broke down to her getting a dose of something nearly every hour from early morning until late at night. What could be taken with food I powdered up and mixed in her bowl. The more palatable things that needed to be taken away from food I powdered up and put in paper to slide into her mouth.

The liquids she took from eyedroppers. I was amazed and encouraged by her level of cooperation and participation. After just a few days, all I had to do was enter the bedroom and sit down on the floor and she'd come crawling out from under the bed and sit waiting for me to administer whatever it was time for her to take.

I had tasted everything I was giving her and believe me, some of those things tasted so nasty, her trouper status rose tenfold in my eyes.

I praised her profusely after every bitter squirt and she responded with the doggy equivalent of, "Yuccckkk!" After the first two weeks, we had another session with Dr. Newman who changed some of the Bach Flower remedies. After four weeks, I noticed a considerable difference in Buttons' energy level. She was frisky all the time and instead of hiding under the bed, she was actively engaged in watching birds and wrestling her chew toys. Her mad dashes to go outside were faster than ever. I was surprised at this, because I hadn't really noticed a decline in her energy. I guess it's kind of like weight gain: you don't really notice it gradually creeping up there until suddenly one day your pants don't fit.

At times, our alternative medical schedule felt tedious, though always essential, and we established a smooth routine. I fell into a pattern of cooking her rice just two times a week and then warming it twice daily with the tofu, which made it a more convenient task. Every morning and every night I lay on the floor next to the bed and sang love songs to her. She would most often just watch me though sometimes she'd crawl over a little closer and let me stroke her head as I sang. Often it made her fall asleep. When she was awake, I talked to her constantly, taking every opportunity to rebuild our connection and let her know that her mom was fully engaged.

Five weeks into the program, Buttons began coming up on the bed to sleep again. After two months, her coat and eyes were shining brightly and there was still no sign of the tumor growing back. Even though she still didn't like to be fondled or petted much, every chance I got, I snuck little feels all over her body for signs of other tumors. There was nothing. Since the moment I'd stepped out of the bathtub the evening after her diagnosis, I never looked back, and by spring, I had a happy, healthy, nine-year-old puppy on my hands.

It certainly seemed that we'd beaten the cancer. Our bond, once threatened by my emotional pain and retreat, was now absolutely indestructible, vibrantly alive, and forever well.

That Mother's Day, 1993, my cousin stopped by for lunch and later that evening, I went and lay on the floor next to the bed to see how Butts was doing. When I lifted the bed skirt to look underneath, there was Miss Buttons curled up napping, and next to her an envelope! I grabbed it and tore it open. Inside was a piece of stationery with the following written on it:

"Dear Mom, I had this card made since I can't write myself
To thank you for feeding me brown rice and kelp
For taking me hiking and de-fleaing my fur
You're such a good mommy, of that I am sure.
I love when you pet me and I love when you kiss
When you're away that's most what I miss.
So when you're away it's these things I think of:
Your compassion, devotion, and perfect mommy love.
Happy Mother's Day- Love, Your Baby Butts"

It felt wonderful to have my parenthood acknowledged. Whether my cousin fully realized it or not, for all practical purposes, my relationship with Buttons, especially since the cancer treatment, was that of mother and daughter. Had Buttons been human, had she suffered some accident, disease, or genetic anomaly that left her unable to talk as a child, our dealings with each other might have been very similar. I know for a fact that my love for her could not have been more vehement or complete.

Buttons had yet to see the Pacific Ocean and so I jumped at the chance when Joe invited us to join him on a two-day business trip just north of L.A. It was obvious by then that Joe and my relationship was mostly sexual and had no romantic future. We had been bickering often about inconsequential things, so I was hoping the trip might mellow things out between us and at least salvage the friendship. I loaded the Coleman cooler onto the backseat of the car so I could easily transport and have access to all of Buttons' supplements, food and remedies. We were taking our alternative health regime on the road, baby!

It all unfolded more easily than anticipated thanks to Buttons' contin-ued cooperation, which I interpreted as further confirmation that I was doing the right thing. There were some days after the initial four months of treatment when she'd just plain refuse to take a certain remedy. I never forced her at those times. Just like I've heard it said that dogs will naturally start eating grass to right an intestinal imbalance, I trusted Buttons' instinctual wisdom to keep guiding me, knowing it was essential that I respect that wisdom and listen to it carefully.

All packed up, we headed to California. Butts was excited and enjoying the extended ride in the car which she hadn't done in such a long time. When we reached Highway 1 in view of the ocean and rolled down the windows, she immediately stuck her head out and then turned to me with a look of pure ecstasy on her face. North of Malibu, we found an empty turnoff with a path that led down to a deserted beach. We parked, got out of the car, and at the top of the cliff where the path began, I let Buttons off her leash to blaze the trail before us. Seconds later she nearly lost her balance from wagging her tail so hard as her snout, fast to the ground, began exploring all the new and wildly fascinating odors. In that moment, watching her ever-emotive appendage, I silently prayed an ardent thank you to the Powers That Be. The Butts and I had come a long way towards helping each other heal.

She adored romping in the sand as she partook of every potent sea smell the beach had to offer. As we walked, Joe spotted a straight, smooth stick about a foot long and bent down to pick it up. Calling Buttons' name, he waited until she stopped and turned to look back at him before he let it fly high in the air above and past her about thirty feet. She took off after it like a speeding bullet.

When she reached the place where it had landed, she sniffed it once and then immediately turned and instead sniffed the five-foot-long piece of driftwood that it was lying next to. Just as I began to vocalize my disappointment that she hadn't retrieved the stick, Buttons dipped her head under one end of the driftwood log, clamped her teeth on one of its broken off branch stubs, and in one gargantuan motion, began dragging the entire log towards us. We stood there for a moment dumbfounded before bursting into uproarious laughter. She was obviously running as hard and as fast as she could, eyes bulging with determination, ears straight back against her head, but because of the weight and length of the log she half dragged, half pushed, she couldn't move it very fast at all. But she didn't give up. The look on her face was pure grit, confidence, and joy all rolled into one. I'm sure if the vet from the emergency clinic back in Chicago could have seen her at that moment, he would have emphatically repeated his question, "What in the world do you feed this dog?" Unlike the last time, I would have answered him knowing that now it <u>did</u> have something to do with the food she ate. Buttons hadn't merely survived the cancer, she was thriving. She was the Lance Armstrong of the canine world, winning the "Fur de France" and <u>her</u> book might be titled, "It's Not About the HIKE."

Joe and I walked the few remaining yards towards her and then praised her exuberantly. I hoped she understood why we couldn't bring her "stick" back home with us—it was simply too big to fit in the car.

A few months after the California trip with Joe, my lease came due and the landlady called to say she was raising the rent. As much as I loved it there, I figured it would be good to leave the apartment that was still so filled with Connor memories, not to mention still only blocks from where he lived.

Since relocating to Tucson, I had kept in contact with a Chicago friend and Lawry's coworker, Makaila, who was now living in Salinas, California, which she described as breathtakingly beautiful. Since I had to move again, Makaila began encouraging me to consider coming to California. I missed the green terribly and was excited about the possibility of moving Buttons closer to the ocean that she loved so much. Makaila suggested we stay with them while I looked for a place of our own. It sounded like a good plan that included a guaranteed full-time waitress job at the popular national chain restaurant that her husband managed in Salinas.

With a mother's joy, I anticipated moving my girl to a place where she could "retire" with soft, green grass under her paw pads, and I excitedly made her that promise. I was anxious to get out of the desert and away from all the places which still called to my grief around Connor. My gut was telling me that moving to the Golden State was the right thing to do.

You'd think by then I would have learned that life seldom unfolds the way one predicts and would have been more prepared for the unexpected. But instead, I was quite surprised when I got a bill from the IRS stating that back when I lived in Chicago and the tax laws regarding gratuities had changed, that my accountant had incorrectly filed my return. Now I owed the IRS not only the back taxes, but also three years of interest and fines. I was no longer sure what to do or how to proceed.

Just before the Christmas of 1993, Joe and I went to see *Schindler's List*, then afterwards had the last of several, all too frequent fights and broke up. As lousy as I felt, I decided not to cancel my plans to attend the family holiday gathering at my cousin's new house in Phoenix. It might feel good to get out of Tucson for a day or two. With Buttons and the gifts loaded in the car, I started up Interstate 10, anticipating the straight-shot, two-hour, through the desert drive ahead. Instead, it turned out more like Gilligan's three-hour tour. Halfway to Phoenix, in the middle of nowhere, midafternoon on Friday, Christmas Eve, my car's steering locked up and it was all I could do to make it safely off the highway.

It's a good thing dogs aren't like parrots when it comes to repeating the words that they hear. Like most people in those days, I had no cell phone, and figured I had two choices: sit and wait until a highway patrolman showed up or hitchhike to the little town of Casa Grande about five miles away. As I sat stranded, an aerial photo I'd seen in the newspaper came to mind. It was earlier that year during the '93 Mississippi River flood and one homeowner had used sandbags to spell out "NO FEAR" on their roof. Gathering up the presents, I put Buttons' leash on her and climbed out of my vehicle.

I'm sure we made an interesting sight on the side of the road. A man who felt untrustworthy to me drove the first car that stopped. I thanked him anyway and said I'd feel safer with a female driver, which luckily was the case with the next car that pulled over. She was a conservatively dressed and coiffed forty-something woman who said she'd never picked up a hitchhiker before, but that we looked so pitiful and cute she couldn't resist. I knew she was referring to Buttons as the cute one, so I just laughed and thanked her profusely for the ride. At the truck stop in Casa Grande, I called my cousin from a pay phone and my Dad (now divorced), who was there from Chicago for the holiday, offered to drive the forty minutes each way and pick us up.

Once at my cousin's, I called AAA and had the car towed to the dealership in Casa Grande, which was closed until Monday, after Christmas. As it turned out, the steering had frozen due to some sort of metal flake/chip problem, common in the transmission of that year and model, but I was still the one stuck with the $3,000 repair bill.

When we finally made it back to Tucson with the Bronco II and now, overwhelming credit card balance, in addition to my Café Terra Cotta catering shifts, I began working lunches at Buddy's Grill, a nice family bistro. A few months later, I decided to sell my Bronco II to pay off the IRS and a portion of the credit card bill. Following Joe's advice (we were still on speaking terms), I bought a gutted 1973 Volkswagen bus. Joe had assured me that because of its simplicity, the VW bus would require the least amount of engine maintenance of any low-priced, used vehicle. Perhaps it was his way of cementing our breakup. In retrospect, it obviously would have been wiser for me to spend a little more and purchase something newer instead, but I was determined to get out of Tucson and make my way to greener pastures. If nothing else, I needed to get away from a town saturated with Connor memories. If I had to, I would do it on a wing and a prayer—or in this case, a couple of pistons and a prayer.

The VW's metal insides sported nothing more than a driver's seat, a passenger seat, and a pop-up roof that housed a built-in canvas hammock. The rest I filled with every box and stick of furniture I could squeeze in and had either Buttons or I gained half a pound once the bus was packed, we would have had to delay our departure. The few remaining items I tied to the roof rack. Most of my bigger furniture I'd already sold. This time I plastered a homemade bumper sticker on the back which read: "Following Bliss."

We left in May of '94. Actually, we left several times in May of '94. The first time we made it a mile from home when the bus died. I had it towed to a mechanic who discovered that it had a rusty gas tank. So after camping out on a friend's living room floor for eight nights, that got replaced. The second time we left, we made it to the city limits before the bus conked out. Again, it had to be towed with, I might add, everything I owned in the world in it. The mechanic took three more days to find and repair an oil leak. I spent another few nights on a friend's floor, frustrated that I had nothing left to do in Tucson and less than thrilled with the integrity of the dealer I'd bought the bus from. Having already said all my good-byes, I worried that the bills were starting to accumulate at Makaila's where all my mail was already being forwarded.

The third time we almost made it to the city limits before the bus stopped running. It turned out to be yet another oil leak, which the mechanic said, would take at least a week to fix. I was running out of money and had already run out of time. Frustration and anger were in ample supply. Three weeks after our intended arrival in California the mechanic called to say the leak was fixed, but that he had found another one and that the bus most likely needed an entirely new engine block. I had my friend drive Butts and me to the repair shop where I asked the mechanic if the bus was drivable in its current condition. He said yes, that it was now a slow leak, but a leak nonetheless. That's all I needed to hear. I'm a

Taurus and when a bull is set to charge, there is no stopping it. I bought twenty quarts of oil and left town.

The bus was so loaded down I couldn't get it past 55 mph on the straightaway. Going downhill, I questioned the brakes. Going uphill, I worried about the mountains later in the journey and wondered if I'd ever seen a VW bus rolling backwards down a steep incline. Buttons was just happy and bouncy as she watched out the window. She loved being able to get out to sniff and pee every couple of hours when I stopped to check the oil level. She was much better at living in the joy of the moment than I was. I was used to living in trepidation. We made it that first day to Flagstaff in northern Arizona and found a cheap motel room. When I called Makaila to assure her we were really on our way this time, she told me that I had gotten a lot of mail, mostly bills. I pushed against the fear rising up in me: after all the unexpected repairs, I only had a few hundred dollars left to my name—that and a still formidable credit card balance.

The next morning Butts and I were ready to hit the road by six o'clock. Even though it was late May, it had snowed during the night. Figuring we'd be okay without heat, I hadn't counted on the fact that I couldn't close the vents, and the air blowing through them was icy. Buttons had her camping sweater to keep her warm, but I had no gloves and my hands were frozen. For an hour, I drove with my shirtsleeves tugged down over my numb fingertips. As we chugged and spurted along, it sometimes felt like a bad dream I couldn't wake up from. But as the sun brightened and we headed into warmer country, my attitude cheered. We were seeing lands we'd never seen together before and life was new and exciting. Best yet, I had finally stopped looking for Connor's car as I had anytime I'd driven anywhere in Tucson. We were now like Lewis and Clark, the ten-year-old, cancer-free Butts and me, headed through uncharted territory and towards a brand new, wonderful life.

PART III

After the Storm

"My love is warmer than the warmest sunshine, softer than a sigh.
My love is deeper than the deepest ocean, wider than the sky.
My love is brighter than the brightest star
that shines every night above and there is nothing in this world
that could ever change my love."

— Tony Hatch

As I got a better feel for the bus and resigned myself to the fact that I would always be the slowest motorist in sight, I was better able to enjoy the trip. We were leaving the desert and starting to see lush vegetation and green trees. What would have normally been a sixteen-hour journey, because of oil stops and lack of horsepower, took us three days. With directions in hand, we finally chug-chugged into Makaila's driveway where she, her husband, and their young son greeted us enthusiastically. Right away, we all began unloading the contents of the bus into their guest room and garage.

I knew they had a young dog named Piper. What I didn't know was that he was a big, excited hound, totally untrained and out of control: the concept of manners existing nowhere in this canine's comprehension. He immediately invaded Buttons' space by sniffing the way dogs do, but there was nothing gentle or tentative about his manner as he forcibly bored right in and shoved her around from the rear. Her facial expression was one of total shock and consternation. As I scooped her up and out of his reach, she gave me a look that unquestionably stated,

"This will NEVER do. We must leave here IMMEDIATELY."

Since leaving wasn't an option, I took a break from unloading and had a long talk with her and myself, promising I would stay very sensitive to the situation and keep her well protected.

When the bus was empty, Makaila's husband drove all of us except Piper to the beach for sunset. Buttons forgot all about Piper as she bounded jubilantly up and down the sandy cliffs. So did I as a giant wave crashed down on me before I could outrun it, prompting everyone to laugh and declare me officially welcomed and baptized by the state of California.

Every morning during our two-month stay in Salinas, I would carry Buttons through the living room and out to the backyard in order for her to avoid Piper's playful mauling. Instead, it was my legs that were constantly bruised from his undisciplined jumping. When Piper was outside, he was put in the dog run, but I could tell that even that was not enough distance between them in Butski's opinion.

In no time, we settled into a routine and when the adults of the household weren't working at the restaurant, we were glued to the O.J. Simpson preliminary hearing on TV. After a few days of that, I closed myself in the guest room with Butts, unpacked some blank canvases and began painting. A week later, after seeing my finished work, Makaila suggested I try promoting my artwork in California. Just before moving, I'd had one small showing in Tucson, at the DeGrazia Guest Gallery, and had sold one painting and some greeting card reproductions of my art. Makaila walked over to her filing cabinet next to her desk, opened the bottom drawer, rummaged around and pulled out a folded piece of newspaper. It was a feature story about a career counselor in Santa Cruz, a University town nestled in the redwoods on the northern bend of the Monterey Bay, and as I recalled, near the epicenter of the last earthquake. Makaila had kept the article because she'd found it so interesting and agreeing with her assessment, I called Daniel, the career counselor, and made an appointment to see him later that week.

The drive to Santa Cruz, about forty minutes away (by car, that is, fifty minutes by VW bus), took me past strawberry and artichoke fields, ocean vistas and towering pines. When I arrived in downtown Santa Cruz, I fell in love. It was cozy and relaxed, quaint without being pretentious, diverse in its vast array of pedestrians, and eclectic and interesting with its many small businesses. One store was completely dedicated to and entirely filled with things about John Lennon. There was even a totally holistic pet supply store. This was a very cool place and I hadn't even seen the beaches yet, but I knew I wanted to live there.

I returned to Salinas with the rental listings and another appointment booked with Daniel for the following week. He was a dynamic man who offered an interesting, in-depth biographical technique to help assess a client's skills, determine career direction, and provide guidance. During that initial consultation, we had touched upon many of the different things I'd done in the past and the marketable skills I'd accrued regardless of whether or not they'd been through employment situations, e.g.: dogwalker, holistic care coach/researcher. Over the next year, working with him enabled me to greatly broaden my outlook of possibilities and gain some wonderful self-promotion ideas, which I still use in many situations.

As I expected, rents in Santa Cruz were much higher than in Tucson, but I did find one listing for a one-bedroom mobile home with a monthly rent close to what I thought I could afford. I called and spoke with the woman who was currently living there, but who was breaking her lease to purchase a townhouse. There was a dog barking in the background as we spoke—a good sign, I thought. She went on to describe the place and answer my questions—and yes, the landlord accepted small dogs. I realized that she'd probably have it rented by the next week when I planned to return to Santa Cruz, so the Poop and I got into the bus and I drove to Santa Cruz for the second time that day.

The place was fine. True, it was a mobile home park, but very well kept by its mostly senior residents and appropriately named, Ocean Breeze Mobile Home Park—close enough to the ocean that you could hear the waves at night. It had a little kitchen and living room and outside the back stairs, a small patch of fenced earth. I paid the deposit and two weeks later loaded up the bus and hauled everything up the coast to the new abode. As soon as I had it set up, Buttons was hiding under the bed and so I gave her some Bach Flower remedies. I knew she had been unhappy at Piper's and that all the moving was traumatic, but I was making the best decisions I knew how to make. Thrilled that we were now living in an affordable, peaceful place surrounded by so much beauty, I figured that eventually Buttons would come around.

We began exploring the beaches. We found one we especially loved south of town where we could walk for miles and on weekdays, rarely see another person. All the exercise and sea air seemed to give Buttons an even greater amount of energy and exuberance for life. On an emotional level, I could feel myself doing a little healing, also. I transferred from the chain restaurant I'd been working at in Salinas to their location in Capitola, the small seaside town on the south border of Santa Cruz and a half mile from our new place. Luckily, Capitola had one shopping mall: typical territory for a chain eatery, an otherwise rare sight in the area.

It was time to make some new friends and at our next session, Daniel suggested that I consider attending Unity Temple, a New Thought church, to meet some local people with similar beliefs. That Sunday as I entered Unity, I was greeted by the angelic voice of a woman my age, seated at and playing the piano at the front of the church. She was singing what I correctly guessed to be original music and I had a strong sense that she and I might become good friends. After the service, I went up to introduce myself and to thank and praise her for her lovely music.

Her name was Pamela Hanson and as fate would have it, she and her dog, Rider, an adorable male Sheltie, lived not three blocks from Buttons' and my new place. Pam and I made plans to get together later that afternoon and walk the dogs. I had conversations with several other people that day, joined the choir and for the next few years, Unity Temple was my social circle. I seemed to resonate much better with the people in northern California than in Arizona. In Santa Cruz everyone seemed softer and more flexible, like the weather and the land itself. Or maybe it was just me. Perhaps my experience with Connor had in some good ways, softened me.

Soon I left the chain restaurant to begin a job doing data entry and on-site duties with a small conference-planning company owned and run by some of the women I'd met at Unity. In addition, I worked with another woman cleaning houses part-time.

A few times a week, Buttons and I hiked a wonderful redwood trail I'd heard about. It began near the railroad tracks, which we'd head down for ten minutes before entering the forest itself, me walking and Buttons prancing. The trail led us up and then down steep, wooded hills of redwood trees, ferns, holly, and bay laurel, through ravines that looked and felt like vaulted cathedrals and for most of the way, we were accompanied by a gently gurgling, crystal clear stream. Our first time on that particular trail, I was blessed to find at my feet, the perfect redwood branch/walking stick. I later wrapped a piece of shammy leather around it near the top and within a few months, the wood above it fit my grip like a reliable old glove.

Watching Buttons on that trail, it was obvious she was rejoicing from the very core of her being. It seemed her paws barely touched the ground as she scampered from place to place sniffing, peeing, then returning to the trail itself. She always led the way, dashing out of sight over the next hill and then returning to its crest and stopping to stare back at me, wondering, it seemed, when I would ever catch up with her. Her smile was contagious. Sometimes she'd run all the way back to me then proceed again as if her being right there could somehow quicken my pace and hurry me along. My heart filled with joy watching her. No matter how much I might not feel like going on a hike in the first place, I was always glad I had. I always felt better watching my sweet baby girl enjoying herself so much—every time—no exceptions. Though she still spent a lot of time under the bed at home, I figured our nearly daily outings at either the redwoods or the beach would surely keep her happy and healthy.

There was only one other person we ever saw on that trail. It was a few days before Thanksgiving, and about a half a mile into the forest we came upon a homeless man who had set up a little tarp shelter to sleep under. I said hello as we passed, and he barely grunted back. He looked to be my age. The next time Buttons and I hiked the trail was Thanksgiving Day. In case the homeless man was still there, I'd packed a bag with some smoked turkey, instant mashed potatoes, canned milk, homemade stuffing, a can of cranberries, a can opener, apples, oranges, and chocolate. When we approached his occupied camp, I said hello again, but this time stopped and reached into my backpack. I handed him the bag containing the food items. He refused it gruffly. "I don't want your charity."

He wouldn't make eye contact with me. I stood silent for a moment thinking, and then I said, "Look, the only difference between us, is that right now I have some pieces of plastic I use to pay most of my bills."

Then I placed the bag on the ground by his feet, turned and proceeded along the trail after Butts and didn't look back.

It was true. I hadn't finished college, opting instead years before for expensive therapy after only one complete collegiate year at Western Illinois University in Macomb, and a few semesters at one of the Chicago city colleges. All through my twenties, when most people my age were finishing their education or building families and/or careers, I was working in restaurants and bars to pay for pricey therapists, personal growth seminars, and workshops. I seldom had more than a few dollars above and beyond what I needed to pay bills every month and rarely spent anything on extras like nice clothes, shoes, or household items. Now in my late thirties, I still hadn't come close to catching up in the worldly achievements. Instead, I was working with the career counselor and hoping that the credit cards, my vehicle, and my luck would hold out until one of my more artistic endeavors eventually panned out. I wasn't lazy and was willing to work hard, but nothing I was trained to do or experienced at, other than restaurant work, which I didn't love, and radio work, which was extremely scarce, would pay me much more than minimum wage. I was living just one step ahead of the streets myself.

In retrospect, it's not difficult to see how much of my adult life mirrored the constant, daily dread I'd grown up with. I'd subconsciously recreated a reality of danger because as stressful as that was, it was still what I was used to deep down. It's still where I lived, vibrationally. Often the only thing that brought me any sense of happiness, peace, connectedness or pleasure was my love for Buttons. More than any therapy or workshop, it was Buttons who was opening my heart. More than any seminar, it was my connection to her that was healing me.

Our first Christmas in California, I borrowed a video camera from one of the girls at work and did my best to capture our entire redwood hike on film. I titled it, "Merry Christmas from Santa ~~Claus~~ Cruz" and sent copies to family and friends. Years later, I am so incredibly grateful to have that tape. As burned into my mind and heart as all the memories of Butts and me on that trail are, it is such a comfort to be able to pop in the tape and see her jubilant face and ecstatic tail as she almost flies through that gorgeous forest.

We accessed our favorite beach from the quiet and serene Seascape Resort in Aptos just south of Santa Cruz. We could park easily in their spacious lot and walk down the cliff on their winding brick pathway to the sand. The beach is wide there at any tide, and always I would walk down to the water's edge, switch my shoes from my feet to my backpack, and then walk south for miles along the fringe of the crashing waves.

Buttons had her habitual behavior too. As I proceeded straight south, she would run from me like a bullet, making a big half-circle up to the cliffs about fifty yards away. The whole way there she'd sniff along feverishly, nose to sand, sometimes squatting daintily to pee before completing her mission by circling back to me at my new point along the shore. You could say it was a series of loops—at least that's the distinct pattern her paws left in the sand. It was her looping trail of paw prints that guaranteed our never losing each other at the beach. I never noticed any other dog exhibiting the same behavior; mostly, the other canines just trotted alongside or ran straight ahead of their person. But not Buttons, who made sure she scouted the full depth of the beach, cliff to water, of every mile I covered. Her favorite part of the entire maneuver was, I'm sure, her final approach back to me at full, beach-running speed, when she would suddenly slam on the brakes just in time to kick up a bunch of sand right at me. Then, fully stopped, she'd look up at me, give her tail a hard wag, and smile hugely before excitedly taking off again on her next spiral-loop.

We were both enamored with the ocean. I loved how the forceful, hypnotic rhythm of the waves, pounding on the beach and each other, pulled at my inner peace. I was comforted by the fact that the actual ocean felt so much bigger than what had for years felt like an ocean of unrelenting terror inside of me. The sunshine, combined with the moist, cool salt air, such a welcome relief after years in the desert, felt soothing on my skin. The unmistakable smell of sea kelp was pleasant and I knew Buttons loved it, too, though she spent much more time with her nose buried in the washed ashore piles of it than I did. Even watching her revel as she rolled around on her first dead fish was enjoyable and the only time I was grateful for having an old VW bus to drive home in instead of a nice car. I know I definitely wasn't grateful for it when crossing the Golden Gate Bridge and feeling I would tip over from the wind, or any of the times I was in San Francisco visiting friends who lived on one of the many nearly vertical streets. There's nothing like a twenty-five-year-old manual transmission as the only thing between you and certain death.

Buttons and I walked that beach at least a dozen times each month, heading south and covering the few miles to Manresa Beach. Once there, I'd pick a secluded spot closer to the cliffs to walk up to and settle in the sand. From my backpack, I'd begin pulling goodies: first a beach towel (mine) to lie on, then the water dish (hers) which I'd fill. After that, a few homemade liver snacks (definitely hers) and then the doggy lean-to which consisted of some nearby sticks of driftwood or bamboo stuck strategically in the sand and then draped with a piece of white jersey covered with black paw prints. The lean-to's purpose was to protect my little skin cancer survivor from the sun when we weren't walking, though she rarely sat under it. Most of the time it just kept her water dish shaded and cool. It was there on several of those beach walks that I came to understand a little more of Buttons' and my relationship, her canine behavior, and the depth of her love and devotion.

Whenever I would sit on my beach towel reading or writing or daydreaming, she would prance around exploring. When another person and dog would walk by at the water's edge, Buttons would run down to check them out as they passed. But whenever I would lie down to nap, she would sit a foot away from me and stay glued to her spot. I mean she wouldn't budge whether I'd slept for ten minutes or an hour. Sometimes I'd wake up and slowly open my eyes, not move, but just watch her—alert as could be and aware of every movement along the beach within her sight. A parade of people could walk by, but she wouldn't move an inch from her post. I could see her ears twitching when another dog would wander close, but she never left my side as long as she thought I was asleep.

Once while I was watching her before she knew I had awakened, she looked over at me. I smiled and said, "Hi, Poop" and that was all she needed; she was off in a flash to let the beach know she was back on patrol. I knew I could feel safe, there with my own little guardian.

Of course like any proud parent, I do have one beach story that stands out from the rest. It was a rather blustery day, the kind I love with only intermittent sunshine, the constantly changing light making the seashore feel exceptionally dramatic. Being a weekday, the beach was empty except for the occasional jogger. I was walking and talking with my friend, Anthony, a fellow choir member, and Buttons was running here then there doing her spiral-loop thing. All of a sudden Anthony stopped walking, pointed ahead of us and shouted, "Look at that!"

I stopped and looked up to see that about twenty feet in front of us, a healthy looking baby sea lion, gray, shimmery, about four feet tall, was sitting in the middle of the beach with his back to the water. He just sat staring at the cliffs, perfectly still, seemingly oblivious to everything else.

About nineteen feet in front of us was Buttons, definitely not oblivious, ears straight up, nose twitching, neck craned towards the side of the sitting sea lion, tail pointed straight back and parallel to the ground, and trembling all over. This had to be way cooler for her than any dead fish or pile of sea kelp!

As we watched, Buttons very slowly and hesitatingly took a step closer to the sea lion who seemed not to even notice she was there. She took another tiny step closer. Her entire body craned forward as it trembled. Then, as his eyelids leisurely closed then opened again, the baby sea lion slowly turned his head and looked right at Butts. She froze. The sea lion seemed to regard Buttons as some annoying fly that had disturbed his regal contemplation. With one easy, fluid motion, the sea lion's left flip-per lifted up and swatted Buttons right off her feet. Then, appearing both satisfied and annoyed, he turned and waddled back towards the ocean.

As the sea lion lumbered along the sand and headed into the wa-ter, Buttons scrambled frantically to her feet, regained her balance, shook herself violently, and then beelined right for Anthony and me. When she reached us, we dropped down to the sand to pet her, console and comfort her, as we giggled away like little children. She was panting and jumping around as if her body just couldn't contain all the excitement it held, and I swear I heard her telling me, **"Oh my God, Mom... you'll never believe what just happened to me... oh, my God, Mom, oh my GOD!"** And then just as quickly, Buttons turned and took off running down the beach again, ready for her next adventure.

It was soon after meeting that sea lion that Buttons settled into mari-tal bliss. Pam the Unity musician, and I had become fast friends. We were both single, thirty-something artistic women who shared some simi-lar history and experiences, enjoyed many of the same things, and had comparable life aspirations. Since meeting and discovering that we were neighbors, Pam, her dog Rider, and Buttons and I had spent a good deal of time together. We were like tribe members: survivors of heartbreak, still looking, still single.

One afternoon we piled into Pam's Toyota station wagon and headed out for lunch at Zelda's, an oceanfront café in Capitola where Pam some-times performed. We took Rider and Butts with us so we could take them for a walk afterwards. Being the responsible dog moms that we were, be-fore going into the restaurant, we made sure their water bowls and treats were easily accessible and the car windows cracked open.

After a fun, relaxed meal and conversation, we arrived back at the car to find Buttons and Rider sound asleep side by side in the back seat, and the rearview mirror tilted down so it faced the floor. Pam and I looked at the mirror and then at each other questioningly for a moment before we burst out laughing. We then proceeded in tandem to create an imagined scenario of canine voyeuristic sex followed by an after-the-act cigarette and a nap, all before we moms made it back from lunch. Then and there we declared Rider and Buttons, husband and wife, so there would never be any question as to either's respectable reputation.

They were an oddly matched pair, especially at the beach or park, Buttons with her speed-of-light running habits and Rider who was much more content with his comparatively slow and steady gait. But they tolerated each other well and Pam and I had fun with our new titles of mother-in-law.

There were other new experiences awaiting Ms. Buttons and me while living on the Central Coast of California, including one minor earthquake, though we weren't together when it happened. She was at home and I was at my new job with the women at the conference planning company. The main office was actually in the owner's home. Her large living room had been converted into a spacious, pleasant workspace where our desks and computers were set up. There was a high, vaulted ceiling and massive picture window that looked out onto a serene, green yard. Sitting at my computer, I faced the middle of the room and my coworkers, with my back a few feet from the picture window.

I was entering data into the computer one morning when all of a sudden there was an odd pain in my chest. It felt like an extremely strong cramp, like a charley horse in my heart, and for a moment or two, the rhythm of its beating changed. Fearfully, I could only guess that I was having a heart attack. Then, just as I took my hands from the keyboard and was about to cry for help, the sensation stopped and the room began to shake. The window rattled and a few little things fell to the floor off tables and shelves. The trembling lasted about five seconds and when it stopped, Lanny, the only other person in the room at the time and a native Californian, delightfully announced, "Cool! A tremor!"

As we went around the room restoring the few disheveled items back to their original places, I told Lanny about the pain in my chest just prior to the earthquake. She instantly validated my experience by explaining to me that some people's heart muscles and rhythms actually are affected by the powerful and sudden change in the earth's electromagnetic field that occurs right before an earthquake. She went on to say that according to articles she'd read, those people always have a few moments of extra warning preceding such earth changes.

At lunchtime, I went home to check on Buttons who as usual, was dancing on her hind legs at the door after hearing me putt-putt into the driveway. She seemed fine and our mobile home with all its built-in shelving and compact storage design was untouched by the day's event.

One of the many great things about Santa Cruz is its proximity to gorgeous nature spots. It sits surrounded by your choice of redwood forest, mountains, or ocean. There are also many little hidden wonderlands tucked in between the neighborhoods. One such gem is Schwan Lagoon. I passed the ocean side of it nearly every day on one of the main roads, but had no idea there was any way in other than by boat. Then one day a fellow dog walker on the beach directed me to its back entrance from a neighborhood dead end street. Upon investigation, we found peaceful, secluded forest surrounding the far end of the lagoon. What made it really terrific was its location—a five-minute drive from our front door—and its wonderful loop trails. Buttons loved the zillion different kinds of birds it was home to, no doubt for her terrier, listening pleasure. We walked the trails there a few times a week on the days when there wasn't enough time for our redwood hike or drive to Seascape beach. Among those three favorite spots and a few others, Buttons and I were able to spend some time every day communing deeply with our natural surroundings.

One afternoon we took our friend Natalie to Schwan Lagoon. She and her husband, Frank, had lived near there for years and had never known about the back way in. Natalie is an incredible Renaissance woman who besides being a dedicated educator is an accomplished musician, gardener, sculptor, and world traveler. She had just participated in an interesting weekend workshop for artists, and I was eager to hear all about it.

As we walked along the trail side by side under a canopy of old-growth oak trees, I listened and asked questions as Natalie described the unusual projects they had done. Buttons led the way a few yards ahead of us. One of the things Natalie described was an art project of self-discovery, which concluded in their creating one sentence to sum up their life as they were living it. This was done in the context of, "what it would say on your gravestone." I can't quite remember now what Natalie's was, but I do remember how difficult it was when she asked me what I thought mine might be. We walked a few minutes in silence as I pondered the question when all of a sudden Natalie said, "Well! It's easy enough to know what Buttons' would be."

"What's that?" I inquired, smiling.

"I love life... let me prance!" was Natalie's response.

Her answer, so eloquent and fitting and true. I couldn't keep from tearing up when I heard it. I loved my friends in Santa Cruz. I loved the ocean, the redwoods, the weather and the open-mindedness there. I loved everything about Santa Cruz except my greatest nemesis—its cost of living.

In 1995, three new things began happening in my life. First, I started experiencing a lot of overwhelming fatigue and allergies. Not only couldn't I identify the cause or source, but I couldn't even control or suppress the symptoms. I never seemed to have enough energy for anything and was always annoyingly tired no matter how many hours I'd slept the night before. I was congested a lot of the time and began having frequent sneezing fits accompanied by nearly constant itchy, watery eyes and post-nasal drip. The second new thing was that people I'd met started buying my paintings. Third, I began a daily meditation practice.

A few years earlier, I had been introduced to the writings of Sri Eknath Easwaran, a professor of English literature. Sri Easwaran came to the U.S. from southern India on the Fulbright Exchange and began teaching at Berkeley in 1960 just prior to establishing the Blue Mountain Center of Meditation (BMCM) in northern California. Besides receiving the BMCM monthly newsletter, I had read many of Sri Easwaran's books on the spiritual life and was especially drawn to his nondenominational, nondogmatic, modern-day approach to Christianity, Buddhism, Hinduism and Judaism.

A couple of weeks before my fortieth birthday (two months after Butski's eleventh birthday), Pam suggested we celebrate by going to San Francisco for the Monet exhibit and dinner. Thrilled with her offer, I asked if we could possibly go on a Tuesday, skip a nice dinner and instead drive another forty-five minutes north to the town of Petaluma where the BMCM held its weekly educational program.

The Monet exhibit was incredibly beautiful and enchanting. Afterwards, we zipped across the Golden Gate and up to Petaluma, grabbed a sandwich, and headed for the Tuesday night program according to the directions on my BMCM newsletter. It was thrilling for me to meet the people from the Center whom I'd read so much about in Sri Easwaran's books. Pam and I sat in on the half-hour workshop, which described Sri Easwaran's Eight Point Program for a happy life:

1) Meditation
2) Mantra
3) Slowing down
4) One-pointed attention
5) Training the Senses
6) Putting Others First
7) Spiritual Companionship
8) Reading the Mystics

Each point was briefly described, with an emphasis on meditation, in this case, the extremely slow, focused, silent repetition in the mind of a memorized inspirational passage. This passage could be from any of the world's great religions, though it was strongly encouraged that beginners start with the Prayer of St. Francis. Beginners also started out following this method for thirty minutes each morning. I had read a lot about this method when my friend Paige introduced me to Sri Easwaran's books in Tucson several years before, but I hadn't felt the devotion at the time for such a commitment. I didn't want to just give it a try and risk it being like some failed diet.

Next, we went downstairs to view a forty-five minute video of a talk Sri Easwaran had given a few years before. I was captivated. Seeing the man behind the books, delighting in his wonderful sense of humor, and hearing his deep, charmingly accented voice was a totally inspirational experience for me. It had been explained to us earlier that when the video concluded, the lights would remain dimmed for a thirty-minute session of meditation. The ringing of a small brass bell would signal its completion. Since Pam and I both already knew the Prayer of St. Francis by heart, we decided to give it a try.

> Lord, make me an instrument of Thy peace.
> Where there is hatred, let me sow love.
> Where there is injury, pardon.
> Where there is doubt, faith.
> Where there is despair, hope.
> Where there is darkness, light.
> Where there is sadness, joy.
> Oh, Divine Master, grant that I may not so much seek
> To be consoled as to console.
> To be understood as to understand.
> To be loved as to love.
> For it is in giving that we receive,
> It is in pardoning that we are pardoned,
> It is in dying to self that we are born to eternal life.

It certainly was challenging during that half hour to sit there, perfectly still, trying to concentrate only on the prayer, when all that my body — not to mention my mind — wanted to do was move around. But an interesting thing happened, too. In the past, I had always interpreted that prayer as only comforting others, loving others, pardoning others, all of which were good things, for sure. This time I felt it in a whole different way. I realized that the places where I hated *myself* let me sow love... the times I had done *self*-destructive things, let me pardon, and the times

I needed comfort, to seek comfort *within* instead of looking for it elsewhere. I realized that I still hadn't learned to be as compassionate with myself as I was with Buttons.

My experience that night was enough to hook me. There was much I could learn and discover here and I was always on the lookout for new ways to heal and grow. The very next morning I woke to sit and do my thirty-minute meditation and for five years after that, I never missed a single morning.

Over the next two years, I often made the six-hour, round trip drive to attend those Tuesday night gatherings. I was able to do this only because of various friends' generosity, mostly Pam's, in letting me borrow their reliable vehicles. Being there offered me a sense of family and belonging: a shared, common goal. Every few months there was a coffee-hour, which Sri Easwaran would attend when his health permitted to give *prasad*, a gift of blessed food, to those who came. Sometimes I would save my portion and bring it home to share with Buttons. I loved those gatherings when Sri Easwaran was present; the room pulsated with joy. Before taking his leave, we would all form a large circle (there were usually fifty or more people in attendance) and receive darshan (gift of energy, or higher vibration transmitted through the eyes of an enlightened or more evolved soul) as Sri Easwaran would walk the inner circumference of the circle and make eye contact with various individuals as he passed. It was never officially announced as his giving *darshan*, but rather, just his taking his leave and saying goodbye. Sri Easwaran never claimed to be some kind of guru, but merely the long time educator he was and one who practiced what he preached. To his devout students, there was no doubt as to his status as spiritual mentor, master, sage.

On the Tuesday nights when there wasn't a coffee-hour scheduled, I often took Butts with me if the weather was conducive to her sleeping in the car during the class, video, and meditation. We'd always drive up early to avoid rush-hour traffic through San Francisco and then have a late afternoon picnic meal at the park or closest beach.

One time Butts and I were enjoying a picnic dinner at Dillon Beach when it started to get a bit gray, cold, and windy so I packed everything and we headed back towards the small parking lot. Off in the distance, from the other end of the beach, I spotted three small figures walking towards me, also headed for the parking lot. As we neared each other I recognized Sri Easwaran, who was in his late eighties at the time, walking arm-in-arm with his wife, Christine, supporting him on one side and one of his long-time students on the other. I quickly scanned the beach for Butts to make sure she wasn't anywhere close to getting in their way or under their feet. When I spotted her I clapped my hands and she came running. Scooping Buttons up in my arms, I headed towards an empty picnic table on the sand a few yards from Sri Easwaran's car. As the three of them passed near me I bowed my head in greeting and as they all nodded a greeting in return, Sri Easwaran looked down at Buttons who was now on her leash and sitting at my feet. His smile grew large and beaming as he looked at her and nodded again before getting into the car to drive away. From then on, I often reminded Buttons how special she was to have received, and perhaps exchanged, doggy *darshan* that day on Dillon beach.

In 1996, Butts turned twelve and I continued delving even deeper into my spiritual study. At Sri Easwaran's suggestion, I lengthened my morning meditation session to one hour and added one half-hour session before bed. Devotedly I read several of the Christian mystics while I reveled in the Buddha's Damapada, and delighted in the Hindu sacred texts of the Bagavad Gita and the Upanishads. I memorized numerous passages from all of them for meditation.

I also began studying the *Science Of Mind* by Ernest Holmes. Holmes founded the Church of Religious Science, a New Thought church—not to be confused with Christian Science or Scientology—combining the sacred teachings and universal principals of both Eastern and Western Christian traditions along with the deep insights of psychology and quantum physics.

At the same time, the allergies and fatigue I was experiencing were getting worse and so were the money problems. So when the workload slowed at the conference planner's, I began looking for another job. I also began attending a therapeutic massage class in the evenings—a skill I'd always wanted to have. There is a creativity involved in doing therapeutic bodywork that really appealed to me. Each body can be likened to a blank canvas, and one of the practitioner's jobs is to determine and feel what that canvas "needs" to restore balance throughout its composition. Many of the people I practiced on swore that their sessions with me were as healing and beneficial as the ones they'd received from far more experienced therapists.

Jobs were scarce in Santa Cruz, but through a friend, I found work at a green-waste recycling center. The pay was low but I got to take Buttons with me every day, support the environment in a good and loving way and learn to operate a tractor, which was kinda cool. It would do until I found something that paid more or could begin building a massage practice. Eventually I faced the inevitable and found a better paying job at a busy, upscale restaurant.

The pace at the restaurant was frantic and demanding. Much to my dismay, their policies and ways of handling things were nothing like what I was used to at Lawry's The Prime Rib. At Lawry's, the management did everything possible to support the staff, in turn ensuring the finest service to each guest. This chef-owner was incredibly talented, his food creative and fabulous, and I loved working with him. But his relatives, who were also the management staff, seemed at war with the servers and bartenders. What had worked at their last, tiny location as far as table seating and timing went, seemed to create insanity when implemented in a venue six times the size.

Seven months later, when I could no longer handle the pressure or the overpowering exhaustion it resulted in, I quit and took a part-time job at a popular little seafood place on the other side of town. It was managed much more sanely and efficiently, but I soon realized I could hardly even handle the pace there.

At times, no matter how hard I tried to push through it, the fatigue was debilitating and because I had no medical insurance, I used my credit cards to pay the doctors as they tried to find the cause. They thought I might be allergic to mold, so I deep-cleaned everywhere. There was no mold in or under my home. I had also become quite depressed. I cried a lot. I had no fuse. Some days I could barely make it to work let alone get Butts out for a beach walk. I gave her lots of attention while I was at home, and told her earnestly that whatever was wrong with me, it was <u>not</u> okay for her to take on any of it. Once a week I took her to a vet who did doggy acupuncture just to make sure she was as balanced as possible. She never really warmed up to the process, but it seemed to increase her energy. For myself, I went to the Chinese School of Medicine to get acupuncture, but nothing seemed to give me more energy. No one knew what was wrong with me. No matter how much I cleansed or fasted, supplements and remedies had no positive affect. No matter how much I slept, I still felt hellishly exhausted, depleted, and drained. No matter how much time I spent in meditation, I was still frazzled, angry and depressed. Mostly I questioned myself and my choices while my frustration grew at being unable to sustain a positive attitude. I would not discover the actual cause of all my symptoms for another seven years.

On the positive side, it was during that same period that I became a licensed, nondenominational minister with the Universal Life Church. My motivation was that a friend of mine, who occasionally performed weddings, was unexpectedly called out of town on a family matter the week before a scheduled ceremony, and had asked me to fill in for her. The ceremony was already written and blocked, she'd gotten the couple's permission for a substitute officiant, and everything else she explained to me in detail before she left. My ordination was done through the mail and the church's only stipulation was that I read through and uphold its list of innocuous tenets. I was not concerned about such lax requirements since my years of personal study had given me such a rich overview and more than perfunctory knowledge of the world's leading religions and philosophies. The day before the wedding, I received my legal church papers in the mail and was all set to perform the nuptial.

I wasn't nervous. I'd always felt comfortable in front of an audience as a child. From the time I was seven until I was eighteen, I studied classical ballet to overcome my alleged clumsiness, and looked forward every year to our performance at the local auditorium of "The Nutcracker" or "Swan Lake". Being on stage was the one place I could shine, let my soul and emotions show, and not fear my mother's cruel judgment and wrath. On stage she couldn't touch me, figuratively or literally, couldn't beat me down, and couldn't squelch my spirit. In front of an audience, I was safe and I felt that same safety, glow, and enjoyment in front of this couple and their guests. The wedding ceremony went off without a hitch. I knew I wanted to do more of them.

Then, in 1997, the autumn of Buttons' thirteenth year, everything happened at once. My VW bus failed emissions inspection and would cost hundreds more than I had to make the repairs for it to pass. A few days later, my landlord informed me that I would either have to purchase my mobile home or move out of it in the next two months when my lease was up. I was miserable, afraid, confused, feeling without options and not thinking clearly. I had little stamina, either physically or emotionally, but without a safety net of any kind, stopping just wasn't an option. And so, I continually dug deeper within myself and pushed my body and mind even harder into well-past overdrive. I had Buttons to take care of. Collapsing was just out of the question.

A week later, my mother was diagnosed with brain cancer and died just a few months after that. I was amazed at the compassion I felt for someone I had spent my entire life terrified of or hating. I attributed those higher feelings to my daily meditation practice and vigorous spiritual study. Since I'd only spoken with my mother a half-dozen times in the last twenty years, it was my cousin and her husband, having had a closer relationship with my mom, who took care of her during her final days. One morning Rachel called, exhausted and emotionally spent. "Your mom hasn't had anything to eat or drink for almost two weeks. She won't let go. Last night one of the women from Hospice who was here said that that usually happens when a dying person has serious, unresolved emotional issues with someone. I thought of you. If I put the phone next to her ear will you talk to her?"

"Of course," I answered and then I heard my mother's weak, dying voice.

"Na...dine?"

I had no idea what I would say.

"Hi, Mom. Mom, it's okay to let go now. You've suffered for too long. Everyone's waiting for you: Grandma, Grandpa, Uncle Arthur. It's going to be okay, Mom. It's okay. Mom? I'm strong because of you."

My words surprised even me. I shouldn't have been surprised at what happened next, though. In a voice I hadn't heard in decades, twisted with anger, revulsion, and this time, Dilantin too, my mother slowly hissed, "You liar!"

Then there was silence and then my cousin, who apologized, thanked me and said goodbye. A few hours later, my mother was dead. I lit a candle. I had mourned for my mother years before in therapy. I hoped her soul could heal now and finally find some peace.

My credit was already overextended, so buying any kind of newer car (let alone a mobile home) was out of the question. I needed to work and live somewhere where I wouldn't need a car. Apartment hunting in San Francisco seemed to be my next option, but I soon discovered that even renting one room in someone's apartment where I could have a dog would cost far more than I could foresee affording. Then I had another idea. On a friend's computer, I made a bunch of flyers that read:

> Friendly, responsible, clean & quiet 42-year-old woman and her friendly, responsible, clean & quiet 13-year-old small dog looking for live-in work. Can cook, clean, manage, organize, run errands, etc. Both have excellent references.

Early one Tuesday morning, I borrowed Pam's car and drove up to Petaluma, which is most commonly recognized for either its free-range chicken or the tragic kidnapping of Polly Klaas. It is a rather sleepy California town surrounded by sprawling ranches, wineries and olive groves. The earthy, feminine hills roll on and on and are blanketed year round with either vibrant green or shocking gold. I plastered the flyers everywhere I could. I figured if I was going to find a live-in work situation, my luck would be better in that community than in Santa Cruz, which has more young professionals than well-to-do families. From most anywhere in town, I could walk to the Tuesday night meditations and get a ride out to the BMCM ashram itself on Sundays when nonresident students were welcome to participate there.

My first time ever at the BMCM ashram, named Ramagiri (pronounced RA-ma-gear-ee, and which in Sanskrit means hills of joy), was when I had driven up from Santa Cruz the year before. I'd looked forward to seeing where Sri Easwaran and many of his very first students, mostly college professors from Berkeley, had lived for the last thirty years.

As I approached the property, I remember thinking to myself, now don't get upset. You are bound to be disappointed. After all, you've spent several years reading about this place and imagining it in your mind and nothing could possibly live up to those expectations. So just be mellow and in the moment and take it for what it is.

Turning onto the half-mile access road that led to the property, the peace was discernible. I pulled into the small dirt parking lot and got out of the car.

The first building I saw was Shanti (pronounced SHON-tee, which in Sanskrit means peace), the ashram's meditation hall. It was a simple wooden chapel with stained glass windows, built by the monks who originally developed the acreage as a working dairy farm decades before. Everywhere there were flowers: wisteria vines, jasmine, and green, lush bushes and trees. A sweet, hypnotic scent filled the air, and I realized that this was one of those lovely times in life when the actual experience of something is better than the anticipated one. It was obvious that the people living there worked hard and lived healthy, balanced, devoted lives without excess or waste. Easwaran's longtime students raised their children to honor their imaginations and to respect themselves, the planet, and each other. Everywhere I looked, that focus was reflected: in the structures, the land, the residents' faces. It felt like heaven on earth and I wished that Buttons was with me. I hoped to return as a volunteer, which I did the following year.

After plastering most of Petaluma's bulletin boards and business windows with flyers, my sore, tired feet drove me over to the church where the Tuesday night program took place. There in the courtyard I saw the church's minister, Rev. Linda, and asked her permission to put a flyer on their bulletin board. As she scanned the paper I'd handed her, her face brightened. "I know of a woman and her husband who are looking for a live-in to help them care for her elderly mother, Ina. Ina's a long-standing member of this church."

Suddenly excited, I followed Rev. Linda into her office where she called Ina's daughter, Breanne, and read my flyer to her and her husband, Turner. After speaking briefly with Breanne, we set up a time for a longer call the following day. Hopeful that my problems might soon be solved, I drove back home to Buttons and Santa Cruz.

Our conversation the next day was extremely comfortable, and we knew we liked each other right away. Breanne, Turner, and Ina lived outside of Petaluma, closer to Santa Rosa, on ten acres of Sonoma Mountain. Breanne commuted to San Francisco for work, staying during the week in their apartment in the city, and Turner was a talented craftsman whose workshop was on the property. We made plans to meet the following week at their home in the country.

Once again I borrowed Pam's car and made the three-hour drive with Ms. Buttons in tow. Turner met us as we pulled up and a moment later Breanne emerged from the main house to greet us also. There were a few other dogs and cats on the property, and I could see they were well loved and cared for. An ample vegetable garden graced the land along with several older storage buildings of various sizes and a small, newer looking shed with a sliding glass door. The shed turned out to be Breanne's art studio, though she said she'd been too busy to spend much time in it since her mother had come to live with them. Then Breanne took Buttons and me into the small guest apartment off Turner's workshop to meet her mother.

Ina seemed a sweet, frail, white-haired lady in her 80's, who kept herself busy with TV, books, and crossword puzzles. Breanne explained that my weekly duties would be to grocery shop, prepare and serve three nutritious meals a day, get Ina dressed in the morning and ready for bed at night, and help her bathe a few times a week. There was another woman, Juanita, who came in twice a week to do all the deep cleaning and laundry.

Breanne continued to explain that I was welcome to be off-property anytime between duties. In exchange they would provide a tiny bedroom in the guest apartment with her mom, space in one of their storage buildings for my furniture and possessions, a small weekly salary and board. The next thing she proposed touched me so deeply I was moved to tears. She said she understood from Rev. Linda that I had recently sold my vehicle (since I couldn't register the bus for an additional three years, I'd scrapped it for $100 cash) and that my original plan was to be in town so I could participate more fully with the BMCM. But because she and Turner lived so far from the ashram and the Tuesday evening church location, if I wanted the position, she would like to also offer a low-interest loan for a few thousand dollars so I could buy a used car. It was clear to me that Breanne and Turner were honest, intelligent, and warmhearted people. There were acres of land for Buttons to explore and enjoy here. We shook hands on the deal.

Back in Santa Cruz, I asked my friend Anthony from the choir, if I could hire him to find a reliable used Toyota for me in my price range. He had good basic mechanical skills and had successfully purchased dependable used Toyotas for several of his family members. It seemed like the smartest thing to do, wiser than trusting myself in the automobile arena. It also eased any added pressure so I could focus instead on packing and moving in my less-than-vibrant state of health and mind. He agreed to help and a few weeks later I was driving a thirteen-year-old Camry. Compared to the VW bus, it drove like a dream.

Even though an independent, certified mechanic had checked the car over and given it the green light, I felt funny that Anthony had found the car at a used lot instead of finding a sweet deal on something in the paper from an original owner, as I had expected. Once again, I should have listened to my intuition, but as the saying goes, we always do the best we can with the knowledge we have at the time. Almost immediately, I had to start sinking more dollars into it than the original purchase price just to keep it running. It seemed I just had bad car karma.

Living in the country there on Sonoma Mountain was certainly tranquil at the start. My tiny bedroom had big, new windows that looked out on the back hill of a neighbor's ranch where there were always several graceful horses grazing. Buttons didn't have any problems with the cats on the property and she loved running around the place, especially in Turner's woodshop with all its wonderful smells. I was able to participate more fully at the BMCM, and though like so many ailing, elderly people, Ina proved to be extremely manipulative and hard to please, she was also intelligent, interesting and well read.

Turner was helpful, kind, had a pleasant sense of humor and was easy to get along with. Breanne, I learned, was an expert organic gardener, calligrapher, soap maker, accomplished yoga student, gourmet cook, cancer survivor, and high-powered corporate success. We became fast, trusting friends.

She had my lifelong loyalty the moment I realized how she totally understood and honored my connection with Buttons. Perhaps the fact that she and Turner had never had children and always had pets was part of the reason. And so, when Ina suffered a stroke a few weeks after I'd moved in and suddenly needed constant, committed, round-the-clock care, I gave it, literally, all I had.

At first we tried just upping all of my duties: after returning from the hospital, Ina could no longer be left alone for more than a few minutes. We worked it out so my grocery store trips were when Turner was available to break away from his work in the adjoining woodshop and check in on Ina. Otherwise, I could no longer leave the property on my workdays except when Breanne was home from San Francisco on the weekends, or Juanita were there to take over.

One way I took advantage of my highly limited freedom was to spend most Sundays at the BMCM ashram. That's when we volunteers worked in the Nilgiri Press bindery, which printed many of Sri Easwaran's books, located there at Ramagiri. We did whatever needed doing: collating chapters, packing boxes, or folding book jackets. It felt good knowing we were making at least a small contribution and being a part of something that would go on to touch so many lives and help so many other people. Sometimes we helped in the office or the organic vegetable garden. Other times, help was requested in the kitchen, which was often overseen by one of the ashram's longtime residents, Laurel Robertson, author of the bible of vegetarian cookbooks, *Laurel's Kitchen.* Cooking under Laurel's direction is one of many fond memories I hold from my time there. Laurel is incredibly creative, and I watched her take the simplest of natural ingredients and expertly turn them into nutritious meals as tasty and interesting as any four-star restaurant I'd ever dined at in Chicago.

After a structured morning of meditation and chores, Sunday volunteers were welcome to partake of that home-cooked afternoon meal. Sometimes after lunch Sri Easwaran would give an inspirational talk, which always left me feeling encouraged and with a deeper sense of inner awareness and peace, temporarily balancing my otherwise increasingly frazzled and exhausted state. Volunteers were then welcome to return for evening mantra chanting and meditation. Often, Sri Easwaran would join us for that meditation. Just his presence in the room seemed to provide an inner atmosphere of extreme focus and intensity.

On one Sunday afternoon during the break between chores and evening meditation, I drove from Ramagiri towards the ocean, turned off on a deserted country road and pulled over. Under a grove of old eucalyptus trees, I sat in my car eating an avocado and sprout sandwich I'd made that morning. Across the road I gazed at a lovely, rolling hillside covered with thick, emerald green grass. Instantly in my mind's eye, I saw my Baby Girl zooming up, down, and across that hill and thought of how much she would love it there. I set my sandwich down, and my eyes filled with tears as I realized that this was how it would someday be for me when she was physically gone. Never in my life would I be able to look at an empty beach or grassy area without thinking of Buttons and wishing I was watching her enjoying it. A wave of bittersweet emotion passed through me.

A movement caught my eye and I looked up to see a speck of white coming over the top of the hill. And then there was more movement and more white as an entire flock of sheep came trotting over the ridge and down the face of the hill towards the road. I chuckled, imagining Buttons on that hillside too, her front end low to the ground, her back end high in the air and tail curled on top of her back while she barked out a warning to the sheep before darting off to do the same thing a few feet away.

I wondered for a moment what was real, our physical bodies that age and die and disintegrate or was it those feelings in our hearts, the love and the connections we make that are timeless? Saint Teresa of Avila wrote, "Everything is changing: God alone is changeless." What is God but love, I thought? I believed that nothing died but merely changed form, evident by standing in any forest and observing. A tree falls, and where it rots, bright green ferns or flowers spring up, fed by the fertilizer the tree has become. The cycle appears endless. And there I sat, several miles from where Buttons was physically at that moment (probably under the bed) and yet I could absolutely feel her there and was cognizant of her feeling me. As a culture we tend to accept this collapse of time and space when it comes to the connectedness between human loved ones, especially in reference to the mother-child bond. I was a pet parent. Did DNA and species really matter, or was it specifically the love we shared that connected us... any of us? After all, deep in the tiniest atom, isn't the energy of love/ God what holds everything together? Wouldn't I feel this same connection with Buttons when her body died? Wouldn't I continue to feel as I did now when she was just in the next room?

And then I didn't want to think about death and love anymore. I doubted that any of those thoughts would matter to me when the time came and I was without her. So I finished my sandwich and returned to Ramagiri for evening meditation.

On my other day off, when I had the energy to get out of bed, the Shtoonkhead and I spent time exploring the surrounding area. We found a wonderful place to hike on the other side of the mountain just outside the town of Glen Ellen, where Jack London had lived, worked, and died. I figured it had to be a good area for dogs if Jack liked it. It was actually off the beaten path, in the 162 acres of Sonoma Valley Regional Park where we discovered a gorgeous lake, which we could access by hiking in a ways from the main road.

There was a trail that wound completely around the water and up, out and through the surrounding hills. The trees, wildflowers and wildlife were teeming. Our two-hour hike led us through groves of maples, live oaks, white oaks, black oaks, madrone, and manzanita. Every color of the rainbow was proudly represented by the clumps of wildflowers growing everywhere. There we saw hawks, blue heron, ducks, and geese. Sometimes I stopped and sat at the water's edge with a sketchpad, trying to capture the opulence of life and feeling of splendor that nature's visual masterpiece bequeathed.

Buttons was blissed out, too. She always got a good, complete workout on that trail and her nose, ears, and tail worked nonstop as she pranced, climbed, ran, and explored.

Once when Natalie came up to visit from Santa Cruz, we took her there for a hike, and the last twenty minutes, got caught in an unexpected, heavy rainstorm. Back at Natalie's brand new white car, I was in a frantic rush to wipe all the mud off Buttons' paws before getting in. It was then I inadvertently left my redwood walking stick on the ground by the trail's head. At two o'clock that morning, I woke up startled and, realizing I'd never retrieved my stick, felt sick with loss. Not only was it a perfect, well-worn, personally fitted walking stick, but it also had miles and miles of "Nadine and Buttons" memories logged into it.

Later that gray morning, Natalie drove me back to the trailhead. It continued to drizzle but I knew there still had to have been a number of joggers, hikers, and dog walkers pass by since we'd been there the day before. I searched everywhere but my wonderful walking stick was gone. Finally, totally disheartened, I got back into the car. Instead of merely waiting, Natalie was leaning forward in her seat and staring with rapt concentration at a wall of bushes near the head of the trail. "What's that?" she pointed and asked.

I looked, saw nothing, and got back out of the car to walk over to the spot she'd been studying. Then I saw it. What she'd spotted was the four inches of lanyard hanging from the leather wrap I had near the top of my walking stick. Someone had stuck the whole stick into the bushes so just the lanyard showed. I was joyous and grateful beyond words for Natalie's keen sense of observation and for the kindness, integrity, and sensitivity of the person who'd found the walking stick and thought to put it in a safe place for me. I also felt disappointed that I would never have the opportunity to thank that person, to convey how important and appreciated their gesture was. I wished there were some way they could know how much sentimental attachment I had to the redwood walking stick that I was now so happy to have back in my possession.

It was about a month later that Buttons and I were able to get away and hike our "call of the wild trail" again. As we rounded a bend where the lake is marshy, we spotted a little girl around the age of five, up to her ankles in water, squatting down and examining some little, hopping toads. There was a hippyish young man with her, long hair, lean, and healthy looking, bending over and talking gently as he explained how tadpoles become toads. I heard her call him Daddy.

Buttons went over to cautiously sniff them and say hello. Then the father looked up as I approached.

"Hi," I said smiling.

"Hi," they cheered back.

And then the most wonderful thing happened. As Buttons and the little girl joined forces in a continued exploration of the hopping toads, the dad stood up, a look of surprise crossing his face before he broke into a wide grin and said, "Oh! You must be the one who lost the walking stick! I'm so glad you found it!"

I couldn't believe it. "Oh, my God—I never thought I'd have the chance to thank the person who found it and left it safe for me! Thank you so much! You have no idea how much this walking stick means to me!"

"Well," he responded, "I could see it was a really great, well-used walking stick. I knew whoever had forgotten it there would be back for it."

I explained about the miles of memories the walking stick held, how close Buttons and I were and about her cancer survival on all natural remedies. We talked about his day and his daughter. We both realized the gift we'd been given. From a world view of random chaos, the chances of our meeting were remote. But from the viewpoint of there being much more to life than what our rational minds can perceive, it was like being a part of a delightful magic trick executed with precision by the universe. We said our goodbyes with huge, grateful grins on our faces. Buttons and I couldn't have known at the time that we wouldn't be returning to Sonoma Regional Park and its glorious 162 acres ever again. Life had something else in mind for us.

Breanne's mother, Ina, became more demanding and disgruntled every day. She was on a lot of different medications for a variety of conditions and Breanne and I knew that most of Ina's negative attitude and behavior were a result of those medications. Still, knowing the reason didn't make her any easier to deal with.

She began ringing the "help" buzzer every couple of hours throughout the night. Usually she didn't need anything other than someone to pay attention to her when she was bored and couldn't sleep.

For a time Juanita, the woman hired to do the heavy cleaning, came to work the day shift and I worked the night shift. Unfortunately, that didn't improve the situation either. Despite frequent reminders, Juanita often seemed to forget that I was trying to sleep just a thin wall away from where she was spending her day. Often, after being up all night with Ina, I'd fall into an exhausted sleep, just to be jolted awake a couple of hours later by the sound of Juanita slamming the microwave oven door or turning on the vacuum cleaner.

Eventually, Buttons and I moved out to Breanne's artist shed. It had no heat or plumbing, but it afforded me some amount of quiet and it was big enough for my own bed, a small desk and chair, and some boxes of clothes. Turner strung a phone line out to it so Ina could call when she needed me. Often she'd call just as I lay down to rest after spending hours with her making sure she had everything she needed. There was always one more thing, though never anything important, and often something I had just offered her that she'd refused. Soon I couldn't please Ina no matter how hard I tried, making it impossible for me to continue. It broke my heart to have to burden Breanne with my quitting, but I just knew that I had reached the end. I was spent and exhausted and I had nothing left to give. I hadn't been hired to provide such involved, intensive care: I was hired as a basic housekeeper and very light caregiver.

And so Breanne found another woman to fill in the hours when Juanita couldn't be there. The new hire was trained, capable, and experienced in full-time geriatric caregiving. Buttons and I stayed in the shed. Breanne and Turner insisted we remain living there until we found a decent situation elsewhere.

Their kindness was unending and I was more than appreciative, but I was feeling a sense of desperation that never went away. The more I worried, the more I berated myself for ending up in such a situation. Knowing that all my emotional angst couldn't be good for Buttons, I pushed myself even harder combing the want ads and dragging myself out on interviews. And yet, my search for a live-in situation resulted in nothing I'd be even remotely comfortable moving into with Buttons.

Luckily, due to the incredible generosity of one fellow volunteer at the ashram, I was able to start doing some outcall massage at people's homes. Jen from Baltimore had a brand-new massage table shipped to me at Breanne and Turner's, after she and I had spent a month working together on Sundays in the bindery. Unfortunately, given my mysteriously failing health, my lack of an advertising budget, and the saturation level of massage therapists in California, I was hard-pressed to generate enough income to cover the credit card payments and my car loan.

As the days turned into weeks, I felt myself sinking helplessly, deeper and deeper, into the hopeless depression that I couldn't seem to prevent from blackening my entire outlook. Every morning I'd wake up feeling more exhausted than I'd been the night before. No matter how many or how few hours I slept, I never woke feeling rejuvenated, but rather, even more overwhelmed and debilitated. Most days I felt like I was trying to swim in mud. My brain was getting foggier and foggier. I could barely stay awake and yet, sleeping never left me feeling refreshed. I was reluctant to go even deeper into debt by getting more medical tests, since the doctors had been unable to find the cause of my physical decline the year before. And creeping around it all, like some pervasive, coastal fog, was that old sense of shame, unworthiness, and powerlessness.

In the meantime, prompted by my worry about Buttons and how all my stress had to be affecting her, I forced myself to muster the mental strength to pick up the phone and the Yellow Pages. I began making the dozens of phone calls and inquiries that after a time, led me to the best-reputed vet in the area who practiced holistic medicine along with his standard practice.

Buttons and I both enjoyed the long drive to the green, lush little town of Forestville: it was good to be focused on taking care of her instead of my seemingly optionless situation. During the course of the exam, the vet mentioned that Buttons' teeth had a lot of tartar, but I was too wary of anesthesia to risk a cleaning at her age. Instead, I would resolve to brush them more often even though I knew she hated the process. Eventually, I started putting drops of colloidal silver on her teeth while she was napping to prevent any infection or danger to her heart from the tartar and bacteria.

Also, while we were there, I had the vet do a complete series of blood and urine tests on the Butts. Two weeks later we returned for the test results. The vet walked into the examination room where Buttons and I waited as he flipped through the pages of her chart. Still reading from the clipboard he held, he sat down, and then suddenly stopped and looked up at me.

"How old is Buttons again?"

With a pang of fear I answered, "Fourteen... why?"

"Well, I'd swear these test results were for a dog no older than six or seven. She's the only dog we've run these types of tests on this month so they couldn't possibly be the results of some other dog. I'd still recommend you have her teeth cleaned, but other than that, she's remarkably healthy. What do you feed her?"

I started tearing up, partly out of relief and partly because by then my system was so overtaxed that just a small amount of adrenaline running through my veins left me feeling as if my very life had just been threatened.

A few days later one of my job seeds sprouted: a part-time opening at Copperfield's, the independent bookstore in Petaluma. I figured I could handle the pace. Even though I'd be making just over minimum wage, at least it was something. A couple I'd met at the Tuesday night meditation class had a room for rent in their house in town. Once again, Butts and I moved all our possessions to a new location.

My last night in the shed, I lay gazing up at the ceiling rafters above my bed and was reminded of a scene from one of my all-time favorite movies, *Shawshank Redemption*. In it, one of the characters, Brooks, who'd been institutionalized for sixty-some years of his life, is finally released from prison and enters a world he is totally unfamiliar with and terrified by. Eventually he realizes he will never adjust to life outside the prison walls or be able to cope with the new world that he's been thrust into and so he hangs himself in his rented room. But before doing so, he climbs onto a table, pulls out his pocket knife and on one of the rafters carves his name and message: "Brooks was here." Some years later, a younger man, fellow inmate, and good friend of his also makes parole and ends up in the same rented room. He, however, chooses to challenge his fear and meet life head-on no matter what lies ahead. When he gets ready to leave the room for the last time, he climbs up on the table and with his pocket knife, adds his message next to his old buddy's: "So was Redd."

I couldn't resist. Despite the kindness, caring, and generosity of Breanne and Turner, and Jen from Baltimore, besides being immersed in my spiritual practice and lucky enough to be studying so closely with Sri Easwaran in what would be the final years of his life, I felt utterly trapped and desperate. This time I wasn't heartbroken as I'd been when Connor left. This time I was just broken. I felt as if I was surviving a life in some kind of prison I couldn't even see and couldn't escape from. And yet I knew I couldn't give up. I couldn't give up because of Buttons. She was the reason I kept going. Grabbing my backpack, I pulled out my Swiss Army knife, climbed up and stood on my bed. On the rafter farthest from the door, on the back side in the uppermost corner I carved, "Nadine and Buttons were here."

It was the spring of 1998, while designing a window display at Copperfield's bookstore, that I had the idea. I'd been thinking about how much better it might be if I could do the live-in housekeeping-cooking thing for someone really wealthy. That way there might be a nice guesthouse or private guest wing and some acreage that I would feel good about moving Buttons to. Of course, I also wanted to be with her as much as I could instead of at a job for eight or more hours a day with her at home alone. I pored over the Yellow Pages during my lunch break. And then there it was—an agency in San Francisco that obviously catered to the wealthiest of clientele. I called and set up an appointment for an interview to register with them.

A few days later, I drove into San Francisco and located the agency, a bustling office on an upper floor of an older high-rise. Given my emotional and physical state, driving to an unfamiliar destination in the bustling city was no easy task, though I knew it was easier in the Toyota than it would have been in the VW bus. Bracing myself to make it through the interview, I put on my best "vibrant and capable" face and entered the building. After filling out a ton of paperwork, I met with the hiring director, Loren, a dynamic and forthright woman who looked to be about my age and with whom I immediately hit it off. She seemed impressed by my experience and maturity, explaining that the majority of her applicants were either very young or much older. Most of her clients wanted someone more my age.

She started listing job descriptions and the names of clients that she wanted me to interview with. I had either seen their movies or owned their albums. She especially pushed one she thought I'd be perfect for: he was an entertainer and movie star who happened to be my favorite comedian of all time. But he needed someone to take care of his city residence in a penthouse apartment. For the second time, I explained to Loren that Buttons was just as much a part of the package as I was and so, again, nothing right in the city would do unless they had a good-sized yard or private beach access. If I hadn't been feeling so desperate and unsettled, I would have gone on that interview just to get to meet the famous comedian, even though because of the unworkable doggy logistics, I couldn't take the job if offered.

As it was, I did get to meet one famous rock star from the '70s. The hallways of his home were adorned with platinum records. He and I got along fine and when the interview came to a close, he insisted I sit and share pizza with him and his fiancé in the TV room where they were about to watch the final episode of *Seinfeld*. It was one of those "damned if ya do, damned if ya don't" situations. Each of my first three polite refusals only met with more insisting on his part and so finally I opted to stay, which I found out later from Loren, lost me the job. As it turned out the rock star wanted to hire me, but the fiancé decided I was "too friendly" and "didn't know my place." I decided it was just as well. Who'd want to work for someone with that kind of an attitude? Plus, the rock star's still-touring band rehearsed in a room just below the guesthouse, which would have been mine. I was never that big a fan.

There were only a few interviews over the summer, since many of the clients who the agency provided staff for were vacationing in other countries. Four months after the rock star interview, the agency called and sent me to the elite community of Pebble Beach—about an hour south of Santa Cruz and four hours south of Petaluma. If I got the job it would take me away from the ashram, but comfort for Buttons and income for me were looming as far more important factors. Mr. and Mrs. D. were looking for a live-in house manager for their estate. They were my age and had no children other than their four big, stately dogs who were with them most of the time and traveled with the D.'s in their private jet. Their seven-bedroom house, located on the 17-Mile Drive, was filled with amazing furniture and incredible art. Next to expansive windows overlooking the ocean cliffs and the crashing waves just below, we sat in their living room talking. They explained that they had recently purchased another large home on several acres also in Pebble Beach and were in the midst of having architects and workmen gut and remodel the inside. Once the remodeling was finished and they were moved in, it would be the house where I'd be working if I were to come into their employ.

The new property included a thousand square-foot guesthouse with a distant ocean view and private yard surrounded by redwoods, which would be where Buttons and I would live rent-free if I got the job. It was early October and the D.'s explained that whomever they hired would, for the next several months until spring, only be responsible for doing occasional checks for damage to the current property during the stormy season. They would be spending the winter at their home in Texas. Until they returned, the only other responsibility for the person they hired would be to stop at the D.'s post office box and forward their mail once a week. Other than that, the job description for the next four to five months was to move into the guesthouse, settle in and be comfortable. When they returned in the spring the new employee would then need to handle cleaning, cooking, shopping, and errands until the remodel was complete and the rest of the staff hired. At that point, the job I was interviewing for would consist mainly of overseeing and managing the new staff while picking up any slack.

I could barely believe my luck. It seemed the perfect situation. The salary was more than twice as much as I'd ever earned before plus I would live rent-free in beautiful, safe surroundings and have full medical insurance. Jackpot.

They drove me up to the new property to see their house and guesthouse. The rolling grounds were old growth, opulent, and impeccable. The two-bedroom guesthouse with fireplace and mantle was classic and lovely. The D.'s explained that not only was I not the first person they'd interviewed, but that they had already hired and fired two other women.

Their voices were laced with irritation as they began telling me stories of dishonesty and betrayal. After a lengthy and enjoyable interview, Mrs. D. walked me out to my car to meet Buttons where she had been patiently waiting. They seemed to like one another. We shook hands and Mrs. D. said she'd contact the agency the following week with their decision.

I really had no idea what my chances were. It was a long drive home and an even longer week waiting. Finally, I got the call from Loren at the agency who said the D.'s would like me to return to Pebble Beach for a final interview that weekend. I drove back down and met Mrs. D. along with her twin brother who worked as her personal assistant. We had a pleasant conversation and then they excused themselves for a few minutes and left the room. I looked around and admired the fine fabrics, wood, marble, and sculpture. I looked out the window and saw a pair of whales swimming not too far out. I felt myself lusting for the security of the job and the much needed initial reprieve it would offer me.

Mrs. D. and her brother walked silently back into the room, sat down on the couch across from me, and then Mrs. D. offered me the position. She told me that I seemed responsible and reliable, had good references, and that they loved my smile. I did my best to disguise the avalanche of relief happening inside of me as I forced myself to appear unfazed. I thanked her politely and inquired once more as to the job responsibilities for the coming months. She reiterated that besides forwarding their mail and checking their first property for damage after any storms, I was on my own in my new guesthouse with pay. I sat silently as if considering for a moment. Then I calmly told her I'd be happy to accept the position as I leaned forward to shake her hand. My old friend at the radio station would have been proud; it was an Oscar-winning performance.

Afterwards, a couple of miles down the road from their estate, I pulled over, stopped the car and cried, yelped and yahooed. I still didn't know what was wrong with me physically, but I knew something definitely was. I knew I needed a lot of rest. I could use my new medical insurance and go for tests until they discovered what was causing the crushing fatigue, depression, irritability and allergies. I could do internal cleanses and fast and cook herbs. I could do all the things I knew to do to build back my immune system and strengthen my nerves. I could walk with Buttons on the beach and not worry about money! We could relax in our pleasing, safe, cozy new home. I could make us both happy and healthy and be my strong, hardworking, energetic self by the time spring came and I had to perform for the D's. I couldn't wait to get home and tell Butts.

That evening Mrs. D. called and told me that they wanted me to move into the guesthouse as soon as possible since they were planning to leave for their winter home in Texas the following week and preferred to have me on the property before they left. All I had to do now was make one more move. Refuge was just around the corner. Most of my things were still in storage, so I knew that with the help of a few friends, I could manage. A week later, I was happily unpacking my boxes in Pebble Beach, while Buttons was enjoying the soft, green grass of her new, luxurious yard. I was almost afraid to embrace all the relief our wonderful new situation promised. And then all hell broke loose.

A week after saying goodbye and leaving for their winter home, the D.'s unexpectedly flew back to Pebble Beach, having decided instead, that they wanted to be around for most of the remodeling. Their new plan was to split their time between Texas and California, a decision that forced me into emergency performance mode. When I wasn't getting everything ready for their arrival—shopping, cleaning, menu planning, cooking, errands—I was following up after their departure—laundry, dry cleaning, changing sheets, house-cleaning. While they were in town I was doing my best to take care of all their needs and meals and cleaning and errands. Once that included a large luncheon with business associates, personal friends, and a famous movie star with his family in attendance. Everything needed to be perfect. I needed a miracle. Somehow, I managed to pull it off, but just barely.

Mrs. D.'s twin/assistant helped a lot, but with no other staff besides the gardener we more than had our hands full. The D.'s didn't want to hire any additional staff until the remodel and move was completed. I felt beat up. I was wired all the time and tired all the time, feeling like I was sound asleep and on several pots of coffee simultaneously. I could barely control my emotions as a result. Where I once felt flexible, now I was rigid. Every request of theirs seemed monumental and totally overwhelming to me.

One morning Mr. D. called from Texas and asked if over the next few days while they were gone, I'd clean out his office closet and reorganize his sweater armoire. Dragging myself out of bed, I drove over to the house and went up to the master suite. When I opened the armoire door, a pleasant cedar scent came wafting out. It held five large shelves of neatly folded sweaters in colors so unusual and rich they belonged in an art museum. When I got to the bottom shelf, I found a pile of sweaters all balled up and thrown in. Sitting on the floor, I began pulling them all out. Their luxurious thickness and softness felt like no cashmere I'd ever felt before and I saw that they still had the price tags attached. The least expensive one read $1,800.00. Carefully I folded them, savoring the feel and sight of each one. It was the most sensual experience I'd had in months. Then I headed for the office downstairs.

I opened the closet door and stood staring at the disarray for a moment before starting to dismantle the precarious pile, topped with never before worn golf shirts and hats now crumpled up and dusty. Beneath them were discarded Tiffany gift boxes containing gorgeous cut glass pieces with the thank-you notes from the friends who'd sent them. Buried deeper, I found plastic bags from music stores holding hundreds of dollars worth of brand new, still shrink-wrapped CD's. As I cleaned and organized the unused items, I couldn't help thinking of the waste and uneven distribution of wealth they represented. I wondered how it must feel to have so much, that gifts worth thousands of dollars ended up in the bottom of a pile in a dusty closet. I began to wonder if I, too, would someday soon end up so easily tossed away and discarded by them.

It was becoming obvious that I couldn't keep up with the new, unexpected job description. Things were falling through the cracks and the more that was required of me, the wider the cracks grew. Of course, I knew before taking the position that I could never have handled such a pace in the condition I was in, but I hadn't seen the need to tell them that. I'd counted on the fact that the original terms were solid and that I'd have virtually no physical labor or emotional stress during the first several months in their employ. The now constant helplessness I felt was like holding a ticking bomb.

January of '99 began a year full of departures: JFK Jr.'s plane crashed, George Clooney left *ER*, and I was given a two-thousand dollar severance pay and let go from my job in Pebble Beach. I had shown up at the big house to work one morning and was in the middle of loading the dishwasher with breakfast dishes when Mrs. D. requested my presence in her office. She asked me to sit down on the couch across from her desk and then simply stated that things just weren't working out between us. She went on to say that I hadn't reached the level of ease and familiarity with their needs and ever-changing schedule that they required. She told me I'd have several weeks to pack and move off the property. I felt both relieved and terrified as I headed back to the guesthouse.

The stress of once again being faced with an unknown future (of course the future is always unknown, but now I felt stripped of even the illusion of knowing) and having to make another major life decision was paralyzing. Even Buttons didn't seem to want to be around me much. And who could blame her? For the most part, she kept to herself except for when we were riding in the car or walking on the beach. And then one day—a particularly overpowering self-pity day—I sat weeping on the phone and telling a friend that not only was I a total failure whose life sucked, but even my own dog didn't love me anymore. There was only a heartbeat of silence on my friend's end before he burst out in uncontrollable laughter. A minute later he was laughing so hard, he was almost crying himself, and pretty soon, I couldn't keep from laughing along with him.

Then very suddenly he stopped laughing altogether and in the most serious tone of voice he asked me, "How can you possibly believe that? Your dog loves you more than most people are loved by anybody. And that is not my opinion, that is fact."

"How do you know that?" I questioned.

"Because," he stated emphatically, "if she didn't love you and want to be with you, she would just leave."

"She couldn't. I watch her all the time. She never has the opportunity to get away."

As if he were explaining to a child, my friend then very slowly and exactingly said, "She absolutely could leave you easily. She would just have the cancer come back and die."

His words stopped me cold, and I knew he was right. My girl was indeed loving me unconditionally, the way dogs so eloquently do, and it didn't matter to her what decisions I'd made, what my life looked like, what I looked like, or what list of accomplishments I could or couldn't boast. She was simply her clear, Buddha-self, seeing only the love in my heart and perhaps the pain and struggle, too.

Calming myself, I did my best to get it together once more. Knowing I could no longer think clearly, I enlisted the suggestions and advice of my most trusted friends. Together they helped me see that the two thousand dollars I had to my name would last me only a few weeks trying to settle back in Santa Cruz or Petaluma. On the other hand, it could last me three or more months in Tucson, Arizona, where the cost of living was so much lower.

I called my cousin, who agreed to let Buttons and me stay in the guestroom of her home in Phoenix until I found a place in Tucson. Then I called a friend in Tucson who offered to begin looking for a cheap apartment for me. With each phone call I made, a part of me died inside, knowing I was breaking my promise to Butts about soft, green grass under her paw pads. Over the next few days, several friends drove down from Santa Cruz to help me once again, wrap and box up everything I owned. As a gesture of thanks, I gifted them all their favorite paintings of mine and hoped they knew how grateful I was for their friendship and help. I would miss them terribly.

I started noticing I was having a lot of trouble breathing—like I couldn't get enough air into my lungs. Everything in my body seemed to just be shutting down, but I wasn't somewhere where I could take the time to stop and care for myself. While still in their employ, I had seen one general practitioner in-between the D.'s visits, and had had a basic physical exam. But the doctor said more comprehensive tests were required to find out what was causing the radical fatigue and other symptoms. I'd been fired before I'd had the chance to set that up.

Knowing my car wasn't sturdy enough to haul all my possessions in a trailer behind it, I rented a U-Haul truck. Even though all my things would fit inside a small pick-up truck or van, U-Haul required that I rent its fifteen-footer in order to tow my car on a tow platform behind it. The thought of driving a thirty-foot-long load across two states scared me. I had no idea if I could handle the challenge.

The day before we left, I rented a video camera and, with a heart full of regret and remorse, took Buttons down to the beach one last time. Proving to me her continued dislike of being filmed, my freethinking, rebellious Poophead refused to run whenever I was pointing the camera at her. Thanks to the zoom lens, I was able to record her sniffing around in some sea kelp at least. No matter what her speed or energy level, her bliss and joy were always evident as she pranced along the sand. After a while I turned the camera towards the waves and just sat there filming. I would miss the ocean so much. Mostly I'd miss seeing Buttons so happy as she romped along the beach. I tried soaking it all deeply into my being: the sound, the smell, the feel on my skin, so I wouldn't forget. I closed my eyes and breathed slowly, knowing in that moment that no matter how bad it seemed things had turned out, many people never get to live by the ocean like we had.

We'd had some wonderful adventures, some glorious times, and

Buttons had sniffed and peed along hundreds of miles of ravishingly beautiful California coastline, each mile forever alive right there in our memories. The tears began streaming down my face. A few minutes later it started to drizzle. I was reminded of the lyrics to a Moody Blues song written by Jeff Wayne: "*A gentle rain falls softly on my weary eyes, as if to hide a lonely tear. My life will be forever autumn, 'cause you're not here.*"

Packing up the camera, I called to Butts and we got into the car and headed back to the guesthouse to finish packing. As darkness fell, my stomach began to growl, but the fridge was already emptied and cleaned so after rousing Buttons from her nap, I dragged myself into the car once more and the two of us headed for Monterey. So I wouldn't have to unpack any of my kitchen stuff, I decided to bring home chicken strips and cole slaw already prepared from the grocery deli. Back at the car, Buttons waited patiently in the back seat. A few blocks away I saw a Blockbuster's and decided to stop, run in, and rent a movie to watch during dinner. It only took a moment for me to make my selection. A few minutes after that we reached the Pebble Beach gate, stopped to show our pass and then headed the last few miles home. Starving and barely able to keep my eyes open, I pulled into the garage, turned off the engine and opened the car door for Butts. She jumped out and ran up the steps to the back door as I gathered the movie, my purse, and the grocery bag.

Once in the kitchen, I laid everything on the table, turned to wash my hands at the sink, and then grabbed some paper towels. Buttons beelined for her water bowl and began lapping. Reaching into the grocery bag, I pulled out the cole slaw and plastic utensils. Then I reached in for the hot chicken strips. However, the only thing left for my hand to retrieve was an empty plastic bag, which no longer contained any chicken at all, but had some very interesting looking teeth marks ripped into it. I couldn't believe it. She'd never done anything like that before. It would take another forty-five minutes and energy I just didn't have to go back into town and get more. As frustrated as it made me and as unhappy as I was about having only cole slaw for dinner, I loved the fact that here, almost fifteen years into our relationship, Buttons was still full of canine surprises. There in the midst of my hungry, dark and hopeless funk, I stood shaking my head and laughing. Perhaps the lesson she was imparting now had something to do with silver linings—with realizing that joy is not contingent upon circumstances, but rather, something to be found regardless of circumstances, right there in the present moment.

The morning of our departure was sunny and beautiful as I drove my car to the U-Haul office where my half-empty, yet fully packed, rental truck waited. The staff there hooked up the tow platform and secured my car onto it. I put Buttons in the cab, signed the last rental paper and climbed behind the steering wheel. This was not a happy event. I hated so many things about Tucson: its politics, climate, and biome, but I knew that an affordable place to rest and heal was essential. As I rolled down the window and filled my lungs with one last breath of salt air, I looked over at Butts who was excitedly standing post at her window. The pieces of my broken heart exploded into countless sharper shards as I turned the ignition key and put the truck into gear. Pulling out into the flow of traffic, I choked down my sobs and we began the next leg of our jour-ney—the one that would take my Poop and me away from our beloved beaches forever.

Our destination that afternoon was a motel near the Arizona-Califor-nia border that I'd found on the Internet. Not only did it allow dogs, but I had called and confirmed that they also had a parking lot encircling the entire building. There was no way I was going to try to maneuver an al-most thirty-foot-long load in reverse. If I couldn't get in and out without backing up, I simply wasn't going in.

The first few hours of driving were uneventful, and I began looking forward to arriving at my cousin's the following day. Then we stopped for gas. As I was filling the tank, the guy on the other side of the pump asked where I was headed. When I said Phoenix he looked upset. "Oh, boy, that means you're probably headed for the Grapevine and I-5 north of L.A., right?" I nodded and he went on to explain that he'd just come from there, and that there were icy conditions on the Grapevine, the mountain pass I intended to climb with my huge load. Great. Well, there was no turning back now. At least I wasn't in the VW bus. All I wanted in that moment was to get to that motel, lie down on the bed and zone out with a good book. Thanking him for the information, I took Buttons behind the station on her leash and when she was finished, we got in the truck and headed back out onto the highway.

So far the roads and the scenery had been pretty flat with rolling hills off in the distance. Soon the terrain became more rugged and then the mountains were looming before us. It was early afternoon and we were right on schedule—I had planned to be well past L.A. by rush hour. It, of course, was not to be.

The traffic had become heavy even though we were in the middle of nowhere and it was the middle of the week. There had been an accident on the other side of the highway on our side of the mountain and people just had to stop and stare. Soon we'd been jammed up for the better part of an hour. Finally, we began moving at the speed limit as we started our ascent.

The highway became steeper and steeper until we were near the slick, icy summit. It was gray and hard to see with the wind gusting and blowing snow and sleet all around us. I was in the middle lane because, along with my fear of snakes, I'm not too keen on heights. Driving such a long pile of machinery made the drop-off from the slow lane on the right more than I could bear. I was going fifteen miles under the speed limit, which seemed the sane and legal thing to do considering the weather and driving conditions. Apparently, none of the semi drivers agreed as they barreled past us on either side with their huge trucks. Every time one did, our truck would shake and start to swerve. I felt frozen with fear. Buttons looked terrified as she pressed herself against the back of the seat and trembled.

A bit worse for wear, we safely reached the bottom of the mountain where I breathed a sigh of relief and petted Butts to comfort her. It was no longer raining or sleeting on the side of the mountain we were now on and so the driving became much easier again. I reached into my back-pack on the seat and gave Butts a treat. A few more miles up the road I pulled over so we could both get out and pee. It was getting late.

By the time we reached the outskirts of L.A. it was dusk and hordes of cars were driving seventy-miles an hour nearly bumper to bumper. For twenty minutes, I felt like Big Bertha trying to get over into the exit lane. I wouldn't consider myself an overly aggressive driver, though definitely assertive when need be, but this was ridiculous. My turn signals were working, on, and yet, nobody would let me in. With turn signal blinking, I would begin inching my way over. My action served no purpose other than provoking an immediate cacophony of horn blaring from the cars in the right-hand lane. I knew my exit was coming soon. No way was I going to miss it and have to negotiate God knows what to get back en route to my motel in the dark.

I spotted my exit sign up ahead. I shot a quick look at Butts. She had her front paws on the passenger door armrest and was looking out her window. "You're a good little copilot, Pooper, come on over here and hang on," I told her. As soon as she turned around, moved closer to me and sat down, I braced myself, made sure my turn signal was on, laid on the horn and aimed right for the exit. At that point I figured one of two things would happen. Either several cars would come plowing into me and we'd all die, or everyone would just move the hell out of my way. Looking back, I think I may have actually closed my eyes, but thankfully, no one hit anyone or anything. A half hour later as Buttons and I pulled into the motel parking lot, I figured I had a pretty good idea of what a nervous breakdown felt like.

After parking the truck, I stumbled out on Jell-O legs. Buttons got out, squatted a few feet away and peed for what seemed like ten minutes. We walked into the motel office, and I gave the lady my name. She told me I looked awful. I thanked her, paid her, took the key and went to find our room. Inside, Buttons started doing her "I am hungry dance" as I fixed her some food and water. Suddenly I was starving and decided to hit the Sizzler Steakhouse next door since it was the only restaurant in sight. When Buttons was finished eating, I took her for a short walk and then back to the room. After petting her and telling her I would be back soon, I put one of my shirts on the bed for her and left. My rumbling stomach led me across the parking lot.

Inside the restaurant, I decided on the all-you-can-eat salad bar, paid, got my tray and proceeded to load up my plate. Sliding into an empty booth, I grabbed a fork and took my first bite only to realize that I wasn't really hungry after all—I was just thoroughly exhausted. Since I always began each day exhausted, it was difficult for me to tell exactly when I'd pushed myself so far that I was on the verge of collapse. Since I no longer had an internal thermostat by which to measure my degree of fatigue, I simply had two speeds: on and off. Tipping the waiter, I told him I was finished as he hesitatingly took my completely full plate and looked at me with a very confused expression.

At the pay phone in the entry, I pulled out my long-distance card and called Pam. In a few minutes, we were laughing hysterically at the events of the day while at the same time she empathized, and I cried in relief that it was over. I couldn't stand all the drama and realize now that what made everything so dramatic wasn't so much the events themselves as my uncontrollable panic over them, my lack of equanimity, and my inability to cope.

At eleven the next morning I woke up with a start. Luckily, checkout was at 11:30 so I had enough time to give Butts some food, jump in the shower and throw on some clean clothes. Even though I had given up caffeine seven years before, I grabbed a cup of coffee in the motel office when I returned my key. This was a special circumstance. I had four more hours of driving to do.

February 12, 1999 was cool and sunny and boasted one other special circumstance: it was also my girl's fifteenth birthday! I had already explained to her that we would not be celebrating in our usual fashion—a long hike somewhere she loved, but would, instead, have to postpone our celebration a few days. Of course, I did sing "Happy Birthday" to her several times and gave her many more treats than she would have gotten on any other day. I was happy to be nearing the end of this part of the move and was not expecting any more hitches in our travels. Ha!

I know it could have been worse. I am so grateful nothing went awry mechanically with the truck or tow platform. What happened instead was a big, violent, blinding sandstorm. One minute we were driving through clear and sunny desert and the next minute, I could barely see the hood of the truck. We passed cars and semis stopped on the side of the road. Giant green and white highway signs were blown partly off their poles and swinging precariously above our heads as we passed under them. Amazingly strong, deafeningly loud gusts of wind shuddered through the inside of the truck as they moved us all over the road and left a fine layer of sand on everything. Buttons couldn't seem to figure out what she was seeing, but just kept staring out the window with a confused look on her face. I kept shouting to her that it was okay.

In my mind, stopping wasn't an option. The shoulder was tiny and what I was driving was huge. Maybe the experienced semi drivers knew how to negotiate such conditions and not get stuck, but I didn't. Not willing to handle one more thing I'd have to think my way through, I just turned on the brights and plowed ahead. Twenty minutes later, the wind stopped gusting, the air cleared, and I took the next exit to a truck stop surrounded by gigantic plastic dinosaurs in the middle of the desert. I found some shade to park under, let Butts out to pee, and refilled her water dish. When I had her back safely in the cab, I walked over to the restaurant to have some breakfast and calm down.

It felt like I had stepped into a Vegas bar. Country music twanged loudly from the wall-mounted speakers and it was so dark inside it could have been any time of the day or night outside. There were rows of black vinyl booths each sporting a multicolored, glass-beaded, glowing light fixture and a credit card phone. I sat down and after a quick glance at the menu gave my order to the middle-aged, gum-chewing waitress. Then I picked up the phone, swiped my phone card and dialed Pam's number.

Serene Santa Cruz seemed like a million miles away. When Pam answered the phone, I didn't even bother saying hello. "It's so dark in this truck stop restaurant I can't tell if it's night or day out. There's country music blaring from the speakers on a wall across from where I'm sitting, in a black vinyl booth complete with totally, tacky-looking multicolored, hanging glass light..."

By the time I got to describing the sandstorm I'd just driven through, she was laughing uncontrollably on the other end. Each wave of her laughter just spurred me on to the next description. She told me it was all so unbelievable that I should write a book. How wonderful it was to have her accepting, compassionate friendship to turn to and her laughter to nurture my heart. I'd needed someone who could help me see the humor of my life as I desperately tried to keep it from completely falling apart.

It was late afternoon when I pulled onto my cousin's street and parked, taking up most all of the cul-de-sac she lived on. Somewhere in my brain, I could not comprehend being back in Arizona. I had shouted, "Good riddance!" out the VW bus window when I'd left Tucson five years before and never expected to be living there again. The air was uncomfortably dry on my skin as I climbed out of the truck's cab. After a nice reunion with my cousin and her family, a home-cooked meal, and a few phone calls to friends in Tucson, I fell dead into bed.

The next morning, after making sure Buttons was as comfortable as possible at my cousin's, a place she was at least familiar with, I headed down to Tucson by myself to drop off the truck and tow platform. Two hours later as the mountains surrounding the city came into view, I felt myself go backward in time. This was the last place I ever expected to be moving to again. I wondered what had gone so wrong, but there really wasn't time to pay any attention to my feelings.

My old friend Linda and her fiancé, Kurt, met me at the U-Haul office to help me unload my furniture and boxes from the truck and into a small storage unit there. Linda and I had met and worked together years before at the radio station. After thanking them, taking care of the paperwork in the U-Haul office, and getting my car disconnected and off the tow platform, I headed out for a lunch date with my old friend Paige and her good friends, Dr. and Mrs. Ryan Lodge. Though I had heard a lot about them, I had never met the doctor or his wife.

Lunch was easygoing and enjoyable and it was satisfying to be making some new friends in Tucson. Afterwards, I headed to my friend Hanna's house. She'd been doing some apartment hunting for me. We drove around for hours looking at places in my price range, a hundred or so dollars above the cheapest available and in neighborhoods we knew to be relatively safe. We saw a lot of horrible dumps. I spent the night at Hanna's, and the next day hit the classifieds and the streets again. Still nothing. That evening, I made the two-hour drive back to my cousin's in Phoenix.

Wrapped in feelings of failure, I went to bed that evening, relieved that at least our stuff was in safe storage in Tucson and that the truck and tow platform were returned. Later that night I woke up with a raging fever.

The next two days I spent sick in bed, shivering, burning up, badly congested, and completely wiped out. My cousin brought me juice, her daughter drew me pictures, and her son complained that I was occupying the guest room where he liked to watch TV in the afternoons.

My third day there, Hanna called about an apartment. She'd already gone to see it and was sure I'd like it. I called the landlady and scheduled a showing for the next day. Still very weak and ragged, I drove down to Tucson. The one-bedroom apartment was half of a duplex in a neighborhood I was familiar with. The inside was knotty wood paneling, which I thought gave it a nice mountain cabin feel. Though more than a bit on the shabby side, the living room had a high, vaulted ceiling and space enough for my living room furniture and a place where I could set up my massage table when I had a client. The room then wound around to a small kitchen that opened to a short hallway leading to the bedroom and bathroom. There was ample closet space and a built-in dresser in the bedroom. The floor was an ugly old dark-brown tile, but the rent was real cheap and, overall, it was heads above anything else I'd seen. There was a side door that led out to an overgrown, partially fenced shared yard and I knew I could block off an area relatively cheaply and easily to make a secure place for Buttons. I made a mental note to buy a Weedwacker.

We were about to move into our ninth home (if you counted our stay at my cousin's) in six years, our fourth move in the last fourteen months, and by now Buttons cowered whenever she even saw a cardboard box. I wondered how I could make this next move as untraumatic for her as possible and decided I would move everything into the new place and have it all set up before bringing Buttons there.

The next morning I met some friends at the U-Haul office in Tucson where we loaded my things from storage into another rental truck. Five hours later we had everything in the new apartment and the truck returned. I drove back up to Phoenix where Buttons waited nervously. Her energy and behavior were different. She seemed hesitant and wary. She knew something was changing again. I gave her some Rescue Remedy, the Bach Flower Remedy for trauma. I did my best to reassure her and make her feel safe by talking to her softly and soothingly. I had no real plan or inkling of what the immediate future would hold. All I really wanted was to rest and recover. My wish was about to come true, more dramatically than I ever would have expected.

I spent the next day at the apartment in Tucson cleaning, unpacking, moving furniture, and getting phone and utilities hooked up. Despite the exhaustion, somehow I just kept moving. Not only did I feel drained of energy, but totally hollow. Each moment felt more torturous to me than the last, like the feeling you get when you're fighting the hypnotic effect of the road while on an extremely long drive.

I discovered that the walls between my apartment and the other half of the duplex were so thin I could hear everything my neighbors said. In my weakened condition, I had become extremely sensitive to smells, especially alcohol-based scents, which gave me headaches that would often turn into debilitating migraines. It was upsetting to realize that whenever my neighbors would spray cologne, deodorant or hairspray in their bathroom, I could smell the chemical fumes in mine. I reminded myself to be grateful for cheap rent. I consoled myself with the fact that for the first time in almost two years since leaving Santa Cruz, Buttons and I were back in a dwelling of our own without being under the jurisdiction of an employer or subject to the habits of roommates.

There was a knock at the door. A friend I'd met a year before moving to California and whom I'd reestablished contact with since landing back in Arizona, had come by with a gift of potted flowers. After seeing my apartment, Trina suggested we get a piece of carpeting she had in storage at her mom's, one that would fit nicely in my new bedroom and cover the ugly brown tile.

Once there, we lifted the roll of carpeting from the garage floor and hoisted it into Trina's car. Then on the way back to my apartment, in the midst of general small talk she abruptly announced that she had something important that she had to tell me. Like a smoldering pile of ash suddenly bursting into flame, for the first time in days, I could feel a sensation inside me other than emptiness. What I felt was a burning sense of impending doom. At the next red light she turned to me and blurted out,

"A few years ago I was involved with a man... it was Connor."

Frozen. Numb. Shock. *Don't feel this*. I stared down at my hands on my lap.

Nervously, she went on, "We met at a concert. He came on to me really strong. After a few dates, I told him we had a problem—that I knew you and that you and I had become friends before you moved to California. He shrugged his shoulders and said there was no reason why that should change anything. That it didn't matter. I'm so sorry, Nadine."

It didn't matter?! I didn't matter. Shrugged his shoulders?!? I really need this carpet. Just get the carpet in the bedroom.

"Say something, Nadine," she pleaded.

A million questions raced through my mind. "How is he?" I managed to ask.

"Well, I don't know. We were together for a few months, and then he broke up with me because I really want to have children and he didn't. I haven't heard from him since. I do know he had been involved with several other women before he and I met, and I heard that he's had a few other relationships start and end since. I'm really sorry."

Of course he didn't want children. I could have told you that. He's Buttons' Dad. SHE'S his child. God, Connor!

"I really don't know how to deal with this now," I told her, "Can we just get the carpet down? I still have a lot to do, and then I have to drive up to Phoenix tonight."

Automatic pilot.

"Sure," she said, sounding very relieved.

We pulled into my driveway and unloaded the heavy roll. I couldn't look at her. Maneuvering the carpet through the twists and turns of the apartment, into the bedroom and underneath the bed was no easy task, but easier than thinking about what she'd just told me. As soon as we were finished I thanked her and she left. Closing the door behind her, I sank into the nearest chair. This was why I'd left Tucson five years before—this feeling here. I knew in hindsight how stupid it was to have moved someplace as expensive as the Bay area with a shoddy vehicle, credit card debt, and no savings. But now I remembered exactly why I'd had to leave Tucson. Since I'd known someone in California and been offered a waitress job and a temporary place to stay, it had seemed the best decision at the time.

I thought about what Trina had said about Connor having been in many other relationships. Maybe he was still searching for that permanent head-over-heels feeling? In a way, her information made his rejection of me feel more personal. In another way, it made it feel less personal. Maybe he was never really in love with me but just in love with being in love?

Dragging myself back up, I unpacked Buttons' bedding, which she always liked under the table I used as a home altar. I put it there now, tucking it lovingly into its new place in front of the picture window. Instead of putting everything that was still out into the cabinets and closets, I folded up all the cardboard boxes and walked them to the storage shed out back. Taking the new Weedwacker out of its box, I cut down all the growth in the side yard, unwound the small fencing I'd bought and pounded it into the hard ground. A detached part of me merely witnessed myself as I performed each task. But the emotional part of me felt like a woman in a Steinbeck novel—pushing on to do what's next because it has to be done, because to not do it is to die.

I locked up the apartment and drove back up to Phoenix, keeping the radio loud and my mind as quiet as possible. I made Buttons her dinner and then sat in the back yard with her for a bit while she ran around. She was unusually affectionate that evening. I noticed I was once again having trouble breathing.

In the morning, I thanked Rachel and her family for all their hospitality and loaded Buttons and the rest of our stuff into the car. I had the distinct feeling that she expected we were headed back home to California and the beach. Guilt clutched my heart as I pulled out of the cul-de-sac and anticipated her disappointment when we arrived instead in Tucson. She seemed more skeptical in each new place we settled. I knew it had been a wise choice to have things mostly in place and no boxes out when she arrived at the new apartment.

When we got there, she entered hesitantly. As she sniffed around and found her own things, I filled her bowl with treats and gave her some water. All considered, she grew accustomed to the new surroundings pretty fast. She was most certainly my little trouper, and I wished I could be as flexible as she was. When she lay down on her bed under the altar, I turned on the stereo and began scrubbing the inside of the dirty kitchen cabinets. I wanted to feel settled and organized. I wanted to avoid thinking about Connor. I was still having a hard time taking a deep breath.

By afternoon, the last cabinet finally filled with items I'd had out on the counter, I began crossing the room so I could organize my paints over by my easel. All of a sudden, I stopped, unable to get enough breath and desperately gasping for air. No matter how deeply I tried to breathe, the suffocating sensation would not stop. Really frightened now, I finally figured out that down on the floor on all fours was the only position I could be in to fill my lungs enough. I crawled over to the phone and called Hanna. No answer. I dialed a few other people. No one was home. Then, hearing my neighbors outside, I crawled to the front door and opened it. Instantly willing to help, they got me into their truck, and answering my plea, drove me to Dr. Lodge's office.

As soon as we arrived, his receptionist paged him. We hadn't seen each other since we'd met at lunch the week before, but from the start, he treated me as if we'd been good friends for years. The first thing he asked was if I had insurance, not in regard to his fee, he assured me, but because he could tell immediately that I needed to be hospitalized. When I shook my head no, he helped me into the examining room and onto the table. He spoke reassuringly as he explained his every step of setting up the magnesium I.V., which he explained would give me a strange sensation of warmth inside while it opened up my lungs so I could breathe normally. Though he was a traditionally trained allopathic M.D. and well-reputed diagnostician, he was also extremely well versed and trained in many alternative modalities. He already knew from our conversation at lunch that holistic was my first choice.

Twenty minutes later the crisis had passed. We talked for the next forty-five minutes. He did a basic exam, and then told me he suspected I was suffering from severe chronic fatigue syndrome (CFS) or adrenal exhaustion or both. He looked me dead in the eye when he told me that judging from my current condition, he believed I should have collapsed at least two years before I did. Maybe he hadn't read much Steinbeck.

Then he proposed that he treat me as if I could afford it, but keep a tab and have me pay it off in massage trade when I was well. God had sent me an angel. He told me to go home and do nothing but rest and drink fresh vegetable juice. I knew exactly which cabinet my juicer was in.

A week later, he called with the results of my blood and other lab tests which all supported his original diagnosis: CFS and exhausted adrenals. It explained a lot: the unending, debilitating fatigue, depression, brain fog, allergies, panic, and breathing difficulty. In truth, I was still several years away from a completely accurate diagnosis.

Dr. Lodge prescribed various supplements and ordered that I not work for two to three months. I couldn't have worked anyway. Making juice, doing a bit of grocery shopping and taking care of Buttons was the most I could handle on a really good day.

I slept, meditated, took supplements, and read. Sometimes I journaled and cried and wrote about how much I still missed Connor and now Santa Cruz, too. At the same time I kept a list of all the things I was grateful for which mostly consisted of Buttons, Dr. Lodge, and being able to breathe. I wrote out plans for increasing my massage business when I was well and reminded myself that although I had made many less-than-good decisions, I had done the best I knew how at the time. I had always kept my focus and direction as far as my personal growth and deepening my spiritual life went, regardless of outside circumstances.

Dear friends called every few days from California, and between their calls I slept. There were many days I had only enough energy to feed Buttons and get up a few times to let her outside and then back in.

Buttons slept a lot too. She was still healthy, vital and strong, yet I knew she'd slowed down some. I knew the stress of all the moves along with time itself had made her older. If we couldn't be in California, I wished we could at least be in a place with a nicer yard for her. We lay in bed together as I petted her and sang to her and loved her. As always, she was a great comfort to me, and I tried not to worry about my precarious situation. I tried very hard not to stress about my dwindling Pebble Beach severance pay. I suspected that my more or less constant fearful thinking was at the heart of many of my physical symptoms.

After two months of supplements, resting and not worrying too excessively, I felt somewhat better. When I finally felt well enough to get bored, I asked myself what things I'd always wanted to do, but had never before had the time for, and two different ones came to mind: learning to play the violin and learning sign language. Because of its affordability sign language won, and I made my way to the library where I checked out twelve Sign videos. It was more complicated than I had anticipated and fun from the start. I tried interpreting some very simple songs, beginning with the ones I sang to Buttons—mostly made-up ditties and popular tunes whose lyrics I'd customized just for her. Her hearing wasn't what it used to be so I tried teaching her a few signs. She quickly picked up the meanings for "outside?", "cookie?", "no!", and "good girl!"

As my health slowly improved, I began taking on a few therapeutic massage clients: first friends and Dr. Lodge, who also began referring some of his other patients to me, and then eventually word-of-mouth referrals. Having the stamina to do only two or three massages a week meant I wasn't earning nearly enough to live on, but at least there was some money coming in. Although performing massage is physically demanding, the next best thing to getting one is giving one, and I was certainly enjoying the freedom of self-employment.

One of my favorite massage clients at that time was a woman named Gayle who started coming to me via Dr. Lodge. Gayle had also been suffering from CFS and many of its accompanying conditions. She came for bodywork twice a month and as those months passed we got to know each other well. I loved listening to her stories about her large, happy, close-knit family including LeRoy, her beloved husband of almost thirty years, their children, grandchildren, elderly parents, sons-in-law, and family dogs. I never tired of hearing of their adventures and interactions so filled with love, laughter, music and singing. Their entire family dynamic was so incredibly different from mine. They were refreshingly open with each other and fully and deeply supportive of one another in every way possible. They also had a lot of fun together, something I have no memory of with my parents, at least not without it ending in some type of argument or tirade.

One day after her massage, Gayle was perusing my bookshelf when she said, "Oh! I see you've read some of Hugh Prather's books."

"Yeah," I answered, "I also saw him speak twenty years ago at Unity Church in Chicago. I remember he started out the talk by saying that each of us were there hoping to find the answer to life, but that we'd all known it since we were small children. He said the answer was simply, 'row, row, row <u>your</u> boat, <u>gently</u>, down the stream.' I guess I've been so busy just trying to keep my boat afloat, I haven't paid much attention to the quality of my rowing!"

"Well," Gayle continued, "Hugh lives here in Tucson and gives free classes a couple times a week at St. Francis in the Foothills Church." She went on to explain that he gave a general class on Wednesday evenings and a class for couples on relationships on Sunday mornings, which she and Leroy often attended. She asked me if I would like to go with her some time, and I agreed enthusiastically.

A few weeks later, I met Gayle and Leroy at the Sunday morning class. Although I'd had a few casual involvements since Connor, I still wasn't in a serious relationship, but I hoped to be someday and figured the more skills and tools I had, the better. From that Sunday on, I attended almost every Wednesday and Sunday class Hugh gave until he took a sabbatical more than a year later. He spoke of how to bring inner peace, kindness and tolerance to all situations and shed light in the dark corners of ego. The classes were always comfortable and entertaining as Hugh wove his delightful humor and insight into every problem or question presented for examination. I especially loved the day he spoke about love in relationship to pets. He said, basically, that every committed relationship whether it is between romantic partners, parent and child or, no less important, between human and pet, is an arena blessed and rife with opportunity to explore and dismantle one's ego. He went on to explain that each of those relationships is a valid and valuable pathway to finding one's way home to God. He pointed out that the depth of love between some people and their pets was just as deep and authentic as that which he'd seen in many human relationships, and just as precious. I felt validated and supported in a way I never had before.

Hugh met Buttons one day when his family was having a moving sale, and I took her with me to check it out. He listened to the entire "nine-year cancer survivor on all natural remedies" story and commented on the independence and sweetness of her spirit. She stood and let him pet her, which, as rare an occurrence as that was, was no surprise to me, and it seemed there was another doggy *darshan* exchange between two very wise, old souls that day.

In the late summer of 1999, I received my invitation to the upcoming autumn nuptials of Linda and Kurt, the friends who'd helped me unload my things into storage the day I arrived back in Tucson. Since a wedding gift was nowhere in my budget, when I called Linda to thank her for the invitation, I asked her who was going to perform their ceremony. She said they hadn't found anyone yet, so I suggested that if they were interested, I'd be honored to help them write their ceremony and would perform it as my gift to them. Linda was thrilled by the offer and called back the next day after discussing it with Kurt to say they'd love to accept my gift.

Linda and Kurt's wedding was held at the Tanque Verde Ranch, an authentic dude-ranch and resort just east of Tucson, and the extra element of their officiant also being their friend added to the experience of everyone involved. There were several hundred guests in attendance, many of whom came up to me afterwards to tell me that unlike most weddings they'd been to, this one hadn't been boring at all. In fact, they added, this ceremony had been extremely touching, interesting, and en-joyable. A few weeks later, I got a call from someone who'd been given my name by one of those guests, inquiring as to my fee and availability to perform their ceremony the following summer. I said I was definitely available and eventually, as word continued to spread, a new part-time business was born.

Around the same time as Linda and Kurt's wedding, Dr. Lodge's wife gave me the name of a friend of hers who owned an apartment that was for rent. She'd always thought the shabbiness and dark wood of my apartment was very depressing and, therefore, noncondusive to my heal-ing. She described the new place as bright, not too far from where I was living, and with a big, fenced, landscaped yard. I told her I didn't think I could possibly afford the rent, but she insisted I at least go look at it.

The next day I called the landlord and met with him to view the apart-ment. He told me on the phone that being a cat person, he didn't nor-mally rent to people with dogs, but since I was the friend of a friend, he'd reconsider and that I should bring Buttons along so they could meet.

When we arrived, I was delighted to find a lovely, private courtyard leading to the front door of the available residence in the L-shaped triplex, which was tucked away at the end of a quiet, dead-end street. When I fol-lowed the landlord inside, however, I had an instant letdown. The living area was tiny. Ignoring my disappointed comments and sighs, he silently led me through the French doors off the very small living room and out onto the back porch. I stood in awe looking out at the 50 x 30 foot, fenced, grass-covered yard, bordered on one side by a hedge of huge Tombstone rose bushes, the other by towering palm bushes, and so private you could romp in it naked. There was an old mesquite tree providing shade in one corner, a previous tenant's live Christmas tree growing in another and plenty of room for a vegetable garden.

As far as Tucson went, the yard was dog heaven. The roof of the back porch was decorative tin and would sound incredible during the mon-soon rains. Turning back to face the landlord who'd been standing there silently, I simply declared, "I must live here."

He smiled, and we began working out arrangements. Instead of the full rental amount, which I could never have afforded, he lowered the price in exchange for some monthly bodywork sessions. Having spent some time with Buttons, he realized she wasn't a yappy barker and actually behaved more like his cats than other dogs he'd known. He wrote on the lease: "one person and one cat trapped in a dog's body."

There were two nice bedrooms with white Berber carpeting, attractive kitchen cabinetry, embossed fabric Roman blinds on all the windows, and a skylight in the little bathroom. A huge plus was its central air-conditioning, but most importantly, this place had Buttons' yard. I signed the lease and went home to start packing.

Two weeks later we were all moved in, and I was once again at Dr. Lodge's receiving intravenous magnesium. I'd tried to do the move at an easy pace and in pieces, but the final shove of large furniture moving and the strain of cleaning the old place was enough to make me collapse again. I'd loaded Buttons up on Rescue Remedy when I had to bring out the first cardboard boxes, and she seemed to be handling things all right.

Most of all, she loved the new yard where she played while I unpacked. Huge, fluttering, orange and black Monarch butterflies and mystifying, brown and blue iridescent hummingbirds visited daily to keep Buttons fully entertained. She especially loved the five-foot-wide area between the side of the building and the fence where tall, old oleander bushes grew, providing a dense, jungle-like look from the bedroom windows. Buttons probably liked it because it was cooler, shady, and smelled of dark, rich compost from all the seasons of fallen leaves. Often I could look out from the bedroom windows and find her there.

She also grew quite fond of the French doors. When it was too hot to be outside, she would sit in front of them for hours keeping watch over her back yard domain. The mesquite tree was home to many cactus wrens and mourning doves and Buttons' twitching ears recorded the flights of all of them as they came and went. I was forever cleaning the inside bottom two panes of glass on each door.

Although no longer her young, rambunctious self, being in this new place seemed to bring my fifteen-year-old Buttons renewed spunk. She'd race, albeit a bit more slowly, every morning from the bedroom to the French doors and bound outside as soon as I caught up and opened them. When she was ready to come back in, I'd see her black nose kissing up against the bottom pane, her pointy ears twitching as if to say, "Well, come on, Mom, I'm ready to come in now... where the heck are ya?!?" I was forever cleaning the bottom two panes of each door on the outside, too.

During our first month in the new apartment, I dug up most of the yard, which was covered with Bermuda grass, and planted winter rye among it. Winter rye is finer and softer while Bermuda grass is coarser and once you've got it growing, nearly impossible to get rid of. Its roots are long and deeply embedded in the concrete-like desert soil. So I did my best to work with it by keeping it watered and mowed so it would be as soft as possible under Button's paw pads. I trimmed the rose bushes so she was safe from thorns and then planted some organic vegetables.

As I got stronger, we began venturing out more. There was a river wash a mile and a half away with a nice paved walkway and while walking it one feels totally in the open desert even though you're right in the middle of town. Often when we'd go and I'd take her off her leash, Buttons would dart ahead at unbelievable speeds, many times outrunning dogs years younger than she was. It was obvious she was older now with her all-white muzzle, and other dog walkers on the path would often ask me her age. I'd tell them and then mention how many years she'd been a cancer survivor on all natural remedies. When they wanted to know more, I'd talk about the organic foods I cooked for her, the daily supplements she got, and sometimes I'd refer them to the natural pet supply store opened by Dr. Lisa Newman, the natural-care pet consultant we'd worked with so many years before.

Then one day I got a call from Dr. Newman. A local trade newspaper was going to do an article on her store and Azmira products and wanted to also interview Buttons and me since Buttons was such a long-term holistic survivor. She had also been the first cancer case Dr. Newman had ever agreed to work with. Besides Buttons, I took to the interview a list of all her supplements, remedies, diet specifications and the original lab report diagnosing the squamous cell carcinoma.

The interview and picture taking went well even though Buttons was as camera shy with the professional photographer as she'd always been with me. Knowing that after fifteen years devoid of recitals or school plays of any kind, my daughter would finally be receiving some type of public recognition by having her name published in the paper, made me as proud a mom as there ever was.

After a week of anxious anticipation, publication day finally arrived and I headed to the neighborhood Circle K store to pick up a copy or twelve. My heart was absolutely bursting with pride as I stood in front of the newspaper rack surprised and staring at the big color photograph of Buttons and me right there in the middle of the front page. My little girl was famous!

Christmas was near, and I had many new friends, clients, and acquaintances. In the spirit of economy, for gifts I bought a bunch of 7-day glass candles from the grocery store, which I decorated with woven ribbon and pictures, each one personalized with the recipient's specific interests in mind. On Gayle's was a smiling photo of His Holiness the Fourteenth Dalai Lama, on Hugh's, a copy of one of my paintings and a favorite prayer of his. On ones I made for myself, I adhered pictures of the doggy of the century.

Gayle liked hers so much, that we began talking about the possibility of starting an on-line company for personalized candles. Thrilled with the possibility of doing something from home that was fun, creative, artistic and possibly quite lucrative, we began researching marketing possibilities and partnership agreement contracts. We met with a business consultant, a lawyer, and an accountant. Calculating all our needs and costs we came up with a simple business plan. Gayle and Leroy put up the money to purchase licenses, computer software, and candle supplies and we began designing labels, order forms, and advertising. At the same time we read books on partnerships and did our best to anticipate the possible scenarios we might have to deal with in the future. For those we made contingency plans.

Gayle and Leroy had been living with and taking care of both of Gayle's elderly parents. Since she would be handling all the order taking, invoicing, and other office and computer duties from her home, Gayle decided she'd show Leroy how to do everything too. She knew that in the event of one of her parents' passing, she'd be unable to carry her share of the business for a time. In preparation, she'd make sure Leroy would be ready to hold up her end of the business.

We also decided that I'd show Leroy how to create the candles, knowing that when Buttons passed, I would also be too incapacitated to work. I was still nowhere near being able to emotionally conceptualize the possibility of her death, instead, it was just something I intellectually knew would someday happen. Like gravity, it existed, but I never contemplated it much beyond that.

Gayle and I figured that by the middle of February, we'd have everything in working order and would be ready to begin our new venture. We were well on our way to a successful and fun home-based business. As I write this, a saying I heard on the television show, "Everwood" comes to mind: "Plans, are like candy to the fates."

On Super Bowl Sunday 2000, I went to Hugh's relationship class and sat next to Gayle, who was there alone, like many of the wives that day. It was an exceptionally fun class and afterwards, Gayle handed me a manila envelope containing our final business partnership agreement for me to look over. Our plan was to take it to a notary for signing later that week. I was very aware of the seriousness of our business commitment, and in a way it felt like an upcoming marriage for me. Gayle and I were committing to this business enterprise together, promising to work together through any snafus, problems, miscommunications, successes, triumphs and most importantly, any feelings that arose. We were entering into an agreement to go through it all—the easy and the challenging alike. It was a big step for me and I was ready to take it. Gayle asked me to call her later that day with any proposed changes to the agreement, and then we'd decide which day we'd go to do the signing.

Throughout the afternoon, I left her phone messages. I called again on Monday morning. It wasn't like Gayle to not return my calls promptly. By Monday evening I was afraid that something was really wrong and the next morning I found out what it was. Gayle's eldest daughter called to tell me that a few hours after Gayle had gotten home from Hugh's Sunday morning class, a policeman had shown up at her door to tell her that her husband Leroy was dead. Heart attack. Fun loving, vivacious, Leroy. Gone. We certainly had no contingency plan for that.

At Gayle's, the street in front of her house teemed with parked cars. Inside, amidst all her friends and family, I found her, and hugged her, but I knew she wasn't in her body. She felt frozen to me, invisible, in shock. And yet it was her voice when she spoke.

"Here's a picture of Leroy. Could you please make five candles of it, for the kids and for the memorial service?"

I didn't know what to say other than, "Of course." Everything else I considered saying seemed wrong. Saying nothing at all seemed wrong. People were busy in the kitchen and bustling around ministering to one another. Gayle sat motionless on the couch, a sweet, but pained look on her face as she watched her grandkids running around wearing their beloved Poppy's tee shirts and ties. Sitting next to her on the floor, I began rubbing her bare feet when I noticed the Dalai Lama candle I'd given her, burning on the mantle. Months later, I found out that she had lit it as soon as the policeman had left and that it had burned continually for several days. Eventually, I got up and went to Kinko's to make copies of the picture she'd given me for the Leroy candles.

There were hundreds of people at the memorial service which Hugh officiated. Relatives and friends shared stories. The grandkids sang. There was plenty of laughter, as Leroy was quite the jokester, and there was lots of music. Sad that I hadn't yet gotten to know Leroy very well, I hated that my friend was in so much pain. I thought it was a really good thing that when she was ready in a few months or so, Gayle would have the candle business to immerse herself in and to generate income. In the meantime, it was all on hold.

Gayle came to me for a massage about seven weeks after Leroy's passing, and as she sat on my living room couch beforehand, she comforted us both with a sweet story from their past. When she finished, I walked over to the bookshelf and pulled out a bound, unused journal I'd gotten when I worked at the bookstore in Petaluma. The manager had let me take it home since its binding was upside-down and consequently didn't match the headings on the paper. Holding it out towards Gayle I said, "You have so many wonderful, loving, funny stories from your life with Leroy. Maybe you should record them all. This journal's probably perfect since like your life, it's been turned upside down."

After only a moment's hesitation, Gayle agreed, took the journal, thanked me, and then walked into the massage room. When she was on the table and ready, I followed her in.

Gayle has a tattoo on her back. It's some happy little cartoon character. As I noticed it again that day, I remembered the program from Leroy's memorial service, which included an exact replica of how he always signed his cards to his family—with a smiley face drawn to resemble Leroy himself, complete with mustache and glasses. "Gayle, why don't you have Leroy's smiley-face signature tattooed on you?" I suggested.

A few weeks later, Gayle did just that. But what I didn't know at the time was that through Gayle's loss, I was beginning to plan the things I would do for myself, some of the rituals I would keep when Buttons died. They were the things that were too difficult for me to think about or face directly from my own emotional standpoint.

Yes, my ButtonsLove was definitely getting old, but her spirit was vibrant and our connection and love, more solid than ever. I knew she wasn't going anywhere yet, and thoughts of the inevitable were far too painful to entertain.

When Gayle came back into the living room after the massage, I broached the subject of candles, wanting only to confirm that at some point in the future, perhaps later that year, we might pick up where we'd left off. She told me honestly that she couldn't even think about the future. She had her parents' care to think about, not to mention the toll the grief had taken on her own health. She also shared that she needed to be alone as much as possible and not deal with any of the world outside of her family and the issues now crowding her plate.

My friend's heart was broken, and I felt totally impotent, wanting nothing other than to stop her pain. Knowing I was powerless to help and feeling terribly disappointed about our now defunct business arrangement, I also deeply respected the sagacity of her choices.

    The next time I heard from Gayle was about a year later, when I came home one afternoon to find the fruits of the journal I'd given her: a completed manuscript leaning against my front door. I stayed up until 3 a.m. and read it straight through. My friend had done well in her year of relative isolation. She had mustered all her inner strength and stayed present with all her grief. Fully honoring herself and Leroy, she'd pulled all her energies inward and connected with his spirit in new and stronger ways. She had cried and prayed and cried and prayed some more as she daringly leaned into the pain instead of running from it, or covering it up, or "getting on with it." She didn't numb it with antidepressants the way our culture would so readily have her do but instead, surrendered to the grief, knowing that somewhere in it was a gift. Gayle had refused to leave the grieving process without that gift, and her pain's unfolding had indeed taken her through an amazing transformation. It was, what I believe Holocaust survivor Viktor E. Frankl was referring to when he wrote, "But there was no need to be ashamed of tears, for tears bore witness that a man had the greatest of courage, the courage to suffer" and "What is to give light must endure burning" and lastly, "When we are no longer able to change a situation, we are challenged to change ourselves." Gayle's choice to fully feel and give life, breadth, and space to all her painful emotions rather than repress them was an enormous act of courage and one seldom embraced in our culture. Deep in my heart, I knew it was a journey I would all too soon be on myself. I placed the manuscript on my bookshelf and hoped to God it would be years before I would have to refer to it for comfort or direction.

I was feeling somewhat stronger by the spring of 2000, and so Butts and I began hiking again. Eventually we found a trail on Mount Lemmon that we hadn't been on before with Connor. Box Canyon Trail is lovely, a combination of flat and steep, rocky and winding, through deep pine forest peppered with outcroppings and vistas as one travels down the mountainside. We hiked it about once a month. As always, one time in particular stands out in my memory as being the most adventurous. Buttons was now sixteen and her hearing had worsened further so instead of letting her run loose, I always kept her on an extendable/retractable leash until we were well down the trail and away from the road.

We had hiked in about three miles, past ferns and boulders and wildflowers, and then wandered a bit off the trail so I could sit and enjoy a half-hour afternoon meditation. It was nice and cool on the mountain, at least 25° cooler than Tucson where it was well over 100° before noon. Near the end of my half-hour sitting, Buttons nudged her cold, wet nose against my arm. I opened my eyes, instantly alert and rather surprised, as she'd never disturbed me during meditation before. Looking around and seeing nothing unusual, I became aware of how cold it had gotten and looked up to see a dark, threatening sky peeking through the trees. I jumped up and stuffed the cotton poncho I'd been sitting on into my backpack, along with her emptied water bowl. Flinging my arms through the backpack's straps, I headed towards the trail with Butts in the lead.

Moments later, I felt the first drops of rain. The two of us scurried right along, but by the sound of the now rumbling thunder, I knew we'd never make it back or even close to the car before the storm broke: it was all uphill, sometimes pretty steep, and even at full speed, we were at least an hour away. The only question now was how bad a storm would it be? I'd heard nothing in the weather report on the news the night before, but sometimes storms in the mountains are unexpected and unpredictable. I was wearing only a tee shirt and some lightweight cotton pants. Even though I knew it would offer little protection if the storm worsened, I stopped and pulled the cotton poncho out of my backpack and threw it over my head. There were only a few other things in my backpack: a Swiss army knife, some tea tree oil and Kleenex, none of which left me feeling too prepared.

Within ten minutes, both Buttons and my poncho were soaked through, the lightening frequent, and the thunder close. I worried, knowing the worst place to be with lightening that near was under a tree, but there was nowhere else but under trees, so we continued trudging as fast as possible up the trail's slippery slopes. Soon the thunder became loud enough to frighten even Buttons, and every time it crashed upon us, she'd turn in the opposite direction and run the wrong way until I caught her and turned her back around. Then there was a lightening strike so close I could feel the wet hair on my arms stand up. Simultaneously, I watched Buttons swerve around like a Blue Angel jet and run past me so fast there was no hope of stopping her. Exasperated, I turned around and took off after her. By then it was raining so hard she couldn't hear me clapping, trying to catch her attention over the din. Even though I chased her as fast as I could, it wasn't fast enough.

Finally, she came to an extra steep part of the trail, which slowed her down long enough for me to catch up to her. I grabbed her and while struggling to hold her, wrestled with the backpack trying to find her leash and collar, but before I could, she squirmed her way out of my hold and once again headed down the trail in the opposite direction from the car. For five minutes I ran, frustrated and miserable, until suddenly it started to hail marble-sized chunks of hard, stinging ice.

As soon as the hail began pelting her, Buttons stopped dead in her tracks. She turned and trembled as she stood in the middle of the trail watching me close the distance between us. Reaching her, I scooped her up and quickly headed away from the trail, hoping for a little more cover from the forest. Crouching against a huge pine, praying it wouldn't be the lightning's next target, I tried to catch my breath, a cold, wet, and terrified Buttons now shivering on my lap. Leaning over, I did my best to shield her from the hail as it pummeled us, surprised at how much pain the pellets could inflict. My legs grew numb and weary. Eventually, I was able to get her leash and collar out of the backpack and on her, and after an interminable ten minutes, the hail stopped though the rain continued. Tethered together, Butts and I headed back up the trail, my glasses so wet and fogged-up I couldn't see. Finally, I took them off and held fearfully onto my end of the leash, hoping I wouldn't fall and turn an ankle on the now, indistinct and dangerously slick rocks.

Two hours from the time she'd nudged me during my meditation, it stopped raining and Buttons and I reached the trailhead where the car was parked. Opening the trunk, I grabbed the corduroy jacket I knew was there and used it to towel Buttons down. I couldn't really tell if she was relieved to be back at the car or angry with me for the whole ordeal. When she was no longer dripping wet, I sat her in the passenger seat, started the engine and turned the heater on full-blast. Starting to relax, I walked back to the trunk, pulled out an old sweatshirt, stripped naked right there by the road and savored the feel of the dry, warm fleece against my cold, wet skin.

Fifty minutes later we were back in Tucson traffic and arid, 100° plus temperature, but instead of driving directly home, I drove straight to the camping supply store where I purchased two, featherweight, pocket-size fold-up, waterproof, emergency blankets. They are still in the bottom of my backpack today.

Doing the candle business alone seemed overwhelming to me, and there was no one else I knew at that time, besides Gayle, with whom I would consider doing it. So instead, in the fall of 2000, I enrolled in classes at the community college, having investigated and then qualified for full financial aid. I was surprised that it wasn't something I'd considered and checked out years before. But knowing that line of thinking didn't lead me in any way towards inner peace, I chalked it up to "everything in its own time" and went on from there. My current schedule consisted of a few weekly massage clients and a wedding every couple months or so. I figured I could handle maybe two or three courses a semester without pushing my still tired self to the point of collapse again and continue to have plenty of at-home time with Butts.

She had begun having problems seeing, I could tell, and the veterinary ophthalmologist, the same one who'd helped us years before with the cat/eye puncture situation, found calcium deposits on her eyes. He said there was no way to remove them without general anesthesia and acid drops. Knowing that at her age I was not willing to have Buttons put under, he assured me that she still had some vision in each eye and that if he could see in, she could see out. Uncomfortably nudged by the reality of Buttons' aging, I returned home and spent hours on the Internet (one of my massage clients had given me her old laptop computer) trying to find a more natural, less invasive way to remove the calcium deposits, but came up with nothing unless I wanted to get rid of the ones on my bathroom tile.

So instead I did the only thing I could think of: never rearrange the furniture or put anything on the floor that she wasn't aware of. Vitamin E drops in her eyes seemed to help when she was feeling discomfort in them. I bought egg crate foam and cut pieces to adhere to the bottom kitchen cabinets so if during her now frequent pacing, she miscalculated and walked into one, it would be a soft encounter. Soon most of the apartment and the furniture, actually anything that had a surface area between 16″—21″ high, was covered with foam. She was sleeping most of the day by then, but with the foam, I felt that she'd be safe.

After having my twenty-year-old college transcripts transferred, I discovered there were still several general classes I needed to be eligible for entry into the Sign Language Interpreter Program. I registered for two of them plus American Sign Language (ASL) 101. It was good to be back in school after all that time. I loved the challenge, and for me it was challenging. Like so many who are unfamiliar with Deaf culture, I was under the misconception that there is only one universal sign language rather than a different one in every country around the world. I was also of the misbelief that signing is the same as English only with hand signals. I discovered that the video tapes I'd watched from the library taught signed English, a pidgin type slang not at all the same as ASL: a complex language with its own structure, form, rhythm, idioms, and syntax. In fact, the only advantage watching the tapes had provided was knowing how to fingerspell the alphabet and gaining some basic vocabulary.

I loved being home with Butts while I studied, and I incorporated her into every assignment possible. When it came time in my required Speech and Public Speaking class to give a presentation on a specific event, I chose "My Daughter's Recovery From Cancer." It included a surprise visit from Buttons herself who'd been outside the door with a friend waiting for my cue to enter the room. Until her appearance at the end of the speech, none of my classmates knew my "daughter" had more than two legs. In ASL class when we were asked to bring in family pictures and sign names, ages and descriptions, it was pictures of Buttons from the previous sixteen years that I brought.

By the time Christmas break rolled around, I was spent but satisfied, having earned A's in all my classes. I was ready for a rest. Some good friends had moved earlier in the year from Tucson to San Diego and invited Buttons and me to spend the holiday with them there. And so, the Sweet Angel and I reserved a rental car (to avoid putting miles on the ever-money-soaking-Toyota) and a few days before Christmas, we were off.

Buttons seemed quite antsy and frustrated in the car, which was very unusual traveling behavior for her. What I didn't realize then was that she was suffering from the beginnings of CDS, Cognitive Dysfunction Syndrome or in layman's terms, doggy Alzheimer's. I had been taking her to a holistic vet for acupuncture, but every time I mentioned new symptoms, pacing and getting "stuck" behind furniture and in corners, he would just pass them off as old age. He told me there was nothing I could do about it unless I wanted to fill her full of pharmaceutical drugs. I knew I didn't want to do that and although I wasn't comfortable with his nonchalant attitude, I unfortunately didn't change vets or research other possibilities until her symptoms worsened.

The San Diego beaches were much different from the Santa Cruz beaches. First, they were smaller. It only took a minute to walk from the car to the water's edge. Second, they were very crowded. Of course, being Christmas week, there were probably more visitors and traffic than at other times, but Buttons and I made the best of it, locating the only dog beach and getting there at the most logically uncrowded times. The beach was never empty, but in the last weeks before her seventeenth birthday, my Buttons was no longer running like a bullet and seemed content to meander along side me through the crowds. I could tell she was very happy, especially when she'd come across a pile of sea kelp and bury her nose in it just like old times. I was grateful to have my girl back at the ocean one more time.

Our six-hour drive back to Tucson lasted almost eight hours. Buttons could only sit comfortably for a few minutes before she'd start trying to pace in the car. Thinking she had to pee, I pulled off every few miles only to stand outside with her. She refused snacks and water. Nothing was right. She just didn't want to be in the car, it seemed. Finally I gave her an extra large dose of Rescue Remedy until it calmed her completely. All the way home the feeling gnawed at my gut and as we pulled into our driveway late that night, I knew deep inside that this would be our last road trip together. Intellectually, I knew these changes were to be expected after nearly seventeen years. They were something my heart, on the other hand, just couldn't comprehend.

A few weeks before her seventeenth birthday, in January of 2001, Buttons and I got a call from a Channel 9 News feature reporter at the local ABC affiliate. They were doing a special report on "Pet Health Food" and as part of the feature, they wanted to interview and film Buttons and me. My girl on TV—I was ecstatic! The morning of the interview, I gave Buttons a luxurious bath, blow dry, and brushing and then proceeded to try on everything in my closet. That afternoon, the crew arrived and one of my favorite news anchors stood in our backyard asking me questions about the cancer, the diagnosis, Buttons' diet and supplement regimen, and my association with Dr. Lisa S. Newman, who they also interviewed for the piece.

The night it was to air, I sat watching Channel 9 for hours, prepared with my blank videotape and remote control. What I wasn't anticipating and was delighted to see was the feature's trailer, which ran an hour prior to the news, at the end of a commercial break. Suddenly, there on my screen were Butts and me in our back yard, her in my arms, me smiling and petting her head, as the voice-over reported, "Coming up tonight at ten... KGUN-9 News looks into the world of pet health food."

Thoughts raced through my head. I couldn't believe how old I looked. I'd have to start dying my hair. Thank goodness the green blouse didn't make me look fat. Why on earth did the cameraman shoot from below me looking up? Didn't he know that is the most unflattering angle for any woman? MY BABY GIRL WAS GOING TO BE ON TV!

I ran over to where she was sleeping, scooped her up and hugged her tight. She opened her eyes and looked at me with that "you are nuts and <u>why</u> are you waking me?" look, but she must have sensed it was a special occasion, and she indulged my show of affection for several minutes before pulling away from me.

Following the break came the national news and then the weather and then, right before the next commercial, there we were once again on the screen as the anchor announced, "Coming up, Julie Myers takes us into the world of health food for pets!"

Tears of joy were already running down my cheeks. All our hard work, the months and months of tinctures and remedies and sea meal, the hours of love songs under the bed, her willingness to have awful, bitter things squirted into her mouth and poured down her throat. Her life was more than enough payment for that. Like the newspaper article, this was a bonus. I always felt wonderful telling fellow dog walkers and friends the cancer recovery story, but this—this would reach tens of thousands of people. It was now my mission and a way to pay homage to my girl's amazing spirit and love, to save as many other dogs as possible through our story.

The piece was about three and a half minutes long. For most of it, Buttons was the one the camera focused on as either the reporter or I talked about her diagnosis and subsequent dietary changes. They also included a snippet of Dr. Newman and her Azmira supplements and food, and some opinions of a traditional vet. As soon as it was over, my phone started ringing. Friends were excited to know such a celebrity: BUTTONS: THE MIRACLE DOG.

In the days after the piece aired, classmates approached me at school with questions about their dogs, and I learned to give answers and explanations in sign language. A few people recognized us on the river walk. Over the next few weeks, I also got a few calls from strangers, wanting to know exactly what I fed Buttons. I loved those calls. These were people who fully experienced the special bond possible with dogs, who unlike human children, always forgive you and never go through that "I hate you" rebellious stage. These folks were unaware of the hazards and un-regulated ingredients in most commercial pet food, and wanted to make sure they were doing all the best things they could possibly do for their beloved animals. I was more than happy to share everything I had dis-covered and learned, and to refer them to the experts I had found. But-tons was no longer here on earth just to give me a place to keep my heart open and focus my love. She was now here for a much greater purpose: contributing to the lives of countless dogs and humans. It seemed singu-lar to me that a mere seventeen-pound body could hold such a Herculean spirit. I felt honored to be her caregiver. That role was about to involve much more than I could ever imagine.

Buttons had started walking with her back hunched-up, which was especially noticeable after a hike. The two things I knew to give her for any joint pain or tissue swelling were MSM and Azmira Yucca Intensive Extract, which helped considerably. For a while I also took her back to the holistic vet I'd found in Tucson for acupuncture treatments, which she still didn't like, but tolerated anyway. Eventually, I grew too unhappy with the vet and his continued nonchalance towards Buttons' health to continue seeing him. Whenever I would mention new problems and ask what could be done, he'd give me some flippant answer like, "She's not going to live forever, Nadine, you can't fix everything."

I wasn't stupid. I knew she wouldn't live forever and that we were headed for more serious issues. But we certainly hadn't gotten this far with her still so active by embracing his kind of attitude. So, I decided that if he wasn't willing to partner with me in continuing to take the best possible care of her, then he wasn't the vet for us. A mile from home was a twenty-four-hour emergency clinic where I made an appointment for Butts to have a checkup, figuring if I could find a vet there that we liked, it would be a good location and setup for the coming years.

We were blessed to find a wonderful vet, Dr. Judith Parker. She had an excellent reputation in traditional veterinary circles and though she admitted fully that she knew very little about holistic or alternative practices, she viewed them respectfully. I believe she viewed them even more respectfully after meeting Buttons. She certainly agreed that Buttons was in amazing health for her age.

Right away I could tell that at every bend, Dr. Parker would help in a way that was comfortable for me and Ms. Buttons. She asked questions and listened carefully as I listed and explained all the supplements Buttons was on. I was concerned that Butts had started to sometimes forget when she was inside and when she was out, or at least, where she should go to the bathroom, a common CDS symptom. I asked about the drugs available for CDS. Dr. Parker gave me straightforward, informational answers and told me she just hadn't seen results dramatic enough to risk the possible side effects. Grateful to hear that kind of honesty from a traditional vet, I chose instead to stop at Wal-Mart on the way home and buy several cases of paper towels. That evening I went online and began researching everything I could find on CDS. There were the drug company's sites and a few senior dog informational sites, but little if anything on natural treatment for it. Knowing that both CoQ10 and ginkgo were good for memory and brain function, I upped the dosage Buttons was already on.

Even with the onset of old age, Buttons was still full of pleasant surprises, which guaranteed our having plenty of that "honeymoon stage" element in our relationship along with the additional "fine wine stage" of deep closeness and flawless, unspoken communication. If she could have finished my sentences, I know she would have, and I had become a pro at anticipating her ever-changing needs. As a seventeen-year-old senior, Buttons decided she liked asparagus tips. Fortunately, I prefer the stalks and so one evening when I put my dinner plate on the floor for her to finish the bits of discarded, hormone-free chicken, I was amazed when she went right for the asparagus tips instead. Shaking my head and laughing, I said to her, "Well, doesn't it figure? Of all the vegetables I've ever tried to get you to eat, it turns out what you really wanted was the most expensive: organic asparagus."

And then in the fall of her seventeenth year, there was what would become known as "The Geriatric Hike." My old friend Paige had gotten married and moved out of Tucson, but called one day to say she was in town for a short time and could we get together? We decided to meet the next afternoon at Catalina State Park and picked the Loop Trail for a sunset hike.

The three of us met in the parking lot and after a warm greeting, crossed the road to the trailhead. Paige, having grown up on a farm and used to aging animals, kindly commented on Buttons' hunched back and slowed pace. Nodding in agreement, I bent and casually unhooked Butski's leash since she seemed to be able to sense the trail on her own. Now perhaps after hearing Paige's observation about her advancing age, Buttons felt she had something to prove, or maybe her French vanity just got the better of her, but in the very next moment, she was off like a bullet, speeding down the trail and out of sight. At first, Paige and I just stood there looking at each other in stunned disbelief. Then we took off after her, Paige shouting and me clapping. Several minutes later we got to a small running wash and Buttons was nowhere to be seen.

"Would she have crossed the water by herself?" Paige asked.

"I certainly don't think so," was my reply. And so the two of us started spreading out on either side of the trail assuming Buttons had left it to explore the underbrush. A minute passed as I searched nervously and then caught a movement in my peripheral vision. Turning, I saw a grinning, panting, Butts, happily sliding to a stop at the water's edge on the opposite bank.

"Poop, you monkey nut! You ARE a miracle dog!" I called.

Paige looked up and started laughing as Buttons came splashing back across the wash towards us. One quick pet was all she granted me before turning to gallop back across the wash in front of us once more. I knew then that the miraculous energy Paige and I were witnessing came from somewhere in Buttons' spirit, for that kind of energy was certainly no longer in her body and yet she was running the trail as swiftly and joyously as she ever had. I recalled the first time she ever crossed that wash, leaving me ankle deep in the water. No, her spirit hadn't weakened one iota, I thought.

Soon we came to another, much wider wash and as we approached the bank, saw a group of eight people including four kids, all spread out and crossing the wash via stepping-stones towards us. The first to finish crossing was a boy of about seven who, as soon as he reached our side and was back on the trail, began running for all he was worth. Immediately, Buttons turned around and took off chasing after him like he had a steak in his pocket.

"Buttons, no!" I yelled while clapping, but that little boy had my girl's rapt attention as they quickly rounded a bend and disappeared from sight. The other four adults had seen the whole thing unfold and giggled the rest of their way across the wash. Deciding that we should go after them so we could catch them before they reached the next wash, we all began trotting down the trail back the way Paige and I had just come. The other adults were calling the little boy's name when suddenly, coming back into sight around the first bend and heading towards us, were Buttons and the little boy. They were both still running at top speed only now Buttons was in the lead and the little boy was chasing HER. We adults stopped in our tracks and began laughing uncontrollably as we watched this reenactment of almost every cartoon we had ever seen on television. Still all smiles when Buttons and the little boy reached us, we parted ways as Paige and Butts and I headed across the wash and on to the rest of our hike.

As the desert air turned cool and heady with the smell of mesquite, the sun lowered itself in the afternoon sky and the stillness of dusk enfolded us. Paige's compelling description of her travels since we'd last seen each other were punctuated every few sentences with another, "Wow! Look at her—the geriatric wonder dog!" as we watched Buttons prancing and bounding ahead of us. It wasn't until after another mile that Buttons began to slow down. As the towering mountains surrounding us turned dark violet and the clouds above us flame red, I felt saturated with the splendor, love, and blessing of my little girl and her indomitable spirit. It would end up being the last time Buttons and I would ever hike that trail together.

For the first time ever, Buttons was becoming a lap dog, so I bought a rocking chair for the bedroom. It was difficult watching her age: her failing eyesight and hearing forcing her to become more comfortable being in my arms where she now felt safe, and making it a bittersweet time for us. She needed me more and more, and when she wasn't sleeping I spent my time consciously engaged with her in some way. Though she maintained her independent air, Buttons now seemed more comfortable accepting a little help. She could navigate the apartment well so long as I didn't move anything, and she quickly compensated for the addition of the new chair, which she absolutely loved rocking in. I'd bought a pretty silk-covered pillow and would place it on my lap before scooping Buttons up and laying her on top of it. That way, we were both very comfortable and she was high enough for me to snuggle with her. Often when the CDS pacing would seem to control her, rocking in the chair with me would calm her completely, and she'd rest or sleep there in my arms.

One afternoon as I sat in the rocker with her on my lap, I positioned my head so that my left temple was resting on her head at the space between her ears. Buttons fell asleep immediately, and as we rocked, I felt myself also drifting off into that peaceful place between consciousness and sleep that's especially noticeable during a nap. Dreaming came instantly. I was in the familiar surroundings of our apartment, but everything looked huge and blurry. It felt like I was only a few feet tall and with a bit of irritation, I realized I would have to jump up if I wanted to sit on the couch. And then it hit me. This wasn't my dream—it was Buttons' dream! I had somehow entered her consciousness and was seeing everything from her point of view.

The moment I fully comprehended what was happening, I felt yanked out of it. My heart beating rapidly, tears sprang from my eyes and I knew my consciousness had joined with hers, just like some kind of Vulcan mind-meld. No one would probably ever believe me, but I knew what had happened.

The same sense of confidence and taste of something sacred I had had in the bathtub a decade before engulfed me now. We had been given an incredible gift and as I stroked her soft fur, I thanked my girl and told her that I would never forget. I knew then in my heart that when the time came and she was no longer in her body, I could just sit in our chair and rock to feel her spirit completely present with me: that we could always meet there.

School was going well and I was now at the point of taking only Interpreter Training Program classes though I was still a long way from completion since I couldn't handle more than two courses a semester. My business was slow but stable with a few regular massage clients and wedding bookings every month from the word-of-mouth advertising I relied on. I had run some bodywork ads in the local paper, but no matter how specific the wording was—that I only offered therapeutic, nonsexual massage—there were still plenty of weirdos who called. At the same time, I continued accruing a few thousand dollars of credit-card debt every year just to pay for basic living expenses and frequent car repairs. Getting another waitress job was out of the question—it was too physically demanding. And since I'd gotten my massage training in California, I wasn't qualified to do massage at a spa or doctor's office in Arizona. My stamina and endurance remained minimal, and any other job I was qualified for wouldn't earn me even as much as I was already making in less than half as many hours per week.

Though I was feeling safe and comfortable in our nice, cozy apartment, my physical health remained a constant challenge. My natural, internal thermostat was still nonexistent, and I had to monitor my exertion mentally since my body couldn't register tiredness in degrees. My diet was clean, whole and organic. I consumed no caffeine, and forced myself to speed walk several miles a day. Even the small everyday stresses felt monumental and overwhelming to me, and combined with my worry about the bigger stuff my stress levels were always high. The expense of a flat tire was enough to send me into suicidal mind games where I felt totally lost and helpless, forsaken and victimized. My life felt like a house of cards between the finances, my health, and Buttons' old age. She was my only comfort, and yet the thought of losing her was ever present in the back of my mind lurking like some boiling volcano, which could blow at any time. And then one day, two months after the Twin Towers went down in NYC, that volcano blew.

It was right before final exams, and I was thoroughly enjoying ASL 3 with my incredibly interesting and inspiring deaf professor. One afternoon after class, I stopped in at the local health food store and ran into Anna, a woman I'd met briefly years before at the natural pet store who was now working on her own as a very successful pet communicator. Normally, I'm quite skeptical of psychics, but I experienced this woman as very down-to-earth and caring so when she suggested we trade a session for a massage, I thought it might be fun and agreed. Besides, every massage I gave was a possible word-of-mouth advertisement. She came for her massage a few days later and then, the following week, came to do a session with Buttons and me.

It was a Friday evening, and as I held Buttons on my lap, Anna sat on the couch with her eyes closed, "tuning in." The first thing she said was that Buttons was very grateful to me for all the love and extreme care I'd given her through the years especially during her illness. Because I had told Anna about the cancer, that didn't surprise or impress me, but the next thing she said left me feeling totally astonished. Apparently, according to Anna, the only complaint Buttons had was the time we'd lived with the big jumping black-and-white spotted dog whom she didn't like at all. I sat speechless. Piper, the big jumping hound dog in Salinas was black-and-white spotted. There was no way in the world Anna could have known about that unless Buttons had told her.

In addition to other interesting things, she went on to say that my deceased grandmother was watching and protecting Buttons and me. When she also said that Buttons wanted me to add some L-5-HTP to her food, a supplement I already had in my cabinet, in order to help curb her CDS night pacing, I planned to do so the following morning. Anna then suggested the dosage that they recommended at the pet store for dogs Buttons' size. All in all, I found the session quite interesting, though I also had the distinct feeling that Buttons did not enjoy having her psyche probed by someone she didn't know, so I decided one session was enough.

The next morning, I gave Butts the L-5-HTP in hopes that it would impact her pacing that night. A few hours later, I noticed she seemed totally out of it and disoriented. Rationalizing it as a mild reaction to the supplement, I kept an eye on her and went about my day. But by that evening, she still hadn't regained any energy so I fed her her dinner by hand, figuring since she was eating, everything must ultimately be okay. She was still woozy when I helped her stand outside to pee a few hours later. Several times during the night I checked her, hoping she'd be better, but she just slept. I lay down next to her then and drifted in and out of sleep myself, concerned, semi-alert, and cognizant of her breathing.

By morning I knew something was terribly wrong and when I called my friend, June, who had several dogs of her own, she came right over to take us to the Emergency Clinic. Buttons' eyes had begun moving rapidly back and forth, her neck was arching at such an extreme angle, she looked like the letter C and she couldn't stand up. I was terrified and my insides felt like marble. Why hadn't I taken her to the vet as soon as I'd noticed something different? Wouldn't I ever learn? I'd always thought of myself as someone who was relatively capable in an emergency, but now I knew that wasn't true. My God, I thought, it couldn't possibly end like this, could it?

June rushed us to the vet, and the girl at the desk led us into an exam room where I lay Buttons down on the steel table, one of her blankets underneath her, and held her tenderly. Soon Dr. Parker opened the door, took a step into the room and after one glance at Buttons, looked at me and said, "Oh. She's had a severe stroke, Nadine." Moving closer, Dr. Parker gently touched Buttons' flank as she peered into her eyes. "We have to give her something to reduce the swelling in her brain as quickly as possible. Is there something natural you know to give her for that?"

God bless her soul, I thought. "Hell, no! You're in the driver's seat now. Please, pump her full of whatever drugs you have that will help her!"

I knew there was a time and place for everything and that this, being an immediate, emergency situation, was the time for a powerful drug: later I could supplement and counteract the side effects holistically. Right now Buttons' life was being endangered by her symptoms and those symptoms needed to be treated and stopped.

Telling Dr. Parker about the L-5-HTP, she said she really didn't think the small dosage I'd administered could have possibly caused the stroke, but I absolutely hated the coincidence and the fact that I would never know for sure. Standing helplessly, I watched them take my sweet girl's temperature and shave a spot on her front leg for the shot of steroids.

Dr. Parker explained what was happening, the effects the steroids would have, and then she straightened and looked me right in the eye.

"In all my years of practice I have never seen a dog recover from a stroke this severe. However, I have never known a person willing to go through what I know you're going to have to go through for at least the next two weeks. Besides, this is Buttons we're talking about. If there was ever a dog who could rally, it's her."

My heart swelled with gratitude and love, for I knew in that moment I was looking into the eyes of the perfect vet for Buttons and me. With the bit of hope Dr. Parker handed me, I felt my internal engines rev up for whatever was next. As she began writing directions on a piece of paper, she continued, "I will give you some additional steroids in tablet form for you to give her every few hours for the next two days. You'll need to go to the drugstore and buy her some Dramamine to stop the rapid eye movements. Keep her hydrated and warm and bring her back in right away if she seems to worsen. You'll need to watch her closely and the next two weeks will tell if she's going to pull through or not. Call if you have any questions."

The bill was huge, and June quietly and generously handed her credit card to the girl at the desk, while relieved and grateful I bundled Buttons up in her blanket, knowing we were surrounded by angels.

Back home, I made Buttons as comfortable as possible and gave her some purified water with an eyedropper. When she'd had enough I lay down next to her. Looking deep into her eyes while petting the side of her neck, I said to her, "I love you my Poop, and I don't want you to suffer, do you hear me? If it is your time to go then you just go and know it's okay. I've never lied to you, Butts, and I won't start now. I'm not ready to be without you, but don't you dare stick around just for me. If you are in any pain, my love, then just let go. Grandma will be there waiting for you."

She stared at me with her dark brown puppy dog eyes, and I kissed the side of her head. Her blanket was wet with my tears as she drifted off to sleep and left me just sitting and watching her breathe.

An hour later she woke up and feeling her sense of panic, I realized she'd peed. It wasn't until several loads of laundry later that I smartened up and layered plastic garbage bags between the bath towels she'd been lying on. All day Sunday I just loved her and kept her hydrated.

In need of emotional support, on Monday morning I called Hugh Prather and told him what had transpired over the weekend. I wrote down everything he said during that conversation.

"Now is the time, Nadine, for you to start focusing more on her spirit. Spend some time every day just gently tuning in to and connecting with Buttons' spirit. This will help you when the time comes for her to release her body... and I'm not saying that's going to necessarily happen soon, but when the time does come, you won't feel such a jarring break or separation."

I thought of our times together in the rocking chair and I told Hugh about entering her dream. And then I protested, "But I love her cute little body so much! Every night she lies on my chest as I watch TV or read and she snuggles her sweet little head between my shoulder and my chin while I hold her. I would miss that so much!"

What Hugh said next stopped me in my tracks.

"But you see, Nadine, it's still her spirit that you're loving. If she were some mean, nasty, little dog, you wouldn't think she was cute at all. You love her body so much because it is imbued with the loveliness of her spirit."

I felt a chord of truth vibrating deep within my being.

That afternoon I looked up the ASL sign for "stroke," then called Paige who was once again living in Tucson, and asked her to come sit with Buttons while I went to class to talk to my teacher. I didn't want Buttons to be alone, especially if she died. I thought that, but I didn't comprehend it—if I had, I never would have left her for a moment. Letting myself feel any of it was totally out of the question. My first final was that Wednesday, and I couldn't see taking it now.

On campus I tracked down my teacher and did my best to explain the situation to him in ASL. He was compassionate and understanding since he had three dogs himself, but he explained that his only option if I didn't take the final was to give me an "incomplete." Afraid of losing my financial aid, without which I couldn't afford school at all, I suggested he fail me on the final and just give me the resulting grade of C but he said it didn't work that way.

That night I stayed for most of the class and then rushed home to Buttons and Paige. It warmed my heart when I walked in the door to see Paige on the floor next to Buttons gently comforting her as she gave her water from the eyedropper. Paige agreed that Buttons' spirit still seemed present and strong and not like that of an animal about to die. I thanked yet another angel as she left us that night to drive back home to her husband.

Over the next few days I washed mountains of towels while Butski slept, waking up every few hours to pee, but not eating. The Dramamine I'd crushed up and mixed with some fruit juice, which she'd taken via the eyedropper. When her ribs began showing, I gave her juice mixed with the contents of her vitamin capsules so at least, I thought, she was getting some nutrition. Studying for my finals kept my terror at bay.

It was a long, slow process, and I hadn't really slept since the Friday night Anna had been there. During it all, I managed to ace both my written and signed finals and luckily Paige was willing to drive across town a few more times to stay with Butts. In retrospect, I still don't understand how I could have put school or work or anything before being right there at Buttons' side. The only explanation I can come up with is that it was my mind's unwillingness to accept the dire reality of the situation. It was as if by pushing to maintain some semblance of normality, I could bring things back to normal.

After a week of never sleeping longer than two hours before being awakened by Buttons needing water or dry towels and bedding, my health was totally shot again. But like a mother who is able to lift the back of an automobile to free her trapped child, I continued to function despite my own ragged condition. By that point, I wasn't even riding on adrenaline, but rather, just love and stubbornness.

Although she was still alive two weeks after the stroke, Buttons had lost so much weight I could watch her heart beating in her chest. As if awakened by the fear of what I was seeing, from the depths of my muddy brain, an idea surfaced that led me to the local natural foods store where I bought something I'd never bought before in my life: all natural, hormone-free, grain-fed raw beef liver. Back home, I opened the container and speared the ugly, slimy mess into a pot of boiling water. As the smell began to permeate the kitchen, long-sleeping memories of childhood dinners ending in my mother's screaming, swearing, slapping, punching and forcing me to eat the putrid, brown liver on my plate came bubbling to the surface. Despite having dealt with it all years before in therapy, the residue remained. I smashed up the cooked liver and mixed it with some warmed, leftover mashed potatoes hoping that Buttons would at least lick what was on the spoon to provide her little body with some much-needed nourishment.

She was asleep on her side when I sat down next to her and put the liver-laden spoon next to her mouth. Out loud I told her, "Okay, Poop, this is how much I love you. Enough to go through smelling this awful stuff." Her nose began to twitch and her eyelids began to flutter. All of a sudden her eyes flew open, and before I knew what was happening, her mouth clamped over the entire spoon. Had I moved my hand a second later, my fingers would have been bleeding.

She swallowed it all in one big gulp and then looked at me with an expression that most certainly said, "Well, hurry up! Where's my next bite?!"

It was as if she had suddenly discovered a new and very important reason to stick around: that heaven couldn't possibly be as good as cooked liver and potatoes. Smiling and laughing and crying with joy, I sat with Ms. Buttons as she ate several more bitefulls. Obviously strengthened by the food, by that night she was trying to sit up and by the next morning, trying to stand. She was unable to keep her balance and was still curved like a C, but I knew this was what Dr. Parker had meant by rally. It was Thanksgiving Day, and I had never been so grateful.

The following day I took Butts to the vet to be checked and although she'd lost almost half of her body weight, her heart was strong and the miracle dog was obviously well on her way towards recovery.

I had a month before school started again so I spent any time when I wasn't working doing research on the Internet. There I found some very interesting articles on the use of a common antioxidant, alpha-lipoic acid, which had been used on stroke victims and Alzheimer's patients for nearly fifty years in Germany: studies had shown it vastly improved both conditions. For years I'd held a great respect for German cutting-edge, alternative medical research and so my next stop was the bookstore where I found similar and supporting data on alpha-lipoic acid, all of which had been tested on animals and documented there in the books. Hopeful and excited, I went to the health food store and purchased a bottle by a company I trusted for their pharmaceutical grade purity. I began adding it to Butski's food. According to the research, they had given stroke victims averaging 150 pounds doses of at least 1,000 milligrams a day to see the results. They claimed this antioxidant-coenzyme was possibly responsible for the regeneration of nerve fibers and improved basal ganglia function: areas in the cerebrum involved in posture and coordination. I started giving Butts 100 milligrams a day. She now weighed ten pounds instead of seventeen, even though she was eating a lot of liver and mashed potatoes.

Then I called a certified animal chiropractor I knew who came to the house to adjust her spine, and within a week she could stand with a little help and go outside to the bathroom. Daily, I massaged her bent neck, which felt hard, like a frozen turkey. Another week on the large alpha-lipoic acid dose and her neck started to relax and she was able to keep her balance for longer periods of time. As another week passed, she began walking by herself.

By January her C neck had disappeared completely and she was able to walk pretty well, her CDS symptoms had lessened and she no longer got "stuck" in corners or behind furniture. The only symptom we couldn't seem to overcome was the nighttime pacing. I figured it might have been too late—that perhaps she'd had the symptom too long for the alpha-lipoic acid to reverse it.

As a result of my on-line research, I was lucky enough to also have secured the advice of a holistic vet in northern California, Dr. Gloria Dodd. After reading Dr. Dodd's website, I emailed her and the next day received a detailed response about her experience working with other CDS animals using homeopathy.

Excitedly, I called her office. Forty minutes later, I hung up from our conversation with a heart full of hope and a list of suggestions. Number one on that list was for me to send a sample of Buttons' fur to a lab for hair analysis. This was something I was familiar with, as a few years before, I had sent samples of both my hair and Buttons' fur to a lab in Texas, which did analysis on people and dogs. Basically, a hair analysis will give you an idea of the mineral levels and their ratios in the body—kind of like how geologists determine natural history by studying layers of rock. Back then, Buttons' had come out normal in everything while my analysis had indicated extreme magnesium deficiency, a common symptom of CFS and adrenal exhaustion. In addition, Dr. Dodd gifted me one of her products called a Healing Halter™, which arrived a few days after our call. It consisted of a green, nylon halter that fit around Buttons' body and neck with Velcro. Sewn into the halter were quartz crystal mandalas and an anti-radiation bead, which also used the principal of pyramid configuration energy, something I was familiar with from Dad's energy plates of long ago. As Dr. Dodd explained on her website, the halter was designed to balance the body's own electromagnetic field (EMF) and in so doing stimulate the immune system and natural healing mechanism of the body.

In our small apartment, Buttons was never too far from the television or the refrigerator, both of which I knew to have large electromagnetic fields. Ten years before, I had gotten rid of the worst culprit, a microwave oven, and I was happy for any protection the halter may have offered her from the other appliances. Again, it was at worst something that I knew couldn't hurt.

When we got the results of Buttons' fur analysis we were surprised to see that her level of aluminum was through the roof. It made sense as far as her Alzheimer's-like symptoms went: the mystery to unravel was the aluminum's source. Dr. Dodd and I carefully went over all the supplements Buttons had been on over the last five years. The water she drank was distilled. The treats were mostly homemade and always contained natural, organic ingredients. I'd never used aluminum cookware, so that wasn't it. And then we found it.

Two years before I had taken a natural-care pet consultant's advice to replace brown rice with barley in Buttons' food. When she heard that, Dr. Dodd jumped on it, explaining that in the past she'd sent several types of grain to the lab and all the barley had tested the same: containing high, perhaps toxic levels of aluminum. Although Dr. Dodd had some personal opinions as to why that was so, all I cared about was finding the source of aluminum and removing it from Buttons' world. So I took Dr. Dodd's suggestion and sent a sample of the organic sprouting barley I'd been special ordering from the health food store to the lab for testing. Sure enough, it came back showing an extremely high aluminum content. Immediately after receiving the results, I threw out the ten pounds of barley I had in the pantry along with the all-natural, dry dog food with barley listed in the ingredients that I kept for travel and emergencies.

Frustrated that even high quality organic products could be toxic, I focused instead on our next step: trying to pull some of that aluminum out of Buttons' brain. I ordered a series of nosodes—homeopathic remedies developed for a specific problem, in this case, aluminum, the probable cause of her CDS. All I could do was pray that they were truly clean and natural.

For the next several months, Buttons was on those remedies and the results were subtle, but sure. The late night pacing continued, but her mind seemed sharper, more alert, and her spirit more present, enabling me at times, to bask in the illusion of staving off time. Most importantly, she never developed the CDS symptom of not recognizing me. In any event, between the pacing and the stroke, there was no denying that we were in the beginnings of our major transition, the one that would take her physical body away from me forever.

PART IV

A New World

"I will admit that the fog of death seems to have rolled in between us
and to have separated us from one another.
But the important point is this; it cannot get into
my thinking and affections,
where you have lived ever since I met you.
Nothing in there can ever harm you or break
the bond of love and understanding between us.
And that, old Pal, is why I know that all is well with you—and us."

– J. Allen Boone

It was nearly impossible for me to stay in the present moment. My mind wanted to either deny the fact of Buttons' impending death or dwell on it. Neither thought process was appealing, so once again I called Hugh for some advice. He reminded me to simply focus more on connecting with Buttons' spirit and went on to say that eliminating the pain of loss was an impossible goal: rather, the goal could be to bring an element of peace to my inevitable grieving.

Often Buttons showed signs of being frustrated with her aging body, but she continued to passionately love eating, being in the rocking chair, and being held. While there were people in my life who tried to encourage me to put her down, I cringed, knowing beyond the shadow of a doubt that Butski herself would let me know if and when the time came to do that. For almost two decades, I'd practiced nonverbal, telepathic communication with this being; I wasn't about to start doubting it now. Besides, her current life consisted of sleeping, eating, being in her beautiful back yard, and cuddling with her adoring companion. How bad of a life is <u>that</u>?

Instead, I embraced our time of transition by going to the second-hand store and buying her a deluxe model baby stroller. After lining it with foam, I brought it on all our walks so that Buttons could ride when she got too tired or stiff to continue walking. We experimented with different brands of doggy diapers, but I could tell that Butts was against the whole concept. Whereas I thought she looked rather cute in them, she obviously disagreed with my assessment and made her way out of them every time. Respect for her quickly led to my abandoning the whole diaper idea for the time being and instead I stocked up on paper towels and natural enzyme cleaner. I also negotiated a monthly massage trade with a friend who owned his own carpet cleaning business.

School was getting more difficult as I was still waking up with Buttons every few hours. After each restless night, she would sleep all day, but of course I couldn't do that with homework, housework, errands, wedding ceremonies, and massage clients to attend to. Each day I dragged myself through every task. The occasional migraine headaches I'd been getting were now full-blown, debilitating ones, occurring two to three times a month. Now and then, I'd discover an herb or hormone precursor, which would offer some relief for a month or two, but then the headaches would return with a vengeance. At those times I felt defeated and desperate, knowing how much my baby girl needed me to take care of her, when what I needed was for someone to take care of *me*. Other than the occasional brief affair, it had been years since I had participated in any kind of positive, romantic partnership with a man; Buttons was my first priority and dearest responsibility and that alone left me little time to socialize. But of the available men I did meet, none of them left me feeling as deeply moved as Connor had, and I wasn't willing to settle for less.

Then around Christmas, I reconnected with some old friends from Chicago, which started me thinking a lot about Dave Heath, a drummer I had been involved with when I was much younger. He had been crazy in love with me, but at that pre-therapy/workshop/seminar time, I was so filled with the self-hate and loathing I'd learned in childhood, his adoration and attention left me feeling almost disgusted. Instead, I was only attracted to the boys who didn't like themselves either and were terrified of my affections or interest in them. Now, thirty years later, I realized how precious and rare Dave's kind of devotion was. What I wouldn't give to have someone like that now, I thought!

One afternoon I heard from those old friends that Dave had been killed in a car accident many years before in Florida. Thinking about him then, time seemed to collapse, and as I sat mourning him and the fact that I hadn't treated his heart with near the tenderness and reciprocity it deserved, I swear I could feel his presence, surrounding me with love. There was a palpable peace in the room, and I could sense him there smiling, as I felt, rather than heard him say, "Well! It's about time!" It was oddly comforting.

Given my short, emotional fuse and attention span, I wish someone had thought to try to convince me to quit school. In hindsight, it would have been the best choice, but at the time all I could think of was securing a better paying, more easily marketable job skill, so I continued to push myself well beyond my former limits.

In other ways, the more practical side of me did show itself. Realizing that I would be in no shape when the time came to research certain things concerning Buttons' body in death, I began making all those investigative calls sooner rather than later. Being a renter, I had nowhere to bury her body and would not have liked it in a pet cemetery, so I began researching pet cremation. First, I found out that there was a company used by the veterinarians in town that came to the clinic or home to pick up the body and then returned a week later with the ashes. That definitely wouldn't do for me. I would need to know that the cremains were indeed hers instead of taking the word of strangers.

A few more phone calls and questions led me to discover where they took the bodies: a crematory in the rear of a funeral home which I'd passed countless times and never knew was there. When I called and asked to speak to the person in charge of pet cremation, they connected me with Sam, a sweet, older gentleman who agreed to let me come down and see the facility, a request he said they seldom got. This was a way for me to prepare and take care of myself: knowing where I'd be going and what to expect when the time came.

Sam met me at the front desk and walked me through the funeral home towards the rear of the building. As we headed down the hallway and turned the corner, I was taken aback when I almost ran into an open coffin containing a man's body, ready to be moved into one of the rooms for his family's viewing. Here, death was not hidden or swept under the rug—here, it was right in your face. I followed Sam through the exit and across a small gravel lot.

As we approached the open, garage-like door to the cinderblock crematory, I could hear the din of the furnace, and once inside, saw two small rooms connected by a short hallway. First Sam showed me the room for the animals with two small chambers, which were thankfully, not in use, and then the room for humans, which looked the same but with bigger cremation chambers. As if we were discussing the weather, I asked him about the cremains themselves, having heard that not all the bone is reduced to ash. Nodding affirmatively, he then asked me if I wanted to see inside the chamber, which was currently being used to cremate a large man. Without even thinking, the word, "yes" flew out of my mouth, shocking me. Standing about eight feet from the doors of the chamber as Sam walked over to the lever that would open them, I tried to breathe. I wanted to scream, "Don't! I don't want to see!" but no word came out of me, and I stood frozen with panic and fear. Why in the world had I said yes? Why couldn't I mouth the word "no" now?

My gut was gripped with terror as the metal doors began to part and reveal their contents. What had been the background noise of the furnace now filled the entire room with its roar. Then, as the doors reached fully open, my terror and panic were suddenly swept away and replaced with a deep sense of calm and peace. Staring into the chamber of glowing, white heat tinged with the most beautiful, deep red, I saw what little of the biggest bones were still left, just barely enough to figure out which way the body had been laid. I felt catapulted back in time, intimate with some ancient tribal memory of when death was an open, natural part of life and everyday ritual, rather than considered something morbid and only the stuff of horror movies. I was looking into the eye of the beast, as it were, and I was not afraid. One of my friends who I later described the experience to, labeled it quite accurately as, "the peace that passeth understanding." I thanked Sam and said goodbye. As we shook hands he told me it had been a pleasure to meet me and that he hoped he would not see me again for a very long time. I nodded in agreement and walked to the car with tears inching down my face.

A few weeks later I heard that they also did cremations at the little pet cemetery in town, and so I called and made an appointment to visit there. Barbara, the woman in charge, was also very kind and helpful. Instantly, I preferred the feeling there as it was lovingly dedicated to only pets and had a private, serene meditation room for waiting and memorial services. On the wall, I saw a plaque with the well-known, touching poem called "Rainbow Bridge":

Just this side of heaven is a place called Rainbow Bridge.

When an animal dies that has been especially close to someone here, that pet goes to Rainbow Bridge.

There are meadows and hills for all of our special friends so they can run and play together.

There is plenty of food, water and sunshine, and our friends are warm and comfortable.

All the animals who had been ill and old are restored to health and vigor. Those who were hurt or maimed are made whole and strong again, just as we remember them in our dreams of days and times gone by.

The animals are happy and content, except for one small thing: they each miss someone very special to them, who had to be left behind.

They all run and play together, but the day comes when one suddenly stops and looks into the distance.

Her bright eyes are intent. Her eager body quivers.

Suddenly she begins to run from the group, flying over the green grass, her legs carrying her faster and faster.

You have been spotted, and when you and your special friend finally meet, you cling together in joyous reunion, never to be parted again.

The happy kisses rain upon your face: your hands again caress the beloved head, and you look once more into the trusting eyes of your pet, so long gone from your life but never absent from your heart.

Then you cross Rainbow Bridge together. (author unknown)

The front room was filled with caskets for pets, which I imagined, were the same as children's coffins, all fancy and full of satin. That was neither my nor Buttons' style, but I could understand why they were there for some people. I knew I would be more drawn to finding a small, simple wooden box for her ashes after her body's death and thought that getting a brass plate and having her motto that Natalie had given her, "I love life, let me prance" etched on it would be a good ritual for me during my grieving process. When the time came, this is where I'd bring my little girl's body. I was doing all I could think of to prepare and support myself, but I knew the truth was that I could never sufficiently prepare for the gut-wrenching pain or the giant crater her passing would leave in my life.

In March of 2002, shortly after Buttons' eighteenth birthday, I got a call from a reporter at the Arizona Daily Star newspaper who wanted to feature us in an article about long-term pet care. She'd heard about us from someone I knew at the Humane Society, and I was thrilled that along with headliners *Harry Potter* and *Lord of the Rings,* Buttons was about to make that year's news. The reporter, with photographer in tow, came to the house and a few days later, a big, color photo of us appeared in the pet section along with a three-column story about Button's cancer recovery, stroke recovery, holistic care and current well-being. In the wake of the story's publication, I got a few more calls from pet parents with questions about their senior canines. Again, I gladly shared what I had learned over the years and referred them to the sources, which were best in my opinion. Even as an old lady, Ms. Buttons continued to help and inspire as she took her place in the ranks of wise Canine Elders.

After seeing the article, my friend, Hanna, whose mother had recently passed, called, and in the course of conversation, encouraged me to borrow a video recorder. She shared that in her grief, the only thing that could bring her any comfort at all was the one video she had of her mom at a recent holiday dinner. She explained that while watching the video, it was as if her mind was tricked into thinking her mom was still alive. Of course Hanna knew intellectually that wasn't true but still, for those few minutes while she viewed the tape, saw her mother in action and heard her voice, she was offered some relief from her otherwise debilitating emotions.

After hanging up I called my friend Laurie who owned a video camera. She was also an avid dog lover. As the mother of a young son, Laurie had once shared with me that after having lost one beloved dog, in her heart, she suspected that the pain was no less than that of losing a human child. I was incredibly moved by her extremely bold and candid opinion. It was something I'd always believed, but having no human children of my own, it was not a statement I felt qualified to make. Maybe it was a more commonly held opinion than many were comfortable with or willing to admit.

The filming marathon began with Buttons in the yard walking and peeing. It continued with her in the apartment eating, drinking, and pacing. Soon, in full Spielberg mode, I set the camera up on a tripod and filmed my waking her up in the morning to go outside, us in the rocking chair while I sang her to sleep, me giving her a bath, drying her, and brushing her. I added the tapes to the Santa Cruz redwood hike video and some earlier tapes of Butts at around three years old in the park and at my cousin's. Deep inside I knew, no matter how many hours of tape I accumulated, they wouldn't come close to filling all the hours of grieving waiting for me somewhere up ahead.

Laurie's empathetic response to my situation showed itself brightly a few days later when she surprised me by stopping by with her digital camera to take some pictures of Butts and me. As I got comfortable on the couch, Buttons snuggled herself sweetly on my chest while Laurie played photographer, and later that evening, she emailed me the great shots she'd taken.

But my friend's true picture-taking motive became clear two weeks later when, opening my front door, I found a big plastic bag hanging from the knob. Inside was the most beautiful, handmade pillow covered in a lovely, cream-colored fabric that perfectly matched my couch. And then I saw the 8"x10" silkscreen of my favorite photo of Butts and me that Laurie had taken. Her thoughtfulness didn't stop there. The pillow was trimmed with three inches of a black, almost furry fabric with gray highlights that looked like dog hair and was dappled with black buttons of every shape and size that she'd sewn on by hand.

Incredibly moved by her thoughtfulness, I somehow managed to dial Laurie's number. I was too emotional to speak when she answered the phone, but she guessed it was me. I managed to blurt out how touched I was and how words could never convey my gratitude for her time, talent and heart. After the call, I let Buttons sniff the pillow as I explained to her that I would only have it to hug when she left her body. She leaned over and licked my tears.

I began seeing a grief counselor who specialized in pet loss. She was a compassionate listener, which is what I needed at the time, and though her orientation was a bit too New Age for even my taste, she was willing to trade for massage, and I was thankful. She gave me a few useful tips on how to become more present with the actual transition Buttons and I were going through and how not to project so much into the future that it ruined what time we had left. Mainly, that meant acknowledging verbally that we were in a time of transition while standing up and stretching my body as I said the words. It was a beneficial, Buddhist-like exercise, which pulled me back from my fear and into the present moment.

One of the ideas I came up with to honor our transition again included my friend Laurie. I phoned her with a dinner invitation and enthusiastically explained what I planned to do with her help. The evening she arrived, I was waiting with a set of silk and cotton pillowcases. After inspecting them and the other supplies I'd gathered, Laurie and I got down to business. She opened the bottle of nontoxic soy ink and poured it onto the spongy ink pad. As she did that, I spread out one of the beautiful white pillowcases onto a towel, and set them on the arm of the couch. When we were both ready, I picked Buttons up in my arms while Laurie gently and firmly took hold of Buttons' one white paw and pressed it squarely onto the ink pad. I then moved Butts over to the arm of the couch where Laurie pressed the paw onto the pillowcase border. Buttons jerked her paw out of Laurie's grasp and the print smeared all over. We swore, giggled and then gently washed the old ink off Butski's paw and tried again. The third time was the charm as the print we laid down came out clear and distinct. Buttons was very glad when it was all over, but not before giving us both that, "you are crazy" look which prompted us both to share some of the evening's organic stir-fry with her.

That Thanksgiving of 2002, I spent the entire day at my eighteen-year-old Buttons' side, sleeping when she did, staying in the yard with her while she was out, and singing, rocking, and holding her while she was awake. I had turned down all the dinner invitations I'd gotten so I could instead cherish my time with my best friend who loved me more than anyone else in the world ever had. Since her stroke, I had bought several disposable cameras and had been taking pictures of her, mostly of her sleeping in her various places around the apartment. When each camera was fully exposed, instead of taking it for developing, I put it in a box in the top of my closet.

Later that afternoon as I gratefully shared my holiday turkey with the Little Turkey, I finally decided that I could no longer continue with school. I had been functioning on what felt like no deep sleep for over a year. Added to that was the overwhelming depression and burnout I was battling every day. There seemed no other choice but to lighten my load.

Successfully, I made it through my final exams, and then Buttons and I spent a quiet and nurturing Christmas together. Since I knew it could very well be our last, I wasn't willing to share any of it with anyone but her.

Our routine became her sleeping all day while I met with wedding couples and massage clients. She'd wake up in the late afternoon, just about the time I was finished working and the rest of the evening we spent getting her fed, taken outside, rocked and held. I had tried keeping her awake during the day, but then she'd start pacing and would sometimes fall and not be able to get up without help. Those were things I couldn't handle and meet with clients at the same time. So I tried Rescue Remedy, liquid vitamin B complex, kava kava, and valerian root to help her relax at night, but nothing worked for more than two hours. As best I could, I resigned myself to the continued catnaps, but instead of offering me the recovery I needed, I continued to feel profoundly tired and wired all of the time. This did not prevent me, however, from cherishing our evenings together—my napping, watching TV, or reading while she lay contentedly on my chest. Every night was the same: her head tucked between my left shoulder and chin, with her one white paw placed always up against the inside of my left arm just above the crook of my elbow. I concentrated on soaking in the smell of her, her softness, and the feel of her weight on me, just as I had soaked the ocean into my being that last day in Pebble Beach.

After making the decision to quit school, I set up a meeting with the principal at one of the Catholic schools in town to implement a fund-raiser with them, selling my candles. I had spent some time on the computer revising the order forms that Gayle had made and included an informational flyer on the same page.

I was still earning less than it took to cover my basic living expenses without the help of my credit cards. Decorating candles was something that combined the possibility of increasing my income with something I could do at Buttons' side. The principal and I scheduled the flyer and order form distribution for the middle of January with me picking them up from the school on February 5. That would allow plenty of time for the parents to fill them out and get them returned. We agreed that I would then have the completed candles ready for pickup two weeks after that so the kids could take them home on the nineteenth.

Right after Christmas I performed several weddings and then spent my time prepping dozens of candles. In the meantime, I took care of massage clients only in the early part of the day as Buttons was waking up around four in the afternoon and needing constant care. She was having good days and bad days. On the bad ones she was having an even harder time getting up, and I would often discover her lying on the kitchen floor in a puddle. As frustrating as that was for both of us, I always did my best to comfort her and make the following, quick bath in the sink as effective and pleasant for her as possible.

Realizing that the diaper thing was now essential, we experimented with different sizes and brands of disposables before settling on Huggies Supreme 3, with comfort stretch sides. I soon made the endearing discovery that if I poked a small hole in the back, right where the picture of Pooh Bear was, her tail fit through and the diaper fit her perfectly.

I had many conversations with Buttons then, asking her to guide me as she always had about her care. Each time I told her that I wanted only to do the best by her and begged to know if she was suffering at all. Inevitably, after each of those conversations, she'd have several extremely good days in a row, and I took that to mean the time hadn't come for me to consider the dreaded option of euthanasia.

Worried that the Monkey Face might awaken and need me, I was scheduling everything so I could go to the walking track during times when she would most likely be asleep. But then I noticed something interesting. Sometimes in the middle of my workout, I'd suddenly be overcome with the sense that I should return home and whenever that happened, I immediately stopped and followed the instinct. Every time, without exception, I'd come home to find Buttons awake and in need of my help to go outside. Never did I return home from the track or running errands, without having had that feeling, to find Buttons needing me. Neither did I ever have that feeling and discover it to be a false alarm. I soon became quite trusting of the knowledge that our communication was strong enough that I could leave without worry, knowing our connection would guide me to her side whenever the need arose. For years I had been feeling her in that way, but now it took on an intensity I'd never known before. Perhaps Hugh was right: focusing more consciously on connecting with her spirit had connected me more deeply with Buttons.

Sometimes when she'd be asleep in the living room and I'd be in the bedroom resting or reading or in the massage room working, I'd tune in to how strongly I could feel her presence in the next room. Often I thought to myself that this is what it would feel like when she left her body... that she was merely in the next room. I could only hope.

The first week of January 2003, I borrowed a baby sling, and with her in it and comfortably swaddled across my chest, I took Buttons to see Dr. Parker. She assured me that The Butts wasn't in any pain, but just experiencing old-age discomfort. Regardless, Dr. Parker also gently warned me that at that point, the writing was on the wall. In response to my question of what I should do in case Buttons had another stroke, Dr. Parker sent me home with some more oral steroids and detailed instructions on what to do before bringing her in under those conditions.

So far, the good days outnumbered the bad. On the worst days, Buttons fell down a lot, though she was still able to stand at her bowl to eat and drink. The second week of January, I swaddled her up again in the baby sling and took her for an acupuncture treatment hoping it would relieve some of her stiffness and improve her strength and stamina.

The following weekend had its difficult energy both globally and personally. The space shuttle, Columbia, had just been launched, a mission that would end in disaster for all on board. Closer to home, there was a big bridal fair on Sunday that I knew I should attend to pass out my business cards. I also knew it was imperative that I get some amount of restful sleep the night before, but it was not to be.

Around 10 p.m. I gave Buttons half of a doggy sleeping pill I'd gotten from the vet for "emergencies." Regardless, just like clockwork, Buttons woke up and started pacing frantically at 1 a.m. After a half-hour of rocking she fell back asleep and twenty minutes later so did I. At 3 a.m. she woke again needing to go outside. We stood in the cold for fifteen minutes while she stumbled around. When she was finished, I gave her a little kava kava extract and by 4 a.m. we were both asleep but it only lasted until 5 a.m. when she got up and began pacing agitatedly once more. And then I lost it.

Flinging myself out of bed, I grabbed a pacing Buttons, stormed into the living room and plopped down on the couch. With my hands under her belly, I held her in the air facing me as I cried out, "WHAT IS IT YOU NEED, BUTTONS?!?"

As the look of shock in her eyes registered in my sleep-deprived brain, I realized how roughly I'd been holding her and as horrible as it is to admit, shaking her too. Granted, I hadn't shaken her hard, but I had, out of frustration, shaken her nonetheless. It wasn't the degree that mattered. What mattered was that I had done it at all. I had scared her. I hated myself.

Immediately, I sat her on my lap, wrapped my arms around her, and began rocking back and forth to comfort her. When she seemed settled down I let myself weep with the mortification and shame I felt consumed by. I thought of my mother, filled with uncontrollable rage, and of all the times she had taken it out on me. I saw a new dimension of my own shadow side and was totally appalled. It is said that as human beings, we are all capable of everything any other human has ever done, that Mother Teresa and Adolph Hitler both reside in each of us, but I guess I never really believed it until that moment. This was my Buttons Girl I'd mistreated, the innocent, unconditionally loving being I cherished most in the world, and now I felt that if anyone should be euthanized, it should be me.

By ten that morning Buttons was fed and sleeping sweetly on her bed. There was now a third presence living in our home: there was a monster and it was in me. The monster and I got ready to go to the bridal fair.

I greeted other wedding vendors I knew, and passed out business cards to couples. Later, I met up with my friend Sarah whose wedding I'd performed earlier that year. She was checking out the fair for a coworker of hers who was planning a wedding, but had been unable to attend that day.

As Sarah and I stood in line so I could buy an exceptionally rare and much needed cup of coffee, I found myself telling her exactly what had happened the night before, for I just couldn't hold in the guilt any longer. As the truth and tears poured out of me, Sarah led me over to a more private corner of the room. She patiently let me finish my entire shameful admission before communicating the following sentiment.

"Nadine, you haven't had a full night's sleep in over a year. Do you have any idea how devastating that kind of sleep deprivation is? Besides, you didn't hurt her; you just lost your temper. Look at me, Nadine: anyone else would have lost their temper months ago. This last year since Buttons' stroke has been a huge undertaking for you. You have to forgive yourself. It was just a slip. My God, the care and love you give that dog are incredible. Buttons knows that, Nadine, she knows how much you love her. Don't you doubt that for a second. Please stop beating yourself up... you are only human."

And then I knew that there was the rub. I had not lived up to the canine standards I was holding myself to. Taking a deep breath, I thanked Sarah with a grateful hug and resigned myself to living with the fact that I was only human. Buttons had no doubt already forgiven me, but I had a difficult time believing she should have.

A little while later I bumped into Jennea Bono, a wedding photographer whose work and photojournalistic style I greatly admired. We had talked in the past about her doing some photos of Butts and me, but had never set a date for a session. She excitedly announced that she was engaged and would love for me to write and perform her ceremony later that year. Agreeing, I suggested a trade for photos, gave her an update on Buttons' condition, and asked if we could do the photo shoot sometime very soon. Jennea whipped out her calendar, and we chose a week from that Tuesday. After giving her directions to our house, I left to get back home to Butts.

She was still sleeping when I arrived; it seemed the sleeping pill had finally kicked in so I slept for an hour myself before waking to make dinner for her. That night we went to bed and, contrary to our usual habit of her sleeping next to me, I fell asleep holding Ms. Buttons on my chest. When I awoke a miraculous seven hours later, my sweet girl was still asleep right there on me. It had been the most peaceful, serene sleep I had ever experienced in my life.

Sarah was right, a little rest brought with it an improved perspective, and though I still harbored some guilt for my behavior, the monster had vacated the premises for the time being. The following week was much better for both of us as Buttons seemed to improve quite a bit and slept for five hour stretches several nights in a row. We cuddled and ate and slept, and I did my best to make up for my previous outburst. Every day that week I held her, cooed to her, and kissed her as we sat for hours in our chair and rocked and rocked—back and forth and back and forth together.

That Sunday I did something social for the first time in months: I attended a Super Bowl party given by my accountant. I've never been a big fan of professional sports, mainly because I've always thought all that money could be spent in so many other, more productive ways on the planet, but I adore my accountant and his wife so I went. Thinking a lot about Gayle that day, I remembered the Super Bowl Sunday a few years before when her whole world changed forever.

The game itself meant nothing to me, in fact, it took me awhile to figure out that most of the other guests there weren't related: all wearing name tags with either Raider or Buccaneer written after their first name. When I felt a strong urge pulling me away, I left for home and ten minutes later when I got there, Buttons was awake with a still-warm diaper that needed changing.

On Monday, I sent out party invitations. Buttons would turn nineteen, two weeks from Wednesday, and I wanted our closest friends in town to help us celebrate.

That Tuesday Jennea arrived smiling with photo equipment in tow. We discussed my wanting some very unposed black and whites to be printed with a ragged border, which would further enhance their dramatic look. We then decided I should wear a long-sleeved, black turtleneck to help create a more artistic feel since Buttons herself was wearing mostly black and was, of course for the photos, diaperless. And then Jennea began weaving her magic, placing us in various chairs and positions in front of windows throughout the apartment. It took over an hour to shoot the roll and by then we were all rather tired, especially Butts who would normally be asleep that time of day. Jennea scheduled a return visit three days later to shoot one more roll.

When she came on Friday, I wore a white turtleneck and she took most of the photos outside. She had me hold Buttons on my right side and then on my left, facing me then facing away from me, over one shoulder and then turned over the other. I had no idea what to expect, but I trusted her artistic eye and ability to capture the emotion between my girl and me.

The next day, Saturday, Buttons seemed worse. She was more listless and by afternoon, wouldn't even try to get up, so that evening I called the emergency clinic, but Dr. Parker was off until Wednesday. Hanging up, I thought about taking Butts in anyway to see some other vet we'd never met, but decided that trying to establish a dialogue with someone brand new who might not be as understanding of our holistic ways would be a waste of energy and money that I didn't even have. I could tell Buttons wasn't in any kind of pain, and she was eating plenty of food so I called back and made an appointment for Wednesday afternoon at five with Dr. Parker. When I called to schedule that appointment, I also asked whether or not it would be wise to give Buttons one of the pills Dr. Parker had sent me home with in case Buttons started showing stroke symptoms. They told me it could do no harm either way. To stay on the safe side, I gave her the pill.

The next morning she seemed a bit better again, and so I went to the Sunday service at the Community Church For Positive Living, one of the Religious Science churches in Tucson. I didn't have the same feeling of belonging there as I had had with the New Thought churches in Santa Cruz, but I liked their minister, Rev. George, with whom I'd spoken on the rare occasions when I was able to attend. He was sweet and supportive and had suggested I bring some of my candle demos for him to display to the congregation. Indeed, that Sunday he showed and discussed the candles at the beginning of the service and encouraged people to meet with me afterwards and place an order. A half a dozen people did, and I told them the candles would be ready for them to pick up on Tuesday at the church.

Monday morning Buttons was still having more trouble than usual, but her appetite remained strong. Since she wasn't able to stand at her bowl, I held her on my lap and spoon-fed her. We went back to the eye-dropper method for her water, and I continued giving her the prescribed dosage of steroids according to Dr. Parker's detailed instructions from the previous month's check up.

On Tuesday, I swaddled Buttons up in the baby sling and took her with me as I delivered the candles to the church, so I could continue monitoring her. Grinning proudly, I held her as Rev. George, captivated by her sweetness, stroked her head while declaring how precious her spirit was. Afterwards, I brought her right back home where she fell asleep.

Later that day, I couldn't get Buttons to eat. At two in the morning I called the clinic to see if I could get in any earlier than my 5 p.m. appointment with Dr. Parker. They told me that the first appointment of her shift was available at 9 a.m., and I took it thinking it would be perfect since I had a haircut appointment at 11 a.m. For the rest of the night I held Buttons in bed, kept her hydrated, and changed her diaper every few hours.

At 8:45 the next morning, with Buttons resting quietly on my lap, I sat anxiously in the too bright and sterile-smelling waiting room of the veterinary clinic. A few minutes after nine the assistant finally led us into one of the small examination rooms where I gingerly set Buttons down on the steel table, her soft blankie underneath her. Then, as I lowered myself onto a chair next to her, I began gently stroking her fur, hoping to offer some comfort while she had her temperature taken. In the past, the assistant had always announced the thermometer reading when she was finished, but this time she didn't say anything before leaving the room except, "Dr. Parker will be right in." Tenderly, I continued petting Buttons, my mind frozen with fear, and a moment later, Dr. Parker entered, said hello, and bent to look searchingly into Buttons' eyes.

I began talking nervously. "She's been doing great on the alpha-lipoic acid and homeopathic remedies, but I think she may have had another stroke. She stopped eating last night. I gave her the emergency, oral steroids according to your instructions. Do you think she needs some intravenous steroids now?"

Dr. Parker asked me to hold on a minute while she listened to Buttons' heart and lungs. As the stethoscope explored, I rested my hand near Buttons' hip. Then the doctor lifted Buttons' lip and carefully examined the inside of her mouth. What Dr. Parker's exact words were after that I can't be sure because the moment she stood up straight, looked me in the eye and began speaking, a little voice inside my head started screaming, *"DON'T LISTEN TO THIS!"*

"Nadine, she has an infected tooth, and I can give her a shot of antibiotics for that, but she's also had another, smaller stroke and more steroids won't help this time. She is most likely in kidney failure. Her body temperature is so low, she probably won't last through tonight. I really don't think there's anything else that can be done at this point. I'm so sorry."

The power of her words detonated an explosion within me and instantly I was crying, the tears literally bursting out of me as if they were projectile. And then, unable to believe Dr. Parker's verdict, and grasping for options, I forced myself back into my rational mind.

"Is she in any pain? What if I start treating her tooth with colloidal silver to kill the infection? Is there some kind of test you can do on her to tell for sure about the kidney failure?"

Dr. Parker looked at me, her empathy tangible as she answered softly, "No, I don't think she's in any pain. I believe she's too weak at this point to fight the infection though I'll give her the shot of antibiotics just in case. And yes, there's a test we could do for the kidneys, but do you really want to put her through all that in what may be her last hours?"

I looked over at my sweet bunny. Her big, brown eyes, so full of love, looked back at me knowingly. "No," I answered. I tried to stop the tears, but they continued streaming nonstop down my face. And then I looked pleadingly at Dr. Parker, "If you were me, what would you do?"

Again, her mere expression reached out to me with love. "Well, if it were me, I'd have her put down right now, but, I don't think that's what's right for you. I don't think you could live with yourself if you did that. I think we should give her the antibiotics, and then you can go ahead and try using the colloidal silver and also a mild salt-water rinse. Bundle her up to keep her as warm as possible, and if she doesn't respond, just hold her for the rest of the time she has left. I'm so sorry, Nadine."

This time it didn't feel as if the world had stopped. If it had, I would have found a way to get Buttons and me off of it. Somewhere in my brain, I knew I just had to keep the world moving or it would all be over. And then Dr. Parker bent down to look Buttons in the eyes and began softly stroking her head. In that moment, my heart ached for them both. After administering the shot, she assured me once more that Buttons was not in any pain. My insides frozen, I thanked her, paid my bill and used the office phone to call and cancel my hair appointment.

With a robot-like efficiency, I bundled Buttons up in a big blanket I kept in the car, laid her on the passenger seat in front and drove to the Catholic school. Today was the day I'd committed to picking up their candle orders. I'd say I didn't know what I was thinking when I didn't go directly home instead, but the truth was I wasn't thinking at all. Had I been thinking, I would have done so many things differently: I would have bought some fresh flowers for Buttons to enjoy the smell of, then brought her right home, lit candles, and put on some soft music. I would have asked Dr. Parker to explain exactly what the stages of dying would look like and sound like, so I would be aware of each part of the path. But like I said, I wasn't thinking. At the school, I parked, ran in, and grabbed the order forms and pictures with no explanation other than, "I can't stay and talk, my dog is dying!" before turning to run back to the car. The women in the office must have thought I was nuts, but I was in extreme emotional shock.

All the way home, I kept glancing over at Buttons who seemed to be resting comfortably. I felt completely fractured. It was as if my body was there doing the driving, but my mind was somewhere totally separate from that and my heart, with all its emotion, was off in some third, remote location. A small, nagging thought kept inching its way from some distant place into the forefront of my mind, *what if she dies before I get home?* I drove a bit faster. Pulling into the driveway, I turned off the engine and ran to unlock the front door. Back at the car, I tenderly scooped my precious bundle into my arms and turned to walk with dread towards the building and the unstoppable events that awaited us there.

This is the last time you'll ever walk into the apartment with her.
NO!

Carefully, I set Buttons on my bed and laid some pillows around her before running to the bathroom, washing my hands, and then flying around the apartment grabbing all her favorite blankets. Lifting her out of the sling, I wrapped her in her soft, furry blanket with the mock buttons of turquoise felt and then wrapped her in another. Clutching desperately to the fragile thread of hope Dr. Parker had left me with, I placed some towels under Butski's head and went to prepare the salt-water syringe they had given me at the clinic. Back in the bedroom I let the rinse slowly run through her mouth before dousing the area with the tasteless colloidal silver. Then I scooped her into my arms and cozy in our rocking chair, I tried to sing to her, but I couldn't make it through any of the lyrics without sobbing. As Buttons lay peacefully on my lap, my emotions flipped on and off like a strobe light. I didn't want to think. I didn't want to feel. I'd spent nineteen years helping her live: I didn't know how to help her die.

Grasping for whatever bit of solace I might find in keeping busy, I reached for the phone, called Barbara the manager at the pet cemetery, and told her what was happening. She sweetly gave her condolences and assured me I could bring Buttons' body in the next day, stay during the cremation, and have complete privacy. Part of me believed that I was only being cautious and that we wouldn't really be needing those services. Then I called Gayle to let her know what was happening. We'd had dinner together a few times recently and since she knew most of the other people I'd invited to Buttons' birthday party, I asked her to call everyone and tell them that the party was canceled.

February 12, Buttons' nineteenth birthday... exactly one week from today, February 5.

My logical mind continued to function. My emotional self had taken off for Bermuda.

During my phone conversations, we'd continued rocking in our chair. I kept checking to see if she was breathing. People and dogs I'd loved had died before, but I'd never been on a deathwatch. I was certainly familiar with loss, but I'd never lost anything that had meant so much to me. I cooed to her and kissed her. All I could tell her was that I loved her and that it was going to be okay. I prayed to God that I was right.

Eventually, becoming incredibly sleepy, I moved us over to the bed, put Buttons on my chest, and pulled the down comforter over us. I continued to try and console us both with my words while also trying desperately to ignore the morbid, crazy thoughts that kept popping into my mind. Thoughts like, *let's get this over with already, I have candles to make.*

Forcing my focus back to the present moment, I told my Baby Butts that when the time came, she should just let go and enter my heart where she would live forever and that Grandma would be waiting for her in the next dimension. I heard myself say the words, but somewhere in me I still couldn't believe that she would die. I was trapped, a prisoner in some void between rational functioning and fervid denial.

For the next few hours, we both drifted in and out of some kind of sleep, though I was always totally aware of her breathing. A little before 3:30 p.m. Gayle called to ask how we were doing and to share that everyone she had spoken with directly had sent their love and prayers, the others she'd left messages for. She then began telling me something about when her father had died the previous year and the family had sat with him beforehand. Buttons began breathing heavily. I wanted Gayle to get to a comma so I could politely interrupt her and end the conversation. Finally I just blurted out, "Something's happening, I have to go!" and hung up.

Buttons was now restless, and it seemed she was trying to get off of me. Thinking she had to pee, I reached for the towel next to us and maneuvered it underneath her. She then inched her way up so that her head was pressing right against my throat as her breathing continued to quicken. I held her close and told her it was okay because of the towel. Still referring to her having to pee, what I actually said without thinking about it was, "You can go, sweetie, it's okay, you can go, Poop," as I lightly patted her bottom.

Then, as I was looking down at her body, everything happened simultaneously. First, I felt a physical, intense cramp in my heart just like I had in California right before the earthquake. At the same moment I felt what seemed to be Buttons lurching powerfully, though her body remained perfectly still. It was the strangest thing: feeling her move, but at the same time, seeing no movement. What I was aware of next was a sudden, powerful feeling that my Grandmother was so close, I could turn and see her, and then I knew. I knew that Buttons was dead, or more accurately, that she had left her body, because I had literally felt her wrench herself out of it.

What happened in the very next moment was that the top two feet of the entire room filled with Buttons. It was so absolutely her energy, and though I couldn't see it, I could feel it there as strongly as anything I'd ever felt in my life, maybe stronger. It was her, expanded to fill the space just below the ceiling, and I felt it more powerfully than any emotion: hate, love, or desire, that I had ever felt before. Perhaps this is why heaven is always portrayed as up, I thought, because the soul, once free of the density of the body, indeed rises.

Dreamlike, and still holding her now empty body, I sat up and felt the towel drop. Part of my brain told me I had to take her into the living room where there was more light and check to make sure she had gone while another part of my brain scoffed, knowing for a fact, she had. But most of me just couldn't fathom that all our years together were suddenly just, POOF—OVER.

As I entered the hall and then the living room, I could feel her essence occupying the top of the entire apartment. Her being, now incredibly expanded and hovering near the ceiling, felt huge as I laid her body on the couch and looked at its lifeless eyes.

Stroking her head, I felt numb and exhausted, shocked, relieved, devastated, and traumatized. I put her body on my chest and lay on the couch as was our evening ritual, but it felt uncomfortably strange. She just wasn't in there—she was filling the top of the apartment. I stood and lovingly laid the warm body on her bed in the living room and covered it from the neck down with one of her blankets.

Over on my worktable was a box of demo candles and reaching in, I pulled out several of them. There were a few different ones with Buttons' picture and one with a picture of the two of us on it. I chose the candle with my favorite picture of her and lit it. From the kitchen cabinet, I pulled out one of her old, ceramic food bowls, turned it upside down on the coffee table in the corner nearest her bed, and set the glowing candle on top of it.

And then I began cleaning the house. My mind had no way to cope with all that had happened that day. It certainly couldn't embrace the depth or intensity of the pain, and so I just kept moving. I scrubbed the bathroom and the massage room, but avoided the kitchen as it was too filled with land mines: her bowls, her rugs, her supplements, the foam on the bottom cabinets. Then the phone rang.

It was Jennea calling to tell me she was at the photo lab up the street and that our proofs were ready. I told her Buttons had just died. My mouth formed the words, but my heart was paralyzed. Jennea urged me to come look at the proofs, sure they'd comfort me and even though I knew I shouldn't be driving, I let myself be swayed. Long before, I'd planned on making announcements to send to friends all over the country when Buttons passed, and including one of the black and white photos would make them extra special. Before leaving, I called Gayle and told her what had happened. To this day I don't remember any of the conversation or have any memory of driving to the photo lab.

Jennea was at the counter when I arrived. She quickly grabbed the proofs and set them in front of me. I felt like I was in some kind of dream or alternate reality, that I was a fragile sheet of thin glass that could break into millions of tiny pieces at any moment. My heart and mind were totally disconnected from each other. Like some observer, I watched myself function, move and talk. Like everyone when they lose someone they love, I couldn't seem to comprehend why the rest of the world continued functioning. Didn't they know the absolute worst had just happened?

Jennea hadn't let me down. The photos were artistic and beautiful, having captured the bond between Buttons and me like some kind of visual, unspoken poetry. I chose the one I wanted for the announcements, ordered copies of it, and drove home.

As I walked through the courtyard towards the front door, my heart began to race and my palms sweat. She would not be there to greet me. Instead, I would walk in and see her dead body on her bed. Turning the key and entering, I could still feel her energy, thick, electric and present at the top of the room. Walking over to her bed, I lifted the blanket, which had trapped her body heat, brushed my cheek against the side of it and then covered it again. I glanced at the clock.

Ten after six, time for *Friends.*

Sitting down I turned on the TV to watch the rerun and a few minutes later felt a wave of hunger. Realizing I hadn't eaten all day, I went over to the phone and ordered a pizza.

Just keep moving.

Back on the couch, I'd glance over at Buttons' bed every so often. She looked exactly like she was there sleeping.

See—this is just like any other night.

The pizza came: I set it on the coffee table and went to grab some paper towels.

Got plenty of those now.

Don't think about it, oh, God, don't think about it.

Sitting back down, I placed the box on my lap, opened it, picked up a slice of pizza and started to take a bite.

Now it's <u>my</u> turn to take care of <u>you</u>, Mom.

For a moment I just sat stunned, my hand suspended in midair as the pizza dropped from it and fell to the box. And then I started crying uncontrollably. I grabbed Laurie's pillow with the picture of Buttons on it and clutching it to my chest, I sobbed.

I hear you, Poop, I hear you! Are you okay?

I'm right here, Mom. You know that. I'm okay. I'm better than okay. I will always be here with you. I will always be your little love bunny. You know that. It's okay, Mom, really.

Within the dense fog of all the emotional upheaval, shock, and fatigue I was feeling, I had some crystal clear thoughts too, as I remembered how I had felt Buttons' soul jump out of her body. Having always embraced the belief of nothing ever really dying but merely changing form, I no longer considered it simply a nice belief to have; now it was something I had experienced, something I knew for certain was true. For her entire life, Buttons had blessed me day in and day out with her gifts, her love, her teachings. And then this day, she blessed me with yet another gift, perhaps the greatest gift of all: that I need not be afraid of death—my own or anyone else's.

And of course she would continue talking to me as she always had. I already knew the difference between her "voice" and my thoughts: I'd had nineteen years of practice.

Certainly there are plenty of people who think such things are silly, hogwash, the wishful musings of a mind desperate to mold an explanation with which to comfort a broken heart. Then again, there are those minds that have thought otherwise:

"I am confident that there truly is such a thing as living again, that the living spring from the dead, and that the souls of the dead are in existence." —Socrates

"The intuitive mind is a sacred gift and the rational mind is a faithful servant. We have created a society that honors the servant and has forgotten the gift." —Albert Einstein

"I look upon death to be as necessary to the constitution as sleep. We shall rise refreshed in the morning." —Benjamin Franklin

"The soul comes from without into the human body, as into a temporary abode, and it goes out of it anew and it passes into other habitations, for the soul is immortal."
—Ralph Waldo Emerson

For nearly two decades of my life, Buttons had been there showing me how to open my heart and trust: how to live happily and lovingly. Now, in the moments when I wasn't completely numb, I hurt like hell, but at the same time, she hadn't gone anywhere. I walked to the bookshelf and began paging through all my old journals, looking for a C.W. Leadbeater quote that I'd copied down years before, one that kept tickling the back of my mind, wanting desperately to be remembered now.

PART V

The Promised Land

"It is one of the commonest of mistakes
to consider that the limit of our power of perception
is also the limit of all there is to perceive."

– C.W. Leadbeater

Feeling validated and somehow safer after finding and reading the quote, I sat back down. Still operating on automatic pilot, I stared blankly at the television and continued eating pizza until there was none left. Some time later I found myself calling the grief counselor and asking if she was available to drive us to the pet cemetery the following day. Somehow, I knew that Gayle had already called her and had told her what happened. The counselor agreed to pick me up about 9:30 the next morning. With little comprehension, I watched the news and when it was over, I turned off the set.

Deadly silence.

Poop, are you there?

I'm here, Mom, you know I'm here. You can feel me, right?

As if following some kind of known, yet unspoken orders, I rose up off the couch, walked into the bathroom, got her special bath mat from under the sink and laid it in the tub. Reaching up, I took the hand-held shower head out of its holder and let it hang down loose and then I moved my "special occasion only" ginger shampoo and conditioner from the shower rack to the floor. Back in the living room I once again lifted the blanket off her still warm body. I bent down and carefully lifted that black, furry body which was now as light as a feather. Walking into the bathroom, I set it tenderly on the mat in the tub and knelt down on the floor beside it. Then I turned on the water and when it was warm, but not too hot, I switched it to shower and grabbed the hand-held. Gently, very, very gently, I began bathing my girl one last time.

That sweet body that I had washed so many times before and would never wash again. That sweet body that had loved life so much, endured so much, survived so much. Her bushy tail, her pointy ears, her white paw. The water and the soap combined with my steadily falling tears as I leaned over the side of the tub cleaning each part of her tenderly, slowly, reverently. Part of my mind thought, *people would think this is weird that I'm doing this.* Instantly another part of my mind answered, *no, people have been doing this for centuries — the women washing and preparing the bodies of the loved ones while the men outside build the funeral pyres.*

Nothing I did that night was pre-planned or thought of in advance. Something deep within me had taken over and made me its puppet. I could barely think at all.

When I had finished rinsing her body, I lifted it out of the tub and set it on several towels on my lap as I sat cross-legged on the floor. With an all-consuming concentration, I wiped her face and toweled the excess water off her fur.

When I was finished, I bent my head so it was next to hers and in-haled deeply.

You smell wonderful, my sweet love.

I'm not in there, Mom.

I wrapped the towels around her body then and carried it and the blow dryer into the living room where I laid everything out on the floor and began drying her incredibly soft, black fur. It took about an hour to dry completely; I couldn't put the dryer on high knowing how that set-ting was always too hot for her.

Leaning over, I reached towards her basket in the corner by the book-case. The moment my fingers wrapped around the handle of her brush, a wave of crushing sadness assaulted me and went storming through my own, otherwise empty body. Over the years, I'd certainly brushed her more times than I'd bathed her. For the last year, I'd been saving the fur from her brush in a satin pouch I kept on my altar. This would be the last time that brush would ever have her fur in it. Rhythmically, slowly, me-thodically, I brushed, and when I was finished grooming her she looked absolutely beautiful, lustrous, dignified, and tranquil. How could this possibly be the last time I'd ever look at her? It was a thought which proved impossible for my mind to wrap itself around.

Following what still seemed like innate orders, I moved her body to the massage table in the next room, reached into my stack of linens and pulled out the white silk and cotton pillowcase—the one with no paw print inked on it. After taking a pair of scissors and clipping a small strand of fur from her white paw, I lifted her body and slid it into the pillowcase. With her head still exposed, I knelt on the floor and stroked the side of her face. Then I kissed her forehead. Trancelike, I got up and walked over to my sewing basket to retrieve a needle and a spool of white thread.

As I pulled the thread, cut it and knotted it, I thought of a movie I'd seen and loved on PBS years before called *Testament*. It was a beautifully acted, moving and realistic account of one northern California family's survival following a nuclear holocaust. At one point, just days after her ten-year-old son dies from radiation sickness, Jane Alexander's character sits sewing together bed sheets to shroud her dead, sixteen-year-old daughter. Sixteen years. Three years less than how long I'd had my adopted daughter. I carefully stitched the embroidered edges of the pillowcase closed. No one else would ever see her body honored in death but me.

Again, as if being led, I picked up her now shrouded body, walked back into the living room, opened the French doors and walked outside to set my precious bundle on the patio chair. After flipping on the white Christmas lights I'd strung along the fence for Buttons when we'd moved in, I picked up the chair and set it in front of the flowerbed Buttons was forever walking through. The night air was cold. Back inside I lit three more of the demo candles with her picture on them, took them outside and placed them on the ground around the chair. *God, this yard will feel so empty without her, so useless, it's HER yard.*

I'm not going anywhere, Mom.

Back inside, I sat down at the desk and turned on the computer. For purely selfish reasons, I wanted to send everybody who knew us an announcement of her death. The more people who knew, the fewer times

I'd have to say the words, "she died," when someone called and asked what was new or how Buttons was doing.

With eyes closed, I could instantly envision the card as if it were already created. On the outside it would read:

"I love life...

February 5, 2003
...let me prance."
        —Buttons The Miracle Dog
        (as told to Aunt Natalie)

It was important to me not to have a dash anywhere between the date of her birth and the date of her death. To me that was far too indicative of something finite. Instead, by having the dates bordering her paw print that I would copy from the remaining pillowcase, I felt it was more symbolic of her time in her body, leaving her mark here on the physical plane. As far as I was concerned, her spirit had existed well before February 12, 1984, and was continuing to exist after February 5, 2003.

A vertically formatted photo would go on the right half of the inside of the card. It was one of the ones where I was wearing black, sitting in a big chair with my feet perched on the edge of the seat. My knees were bent and drawn close to my body, and I held Buttons in my arms between my chest and my thighs so that her head was just below mine. The photo showed me in the background from the waist up and softly out of focus. In the foreground, and in sharp focus, was Ms. Buttons, defined clearly by her snow-white muzzle, chin and eyebrows, the light reflected in her eyes and the shape of her head and pointy ears. The rest of her black body faded into my black shirt so that it looked as though we were two parts of the same being.

After measuring a space where the photo would go I created its caption:

> During this, our time of deep transition, we would be most grateful to you for holding us gently and peacefully in your prayers, your light, and your love. Thank You. Nadine and Buttons

On the left half of the opened card, I knew I wanted to have the lyrics to *Forever Autumn*, the Moody Blues song I'd thought of my last day in Pebble Beach. I found the cassette it was on and sat down in front of the tape deck with a pen and a pad of paper.

At 1 a.m., the time Buttons normally woke and started pacing, I finished everything on the computer that I would take to cut and paste at Kinko's for the final master announcement.

Contrary to my normal routine, I left the living room drapes opened instead of closed over the French doors. The candles with her pictures were luminous beacons glowing in the otherwise dark desert night. I grabbed another candle from the box with a picture of the two of us on it, lit it, and used its light to guide me into the bedroom. Still feeling her energy intensely near the ceiling of the entire apartment, I set the candle on my altar, took off my clothes and crawled into bed. I bunched up her blanket that was still there and wrapped my arms around it before falling instantly into the second most peaceful sleep I'd ever experienced in my life.

The next morning I woke up and lay there just trying to breathe. For the first time in nineteen years I didn't have to get out of bed, a fact I absolutely hated. She wasn't there waiting for me to let her out, kiss her, and make her her breakfast. My gut felt bruised. Finally, I got up to use the bathroom. Next, I walked into the living room and looked out the French doors into the yard; relief swept over me as I saw that all the candles were still burning. Other than that, all I felt was shell-shocked. I called Pam in Santa Cruz, got her voice mail and left a message. Explaining that Buttons had died in my arms the day before, I asked Pam to please pray for both her friend and her daughter-in-law whose spirit was alive and well. I knew Pam would understand and that she would actually start praying for us, holding us in light, as soon as she got the message. Then I went into business mode and called all the clients I had scheduled for massage appointments over the next seven days. Thank God I didn't have any weddings that weekend. Luckily, I got everybody's voice mail and was able to simply leave messages that an emergency had come up and I would call them the following week to reschedule. With that task completed, there was nothing left for me to do other than take a shower and get ready to go to the pet cemetery.

Oh, God, please, I can't do this.

It's okay, Mom. You can do this. It's just my body. I will help you do this.

As the water pounded against my skin, I stood numbly in the shower trying my best not to think about what I had used it for last.

When the grief counselor showed up, I continued in my robot-like state, feeling totally disassociated from myself as I answered her questions about the day before. When it was time to leave, I set Buttons' shrouded body on the pillow from the rocking chair, picked them both up and walked out to the car.

At the cemetery, we were led into the meditation room where I set my bundle down on the low table/altar by the window before sitting down on the floor in front of it. Soon the door reopened and Barbara, the manager, who had received one of my canceled birthday party invitations the week before, entered the room and walked directly towards me like she was on some kind of mission. Without hesitation, she dropped to the floor next to me, threw her arms around me and began rocking me as I cried. For a few moments I surrendered to the comforting movement and her, "I'm so sorry, Nadine" mantra. The force of the pain wanting to escape from my insides threatened to destroy me totally when I blurted out, "I wanted you to meet her when she was alive! I wanted you to meet her before this!"

I could have stayed sobbing and rocking in her arms forever. Then my "internal switch" turned off again and took with it, the tears. We had business to attend to. How much the cremation would cost depended on the body's weight and so Barbara lifted it off the altar and took it out of the room to be weighed. When she brought it back to me and asked if I was ready, I told her I knew that OSHA rules prevented me from doing it myself, but could I please be there to see them put the body into the furnace? Buttons and I had come this far, through so much, I just wasn't willing to stop tending to her body until there was no body left to tend to. She was still my responsibility. Showing nothing but understanding, Barbara led the way out of the room and around the outside of the building to the garage-like door of the crematory.

When it was time for me to let go of Buttons' body and hand it over to Barbara, I had to literally, and with force, fight against my own body's urge not to do it. Barbara stood for a moment facing me before she turned to walk away with my precious bundle. I saw her place it onto the metal bed and then, feeling more alone than I ever had in my entire life, I watched as it disappeared forever behind the slowly closing door.

When the door was fully shut, I turned and walked back around the building and into the waiting room. We sat down at the table and Barbara and the grief counselor began chatting and networking. They continued as I sat writing out the check and signing forms. Inside myself, I felt the urge to scream at them to shut up and quit talking about such unimportant, trivial things. I felt like some kind of skeletal, bomb-blast victim sitting there bleeding, but feeling invisible since no one seemed to notice. I remember wishing I could just be with Buttons in whatever realm her spirit was in instead of where I was. She'd understand.

Finally, the counselor asked if I wanted to stay during the cremation which would take a few hours, and have her pick me up later to take me home. "No, there's no point." I said, realizing Buttons just wasn't there. Instead, I suggested we go back to my place and watch the Santa Cruz redwood hike video when Buttons was alive and happy, and that's what we did. I could still feel her at home.

After the video, when the counselor left, I gathered all my computer stuff from the night before and headed to Kinko's. Again, being out in public felt totally bizarre, as if the world had come to an end and because of some horrible disaster, life as we'd known it on the planet was over, but I seemed to be the only person who knew about it.

A part of me simply observed everything I did as the rest of me went through the motions. I noticed that my mind kept trying to torture me with thoughts like, *she's dead you know, that's why you're having to make these announcements.* But in-between my anguished thinking, was the miracle of my connection with Buttons, who had been talking to me almost nonstop. I think it was in *Tuesdays With Morrie* that I'd read "Death ends a life, not a relationship." I wanted more than anything to know it was really her I was listening to.

As I endured that first surreal afternoon, Barbara's phone call finally came telling me Buttons' cremains were ready and I could come to the cemetery and pick them up. Instead, I opted for the next morning, feeling like I couldn't bear to leave the house again so soon.

Pam called later that night and for an hour we cried and laughed as she shared her favorite Buttons memories with me. Sharing the pain gave me a safe place to unravel some—a bittersweet balm on my open wound. At one point Pam suggested I buy a special journal to record all the things Buttons was saying, so that I wouldn't forget them or worse, in case they stopped.

There was no question in my mind that Pam had no doubt that it was Buttons' communications I was "hearing." What a great mother-in-law. What a special friend. The candles continued to glow throughout the apartment as I fell asleep that night, praying I'd dream about my little Monkey Face.

The next morning I awoke from a dreamless, fitful sleep and headed back to the cemetery. On the way there, I stopped at a small, upscale shopping plaza. I found the stationery store where I walked around in a kind of shocked daze until I found envelopes to match my announcements and a small, bound journal of handmade paper.

At the cemetery, they handed me a plain, black plastic box sealed with a red and white paw print sticker and a label with Buttons' name and the date written on it. They told me that inside there was a Ziplock bag containing her cremains. My mind wasn't willing to register anything other than that I liked the fact that the box was black like my girl.

Back home I decided I wanted some sort of jewelry, a silver vial or something, to wear around my neck with some of her ashes in it. I pictured the vial on a black satin cord dangling just near my heart. Using the Yellow Pages, I found no jewelry stores that carried what I was looking for so instead I began calling bead stores, knowing they often sold various jewelry-making supplies.

One store said they indeed had several mini-prayer boxes and vials in silver so I drove over to see the selection. Looking over the case, one vial about an inch in length with a hinged and locking cover caught my eye. It had been made in Bali with Balinese silver and was hand-carved all around with hands clasped in prayer surrounded by little doves. It was rather delicate-looking while at the same time very solid—very much like Buttons herself had been. Though the carving was a bit heavier in specifically Christian symbolism than I would have liked, it was otherwise perfect so I bought it.

When I got home it was already dark, but walking into the apartment and seeing Buttons' candlelit picture was comforting. At least it wasn't as brutal as seeing nothing. It felt disconcerting not to have to be home before dark to fill her bowl with dinner. I hated not being needed by her. I hated the complete upheaval of a schedule I'd lovingly followed daily for nearly twenty years of my life.

That evening I called Breanne and Turner in Santa Rosa. Breanne was incredibly empathetic when I told her my news. After a little while she put Turner on the phone who immediately began telling me how sorry he was and how much he'd enjoyed Buttons and all her antics when we'd lived there. I asked him for a favor then, telling him I needed a special wooden box for her ashes. Without hesitation, he began asking me for dimensions as I measured the black, plastic box on my desk. Thanking him profusely and tearfully, I told him how much more it would mean to me to have it made by him rather than just buying something somewhere. Of course, there was no need for explanation. He already understood completely.

After hanging up the phone, I carried the still-sealed plastic box into the bedroom and set it on my altar. There I surrounded it with framed pictures of Buttons in her younger days, her <u>Healing Halter</u>™, the satin bag containing the fur from her brush, along with the piece I'd cut from her white paw, and the lit candle with the picture of the two of us. Then I lay down on the bed and stared at nothing. Why in the world had I driven to the church from the vet's office to pick up candle orders when I knew she only had hours to live? Why hadn't I surrounded her with sweet-smelling essential oils and soothing music as I held her those last hours? Why hadn't I taken her to the vet a week earlier so someone could check her out even though Dr. Parker wasn't there? Why had I treated her so roughly the night before the bridal fair? My mind reeled from the agony of my guilty thoughts as it simultaneously cried out, *BUTTONS, PLEASE FORGIVE ME!*

I turned on the light, reached for the new journal on my nightstand and opened it to the first page. There I simply wrote, *Buttons can you forgive me?* And then, I could barely write fast enough to keep up with the dictation:

Mom, there is nothing to forgive. You were tired. We were both frustrated. It was difficult and after all, you're still only human (a definite bit of doggy chuckle here). **I always knew you loved me. I never doubted that for one second ever. Please, please, please don't use me or this to tear yourself up inside. You've been beaten enough already. You never, ever hurt me. You were just exhausted.**

And then I wrote, *How can I forgive myself?*

It surprised me to hear her immediate and simple response:

Go walk by the water.

In Santa Cruz?

Yes.

How can I forgive myself until then?

Cry and know I love you. Just keep loving me now and trusting and having faith. I will help you and guide you. I am still watching over you—like always—like at the beach when you'd sleep. You are my person. I love all of you through and through. We sizzle.

I closed the journal, turned off the light, and cried myself to sleep.

The next day, Jennea dropped off the pictures I'd ordered. As soon as she left, I began assembling and addressing the more than fifty announcements. Buttons had a lot of friends. When I was finished I checked my e-mail for the first time in several days. There was a message from Hugh and his wife. Gayle had called them to tell them what happened. Their e-mail read:

Dear Nadine,
We are so very sorry that you have lost Buttons in the wonderful and physical way you have known and loved her for so long. We hope you soon begin to feel her loving presence and that your grief is not too great. When you feel up to it, I would like to take you to lunch. Just whenever you feel like it. We will be holding you and Buttons in our prayers.
We love you.

Picking up the phone, I called Hugh at home, thanked him for their understanding words, and told him that not only was I feeling her presence already, but that she wouldn't shut up! He chuckled and wisely suggested I be selective about whom I shared that information with. Thanking him for his luncheon invitation, I asked if we could get together on Wednesday, Buttons' birthday?

We made plans to meet then and hung up. I expected it to be an even more difficult day for me emotionally, perhaps the day I lost it all together. Of all the people I knew, I thought Hugh would be the best one to be around if that happened.

Alone again, I reached for the pile of pictures Jennea had dropped off, and started leafing through them once more. I couldn't believe that she had taken them less than a week before. Had I known then somewhere deep inside of me that these would be the last photographs ever taken of Buttons? Thank God I'd run into Jennea when I did. Thank God we hadn't scheduled the shoot for a week later. I opened my journal and wrote the date, 2/8/03, and the rest came flooding through almost faster than I could write:

That was the gift I gave to you, Mom. I couldn't stay for the party. It would have been too hard for me. But I stayed for the pictures. I wanted you to have them. Of US. Look at them closely. You will see. It is only the body's pain. The rest of me is okay! I am with you now. You can hear me in your head. You can see me when you close your eyes and you will carry me in your heart. That is where I live now. You will still feel some disjointedness for a time. I like that you have the candles lit day and night. I am loving you, loving you, loving you and it is all okay. I will always be here. I am never leaving. Go slow, Mom. Be gentle with yourself. Take care of yourself like you took care of me. I will help. Just think of me and I'm right there with you. I love you sweetly. I love you dearly just like you love me. Cry if you must, and I will lick your tears. Know that I am here beside you prancing and dancing. I will guide you and protect you just like always. You are not making me up. We are a team. Forever.

Was she really speaking to me or was it just some survival trick of the mind? I didn't care anymore as long as it continued. This was how I wanted it to be, a continued connection with my girl, as real and alive and poignant in my life as it had always been. I was going with it.

In the days that followed, my attitude with most of my friends bordered on cheerful and composed, which I came to understand later was merely an indication of the serious emotional stress I was under. In addition, I noticed I felt much colder than normal and that my heart was now racing all the time, more symptoms of the same.

With candles still flickering throughout the apartment, I sat for hours just staring at nothing. Sometimes I'd rock in the rocking chair with Buttons' blanket wrapped up and clutched to my chest. It smelled like her. How could I ever bear to wash it?

My physical reality had been drastically changed. A part of me was missing, no less than had I lost an arm or a leg. No longer were there certain foods to shop for and prepare or a water dish to clean and fill several times a day. The floor was no longer a shared space where I needed to consider that Buttons had dominion. I never saw a beloved, black shape out of the corner of my eye. I could go anywhere at anytime, and it didn't matter when or if I came home. Never again would I hear her walk into a room or out of it.

One of the worst moments was one evening as I sat on the couch finishing my dinner. There I was, confronted by the last few bits of chicken sitting on my plate. Buttons always got those last, gristly bites, but now they just sat there like some kind of bitter proof reminder with nowhere to go but the garbage. Once again, I was reduced to tears as the reality of her physical death came crashing in on me.

That first weekend, Gayle had me over for homemade soup. Since she had experienced extensive, intimate communication with her husband Leroy's spirit since his body's death, I knew she'd understand when I excitedly shared with her the comforting realization I'd had on the way over: that even though every day was one more day since I'd seen Buttons, it was also one day closer to my own death when I'd be with her again in a more complete way.

The look on Gayle's face registered shock, confusion, amusement, and understanding. She commented on how utterly strange it felt seeing the sheer joy on my face as I shared being excited about the prospect of my own death. Her words made us both laugh until I, of course, started crying again. Somewhere through the tears and laughter, I said to her, "HEY! With any luck, I'll get hit by a bus on the way home!" and we laughed and cried some more. It was precious having a place where I could be comfortable sharing everything I was feeling. We are so careful in this culture to ignore death and anything associated with it as much as possible; it is so uncomfortable for us to have it in the open. Grief is such an isolating experience in and of itself, it's a shame that our mores about it are so quick to support and intensify that isolation.

After dinner, Gayle and I went into her office, logged on to her high-speed computer, and searched the Internet until we found a cheap, round-trip airfare to San Jose. I was going to take Pam up on an offer she'd made for me to visit, and Buttons' advice to walk by the water, knowing also that some of Buttons' ashes belonged in Santa Cruz. In six weeks I would return to Santa Cruz and stay for seven days. I wondered if everything I did would still be feeling so bittersweet by then. Gayle made sure I left that night with a grocery bag full of books about grief, loss, death, and after-death communication that had helped her when Leroy passed.

Very late that evening, I began working on the candle orders for the Catholic school. I left for Kinko's, knowing it would be fairly empty, and copied the photos for the candles. It didn't matter what was happening in my life, I had obligations to fulfill. The busier I kept, the less danger I was in of feeling anything.

When I returned home, I decided it was time. Gathering all the lit candles in the apartment, I set them on my desk along with the Balinese silver vial, a length of black, silk cord, and the satin bag with Buttons' fur in it. Then, back in the bedroom, feeling like my blood was slowing in my veins, I stood staring at the black, plastic box sitting on my altar. After several long, deep breaths, I finally picked up the box, carried it back to my desk, and realized I was feeling the same kind of stomach-gripping fear I had felt at the funeral home prior to the doors of the operating cremation furnace opening.

Sitting down ceremoniously, I cut the seal on the box, opened the top, pulled out the Ziplock bag and opened it. As I sat looking at the two and a half cups or so, of light gray, sand-like contents, I felt the fear drain out of me. These were the crushed and powdered bones of my sweet, baby girl. Her whole history was here in these bones: every organic meal I'd ever cooked for her, every treat, every supplement and herb, every remedy she'd ever taken.

Placing a few strands of the soft, white fur I'd cut from her paw into the bottom of the vial, I then dipped the coconut-shell spoon, the one I'd used to feed her her last meal, into the bag of cremains. As I carefully let the ashes pour from the spoon, and watched them cover the white fur, I knew what I was filling that vial with. If anybody ever asked me what was in the vial I wore around my neck I'd just tell them the truth: "nothing but pure love."

On Monday morning, I went to my rescheduled hair appointment. The owner of the shop was an old acquaintance who'd been understanding when he'd heard what happened and agreed to squeeze me in right away. As I sat drinking tea in the lobby and waiting for him to arrive, I noticed the CD that was playing. I couldn't remember the artist's name as he crooned a lovely Italian ballad, but I'd seen him on PBS and been deeply affected by his powerfully moving voice; it had a healing quality that was undeniable. When the receptionist looked up, I asked her if she knew the CD.

"Sure. Josh Groban. He's got an incredible voice, doesn't he?"

And then the song ended and the next song began to play:

> "Who can say for certain, maybe you're still here?
> I feel you all around me, your memory so clear.
> Deep within the stillness I can hear you speak
> You're still an inspiration, could it be?
> That you are my forever love
> and you are watching over me from up above...?"

I jumped up and ran from the building. Out on the sidewalk, bent over, my whole body shook as I forced myself to hold in the tsunami of emotion that threatened to destroy me. I stood waiting and breathing as deeply and as slowly as I could until I regained the feeling of numbness that allowed me to stay in control.

When I estimated the song to be over, I walked back into the salon and soon René arrived to cut my hair. He agreed to let me borrow the Josh Groban CD though it took awhile for him to find it in the full CD player which held more than a hundred CD's in its playing rotation. What a nice "coincidence" that out of the thousands of possibilities, that particular song had played while I was there waiting. Safe at home, I listened to it privately.

> "Fly me up to where you are beyond the distant star
> I wish upon tonight to see you smile
> If only for a while to know you're there
> A breath away's not far to where you are.
> Are you gently sleeping here inside my dream?
> And isn't faith believing all power can't be seen?
> As my heart holds you just one beat away
> I cherish every moment every day.
> 'Cause you are my forever love watching me from up above.
> And I believe that angels breathe
> and that love will live on and never leave.
> Fly me up to where you are beyond the distant star
> I wish upon tonight to see you smile
> If only for a while to know you're there
> A breath away's not far to where you are.
> I know you're there—a breath away's not far to where you
> are."

I knew instantly that I needed to learn to sign the song. It was so moving and it so perfectly expressed my feelings, it could only be healing for me to "sing" it with my entire body the way only sign language would allow me to. Plus it would give me one more thing to concentrate on which didn't take me away from thinking about Buttons, but at the same time didn't plunge me face first into all that grief. I called my friend, Jennifer, who's been fluent in ASL for decades, and asked if she'd come by that week and help me interpret the song. A few nights later, we spent several hours working on it together and were feeling so impassioned that much of the time we were wiping tears from our faces.

The reason I wanted Jennifer's help was because interpreting lyrics can be quite involved, and I wanted to do it right. American Sign Language is very literal and therefore lends itself in a whole different way to music. For example, if I signed exact English, "you broke my heart," I'd have to sign, "PAST MY HEART YOU BREAK" and what I would be telling you is that my heart muscle was literally broken, or not functioning and you caused it which might be even more confusing to you if you weren't a heart surgeon!

Instead, using ASL, I would sign something like, "PAST YOU GO MAKE ME SAD." Any metaphor or concept's meaning must be interpreted correctly to be communicated accurately. What we came up with was wonderful. Without being able to sign it here, I can only give an English written translation (called GLOSS) since ASL is not a written language itself and some of what is signed is also mimed. That combined with facial expression and the size, speed, tension and placement of each sign is what replaces voice inflection, tone and volume.

> YOU(honorific/right/above) NOW DEAD GONE BUT
> MAYBE SOUL STILL HERE
> ALL-AROUND-ME REMEMBER CLEAR
> HAPPEN. PEACE. TWO-OF-US-TALKING
> STILL YOU-HELP-ME INSPIRE-ME
> QUESTION. YOU MY FOR-ALWAYS-STILL LOVE?
> YOU-WATCH-ME YOU-BLESS-ME
> I-MISS-YOU I-WANT VISIT HEAVEN
> TONIGHT YEARN I-SEE-YOU SMILE
> I-WANT KNOW YOU HAPPY, SAFE
> LONG AGO YOU-BY-MY-SIDE
> NOW YOU IN MY-HEART.
> DURING SLEEP I-DREAM YOU
> FAITH MEAN WHAT? CAN'T-SEE BUT BELIEVE STILL
> MY LOVE FOR YOU ETERNAL LIVE
> EACH MEMORY TWO-OF-US SHARE I-CHERISH EVERY
> DAY

WHY? YOU MY FOR-ALWAYS-STILL LOVE
YOU-WATCH-ME, YOU-BLESS-ME
I BELIEVE YOU MY ANGEL
REALIZE LOVE ETERNAL END NEVER
I-MISS-YOU I-WANT VISIT HEAVEN
TONIGHT I-YEARN I-SEE-YOU SMILE
I-WANT KNOW YOU HAPPY, SAFE
LONG AGO YOU-BY-MY-SIDE
NOW YOU IN MY HEART
I-KNOW YOU HERE
YOU-AND-I-TOGETHER, JOINED,
FROM-NOW-ON.

Day and night I practiced until I had it committed to memory and I could sign the ASL while simultaneously listening to the English lyrics. Once memorized, I could begin to let all my emotion flow into it, and express through it, until it felt like I became the song itself. As the music and the movement combined somewhere in my soul as a healing thing, I could feel Buttons watching me as I practiced, and I knew she was pleased.

For the next few days I was either signing the song, working on the candle order, crying wretchedly, reading Gayle's books or writing down Buttons' messages in my journal. Sometimes I watched her videos. Hanna was right, for those moments my mind was tricked, and I felt as if Buttons was alive and well and with me physically in the room. The rest of the time, my mind could only process so much of the pain. I no longer felt her essence or energy hovering near the ceiling, but rather more contained and right next to me, usually on my right side. I began to suspect that the dimension she was now in was just next to the one I was in, maybe even occupying the same space, but at a much different frequency. These weren't things I necessarily thought about intellectually, but rather seemed to be able to sense in the heightened state of awareness the shock and pain had left me in.

At 8 p.m. on Tuesday, the eve of Buttons' birthday, Gayle picked me up and drove me to the appointment I'd made a few days before. I'd wanted it scheduled on Buttons' actual birthday, but the person who'd been recommended to me didn't have any openings that Wednesday. We entered the building, I filled out the required paperwork, and after a short wait, Adam, the man I'd come to see, came to the desk where we all introduced ourselves. He then led Gayle and me into the back office, a cramped and colorful room, and directed me to sit in the big, adjustable vinyl chair in the middle, while moving a folding chair along side it for Gayle. When Adam took his place, sitting at the brightly lit worktable in front of my chair, I handed him a package. It contained one silk and cotton pillowcase, folded and in plastic.

As he hunched over the table and inked an exact replica onto tracing paper of the one paw print from the pillowcase's border that was not smeared, he and I discussed exactly where on my body I wanted my first and only tattoo. It was to go on the very spot Butski's white paw always sat when I held her—on my left upper arm, just above the crook of my elbow. Gayle found some matches, lit the Buttons candle we'd brought, and set it on the shelf in front of us. I apologized to Adam for the simplicity of my request, having seen a big binder filled with photos of his freehand work and knowing he was certainly a talented artist. He told me then that the design was of no consequence to him in matters like these; he was honored to be a part of my ritual and show of dedication

to the being I loved, rather than his regular fare of teenage body art for
the fun of it.

It didn't hurt, and I was still too numb to feel fear, but I liked the fact
that Gayle sat holding my hand anyway. Adam first applied the ink replica to my arm, and then he went over it with the needles and permanent
black ink. The aftercare instructions seemed to take longer than the tattoo
itself as he explained the three-times-a-day washing and moisturizing
with only certain products for the next five weeks after removing the
pressure bandage in twelve hours. I loved the fact that to create a tattoo,
the artist must inflict an actual wound to the skin with his needles that, as
it heals, becomes the finished product. It seemed natural that for a time,
my body show a representation of the wound my spirit carried. Buttons
had left her permanent mark there, why not on my body too? Tattoo—
from the Polynesian word, tat, meaning "open wound" and just as ap-
propriate for me I felt, "the ancient initiation to becoming a warrior."

What I began to realize in the depths of my despair was that my pain
was, logically, in direct proportion to the love I felt for her. It had nothing to do with whether she was an animal or a human, but rather how
passionately I had experienced her friendship, caring, dependence on me
and yes, my dependence on her. In my more critical moments I concerned
myself with appearing to others to be a stereotypical, single, middle-aged
woman, emotionally damaged by an abusive childhood who'd ended up
living alone with only her dog to love. When clarity replaced those judg-
mental moments and I simply surrendered absolutely to my grief, what I
knew was that I had loved (and still loved) Buttons as completely as any
soul is capable of loving, which is one of the most important things I believe we are here to do. If that was true, then I had done a darn good job
and so had she. She'd helped me open up my closed and armored heart
the way no human being could have.

Sometimes, in those moments of melting into the sheer agony my
heart held, I no longer felt grief or sadness as much as just intensity. It
was as if the sadness and the love merged and became something else
entirely, and I found myself in that place where the agony and the ec-

stasy become the same thing. I wasn't sure, but in it there seemed to be a feeling of complete, authentic freedom. It only lasted for moments at a time, but those moments were powerful. My suffering had led me directly and completely into the magical beingness of the present moment. Without past or future, ego, worry, or fear, I could feel what Eckhart Tolle so beautifully describes as "The Power of Now." Embracing my grief fully, surrendering to it instead of trying to feel better or push it away, left me spiritually chaste—my soul completely naked. Deep within the pain I just WAS: right here, right now, totally connected to my Being, to Source, to love and…to my girl, Buttons. Not her body, of course—bodies die. But as Einstein said, you cannot kill life; energy doesn't die, it only changes form. When, instead of fortressing myself against it, I yielded to the landslide of pain, it carried me directly to a place inside myself where my girl was waiting for me, and I could feel her there as vibrantly alive as ever. Heck, I could even smell her. And then, with a single worrisome or doubtful thought, I'd instantly lose the awareness of her presence. I had slipped back into my misery via my mind which only wanted to resist the pain and push it away. I hadn't learned yet how to sustain the connection, but that was okay. I had plenty of grief as the vehicle to lead me there again and besides, you can't unring a bell.

On Wednesday, Buttons' nineteenth birthday, I met Hugh for lunch and found being in his calm presence wonderfully soothing. The safety of his acceptance and compassion allowed me to share some of the feelings of guilt I was experiencing: the things I thought I should have done differently. He responded with the following comments, which have helped me in so many ways since. "Nadine, instead of torturing yourself with the ego's thoughts, why don't you use that same energy to bless Buttons in her transition? Remember, any thought that does not bring peace with it, is not from God." I was grateful to have heard those caring words of wisdom, especially later that week when I began receiving responses to the announcements I'd sent.

Several people sent sympathy cards, and some people called. I knew they all had good intentions; however, a lot of what they said to make me feel better actually made me feel worse. Mostly, it was people's timing that gave their words their sting. It was difficult in that first week or two, for me not to hurt when people said things like, "You should start a business giving alternative health care advice for dogs. You might make a lot of money." Money or a new business were the last things I was interested in at that time, let alone had the mind for. I wondered, would one ever say something like that to a mother whose human nineteen-year-old son or daughter had just died? Some people called and left perky, bouncy messages, and others, in silly accents, as if some clowning around was all I needed to cheer up. Desperately I wanted and needed the comfort I knew they had intended, but instead, I felt incapable of reacting in any way other than feeling wounded and trivialized. Often, those communications felt like a knife in my gut or a bucket of ice being thrown at me. Such comments weren't always from casual acquaintances either, but from friends who'd long known the special bond I'd held with Butts and how dearly I cherished that bond. I remembered how uncomfortable I'd felt not knowing what to say to Gayle when Leroy died. But mere empathy towards my friends when they called, proved no shield or antidote when their comments came.

About five weeks after Buttons' passing I was getting a massage from a therapist I'd been trading with for over a year. She was working on a very hard knot on the side of my head while I wept in gentle release. Breathing deeply, I began softly chanting, "God, I miss her so much..." when the therapist, a self-proclaimed animal lover, suddenly blurted out, "When are you going to get on with your life?!" That was one of those ice bucket experiences. And then there was the inevitable, "So when are you going to get a new dog?" or after three weeks one friend asked, "Aren't you over it yet?" and "You were lucky she lived as long as she did, you should be happy about that" and so on. Soon I learned that I could take better care of myself by screening all my calls and not even returning some of them.

What I learned was this: there is only one thing to say, in my opinion, when someone loses someone they love and that is, "I am so sorry. I love you and want to help. Tell me what needs doing that you can't handle right now." That, and like all the grief books say, be there to listen. If they want to tell you the death story forty times, let them. That's how you can be there for them and support their healing. That's how I knew I must be there for my friends in the future when they lost someone. I wondered why we aren't taught about grieving in school, why as adults, we still don't know how to deal with it or behave with others who are dealing with it. Death's loss, the one thing we know for certain we must face, and yet most of us are clueless when it comes to helping each other through its devastating wake.

A few times over the next month or so, I attended the Pet Loss Support Group in town. It was beneficial to see that other people had also dealt with their dog's late-night pacing, their own sleep-deprivation, and current feelings of guilt.

I read every book on pet loss I could find, but none of them adequately addressed the profound sense of loss I was experiencing. So rather, I turned to books written about the death of a human child, and found them to be more helpful. I also came across a copy of Suzanne Clothier's book, *Bones Would Rain From the Sky*, which touched me deeply. It is my belief that no person should even think about living with a dog before reading Clothier's book. Another helpful read as far as my grief was concerned was a book Gayle loaned me entitled, *Signals* by Joel Rothschild, which fully supported my continued communications with Buttons.

When I went online I was comforted to find thousands of wonderful web sites relating to pet loss and was rather surprised at the countless number of tribute entries and memorials, mostly from men, writing things like, "Skipper, you've been gone for ten years and I still miss you so much. My life will never be the same. I am glad I can express that here."

I realized then that there were many other literate, intelligent people who were not of the belief, "it's just a pet." Those people were in the closet with their pain, mostly I believed, because we live in a society that is not supportive of the sanctity of the human-animal bond. Instead, we live on the planet as if we are superior and have nothing to learn from anyone else or from any other species. Once I saw a cartoon saying, "Man is the only species on Earth that has no natural predator... He doesn't need one since he is his own worst enemy." You don't have to look any further than today's newspaper to agree with that truth.

His Holiness the Fourteenth Dalai Lama teaches that simple compassion and kindness will change the world. If one person reading this is inspired to be just a bit more gentle and patient with someone they know who has lost a beloved animal, or any other family member, then I believe we are further along our way to contributing to the healing of the entire planet.

I found it difficult going anywhere I had gone regularly when Buttons was alive, but after a few weeks of no exercise, lots of sleep, and a still-racing heart, I ventured out for some intentional cardio. On my first return trip to the indoor walking track, as I began doing laps, I found myself frantically fighting back an onslaught of tears. How many times had I been walking there when I'd feel Butts calling me, causing me to stop and run home to her? She would never need me to come home to her again. Here I was doing something from my old routine as if nothing had changed, but of course, everything had. A feeling of such acute despair swept through me then, that it left me feeling faint.

Desperately, I walked faster and faster in my lane, trying to somehow outdistance the pain, when I suddenly felt lifted up, as if my feet were no longer quite touching the floor. In that instant, the despair inside me was replaced with the most potent feeling of love and safety imaginable. I kept having the sensation of being gently lifted by some kind of energy or force on either side of me, underneath my arms. Out of control, I no longer felt attached to or of this world. As I felt myself surrender and relax into whatever it was I was feeling, something I certainly couldn't explain and didn't understand, I suddenly knew what was happening. In my mind's eye I could envision Buttons prancing up ahead of me on the track. Every now and then she'd turn around and look at me with her vibrant, joyful smile. I smiled too.

Also with me was my grandma and Dave, the drummer who'd loved me so ardently years before. I just kept moving though I didn't seem to be exerting any effort at all and my heart felt... well, for the first time in weeks, unburdened of its grief. My mind was empty except for one mantra-like thought that chanted itself over and over in my brain, "I am being ministered to." I drank in all the good feeling and peace I felt saturated with and surrounded by. When eventually the sensation began fading and I once again felt the heaviness of my own body, I looked over at the clock and saw that forty-five minutes had passed. I could feel the pain again, but now added to it was a sense of serenity that hadn't been there before. Driving home, I felt grateful, humbled, tired, and awed by the enormity of possibilities that we as humans have no conception of or explanation for.

The time had come for me to start preparing for my pilgrimage back to Santa Cruz. It wasn't that I was trying to prolong my grief or dwell in it, I just wanted to move through it with some measure of grace. In honoring Buttons, I wanted everything I did to be as symbolic and meaningful as possible. My plans included some beach time to spread not all, but a portion of her ashes, our redwood hike, which I would do for the first time alone, and some time visiting old friends. I looked forward to spending some time with Pam, since I'd be staying at her house, a ten-minute walk from the beach that Buttons and I had always considered ours.

In my freezer at home there were still a few pounds of Buttons' frozen, organic, ground turkey which, for the last month, I had continued to defrost, cook and mix with millet, but since she was no longer there to serve it to, I ate it. I just couldn't bring myself to stop all of our routines. Then it dawned on me. The final two pounds of turkey, I'd cook up with veggies from my garden, make lasagna and take it with me to Santa Cruz to have for dinner one night at Pam's. It was only fitting that I share the last of Button's food with her beloved "mother-in-law." Besides, unlike Buttons, I was getting bored eating turkey and millet every night.

Getting it on the plane was a different story. I certainly wasn't interested in serving organic, X-rayed lasagna; all that radiation just takes the fun out of it somehow. So I called Tucson International Airport and asked to speak with the head of security. My heart pounded as I waited on hold and then launched into my story. The gentleman they'd connected me with was truly goodhearted and obliging when I told him the situation: that I was traveling to California to spread some of my daughter's ashes—that she'd died recently, and I wanted to take some frozen lasagna made with veggies from the garden in her yard, to her mother-in-law. He was so sympathetic and helpful, I wished that I could tell him the entire truth, but I was too afraid he wouldn't understand the importance it held for me if he knew my "daughter" had been a dog.

He told me it would be no problem for me to merely request that my carry-ons be checked by hand rather than going through the X-ray, though it would certainly take longer. So that's what I did. While I was at it, I had them hand check all my cosmetics too, so that anything I used every day internally or topically would also remain relatively radiation-free. Now, I don't know anything at all about plastic explosives, but I must admit, as grateful as I was to arrive in California with nonradiated lasagna, I couldn't help but be a little concerned that my frozen love-offering had made it through security so easily.

The final leg of the flight was bittersweet as I peered out my window and found landmarks to help me retrace Buttons' and my journey back through Pebble Beach, Salinas, Seascape beach, and then finally, Santa Cruz. Pam was there to meet my plane when it arrived just after sunset in San Jose. It was so good to see her and know instantly that I was looking into the eyes of someone who truly understood the depth of my pain. How odd it is, I thought, to feel such happiness and sadness both at the same time. On our way to the baggage claim, Pam just smiled and shook her head as I handed her the frozen lasagna she'd been told was coming. She laughed, when after picking up my suitcase, we stepped outside into the night and I stopped, took a huge gulp of air and exclaimed, "Oh, my God! It smells incredible here!"

Of course, I was referring to the tangible moisture and faint sea smell which hit me like Beethoven's Fifth when we walked through the doorway, but as Pam pointed out, those were probably words never before spoken at the San Jose airport.

I felt like I was home. From the sides of the headlight beams, the redwoods seemed to reach out and hug me hello, celebrating my return, as the car wound along Highway 17 over the mountain from San Jose and into Santa Cruz. I rolled down my window so I could return their greeting. The air was cool and moist and smelled earthy and green.

Oh, Poop, I'm so sorry I took you away from here.

It's okay, Mom. You always did the best you could. Anyway, we're back now.

But you can't really feel it, my sweet love.

I can feel it, Mom. Now I AM it.

The next morning I loaded my backpack and headed down the narrow lane, bordered by pungent eucalyptus trees, from Pam's house to the ocean. I had intentionally planned my arrival so that my first day on the beach would be a weekday when I knew I'd see few if any people there. As the vast, turbulent Pacific came into view and I headed down the concrete boat ramp, I braced myself for the sadness I knew I would feel. What I wasn't prepared for was the shock that hit me the moment I stepped onto the sand, and the force of it nearly knocked me off my feet. Her paw prints weren't there! They had always been there before because she was always flying on ahead, laying her tracks down first.

I stood rooted where I was, feeling sick to my stomach and as if the wind had been knocked out of me when suddenly I heard the strangest noise. It was like nothing I'd ever heard before, not loud, but deeply disturbing—some kind of primal, mournful wail that sounded like someone was dying. And as I looked all around me trying to locate its source, I suddenly realized it was coming from me. I couldn't stop it... rising from somewhere so deep within me, nor could I find it or control it. I just wailed. So I started walking. I walked and cried and wailed until some time later the wailing stopped on its own. Finally, too tired to walk anymore, I turned up towards the cliffs and nestled a seat in the warm, soft sand. Opening my backpack, I pulled out my journal and wrote: *Baby Butts- why was I so devastated when I reached the sand and didn't see your paw prints? This awful sound came out of me and I couldn't stop crying.*

It feels so different when you're in the physical world—and the ocean, sand, cliffs, wind, sun are so physical. How could you not miss me even if I was still right there with you?! You are crying here because your heart is here. Here, you know you are blessed by the earth. Here, the trees enfold you, comfort you, nurture you. Here, the ocean sparks your passion and opens your soul. Here, you know love and now, for a time, you'll embrace pain. It's okay. It's growth and it's change and it's deeper in the silence. It's love.

That evening, I asked Pam if she'd like to see me sign the Josh Groban song I'd been telling her about. I was anxious for my friend to witness my newly acquired, hard-earned skill. We set up a little spotlight in her living room and then she sat on a kitchen chair in the "audience" as I put the CD in the stereo. It was the first time anyone had seen me sign, "To Where You Are" since Jennifer had helped me with the interpretation, but I could not have anticipated Pam's reaction. Because of the bright light, I couldn't see her face and when the song ended she said absolutely nothing at all. Reaching over, I flipped on the overhead light and my dear friend... Buttons' dear friend, was just sitting there, her entire body wracked with silent sobs. And then, after crying together until our tears finally turned to sweet laughter, we did what any two, red-blooded, forty-something, female friends would do under the circumstances. We drove to 7-11 and bought ice cream: Ben and Jerry's... two quarts.

My time in Santa Cruz was not all maudlin. My ceremonies were punctuated with good times as Pam and I visited several of my favorite haunts and restaurants. I surprised Frank and Natalie, who didn't know I was in town, and ended up sharing some delicious meals and conversations with them. Seeing all of Natalie's latest sculptures was a thrilling adventure and she'd taken up (of all things) the accordion since I'd seen her last.

Before I left town, Natalie told me she wanted to gift me one of her sculptures and that I should pick any one I wanted. Bedazzled by her generous offer, I walked slowly back through the room filled with emotive and engaging figures. Soon my eyes came to rest on the one I knew was mine. She stood less than eight inches tall and yet she was an imposing female. Hands on hips and faceless, her hair melting into her highly held head, which then melted into her body and in turn became her gown. She was solid and strong and fluid. The entire figure was covered with the same glaze, one arresting color made up of many colors: pinks, reds, purples, blues, and between her breasts, a gaping hole... right where her heart should be. It was exactly how I felt as I continued to move through my life.

Midweek, I borrowed Pam's car and drove out to the little road up by the railroad tracks where Buttons and I had always started our red-wood hike. What was missing besides Buttons was my walking stick. I'd figured I'd been pushing it with the lasagna and knew I'd probably never get the walking stick through security and onto the plane, too. As I headed down the tracks, secluded and banked by towering trees, I felt my guilty thoughts begin to bear down on me like some runaway train. Why had I ever taken her away from this beautiful place? I should have done anything to make enough money to stay here. And as I fell into the rhythm of my walking, my thoughts took an unexpected turn.

Picturing what it would have been like if money hadn't been a fac-tor—if I had had all the money I could ever want or need, I imagined having bought a cabin in the redwoods and perhaps a cottage by the sea. And as that scenario played out in my mind, I saw that even then, anything could have happened, much of which I still wouldn't have been able to control. We could have stayed and Buttons could have been run over by a car or gotten into a neighbor's weed killer or any number of other possible tragedies. In fact, maybe we had actually avoided some-thing like that because we weren't there! Maybe moving had saved her life and given us our years together.

I realized then that Buttons had always been showing me how to be flexible and accepting and, as with most things, she'd been much better at it than me. She was consistently happy regardless of outside circum-stances, focusing instead on the simple joy and peace available in each moment. My belief was and is that all our beliefs, thoughts, actions, and intentions have a radical effect in creating the events of our lives. But as

I left the railroad tracks and entered the silent, vibrant forest that day, I also saw that life just keeps coming at you, and like the surfers in the bay just a few miles away, I'd do better to simply keep my balance and find a way to enjoy whatever wave I was on.

The soft earth with its thick blanket of fragrant pine needles, gave slightly beneath my feet with each step. It was quieter than I remembered. Absent was the rustle of Buttons scampering up and down the hills on either side of the trail. Gone was my constant commentary: "Wait for me, Love Bunny... look at you, ya little Poop, you're so cute... come on, this way... it's okay, keep going...uh, what is it? You hear them birdies, Poop? You are such a happy girl, my love!"

At the bottom of one of the biggest hills the trail climbs, I stopped. Opening my backpack, I pulled out the jar containing some of her ashes. My favorite part of the Santa Cruz Christmas video I'd made years before was of Buttons flying up that hill, disappearing over its crest and then a few moments later, coming back into view and standing at the top looking down at me, her body nearly bursting with excitement and anticipation. Anyone watching that video can almost hear her say, "Come on, Mom! What's taking you so long? Let's go!" I sprinkled some of her ashes along the side of the trail as I climbed the hill.

Next, the trail led me down below the ridge and then wound back and forth across the rocky creek for another twenty minutes. I realized I wasn't as passionately in love with hiking as I thought I was. The earth and the trees could certainly touch my heart and fill my soul: who wouldn't love being surrounded by such beauty? But it was witnessing all that uninhibited, blissful joy Buttons exuded, that created the bulk of pleasure my hiking memories held.

When I reached the series of small waterfalls where the trail twists and enters one of the forest's cathedral-like ravines of redwoods, I stopped and put my backpack on the ground. Once again, I unscrewed the lid on the jar. I poured some of its contents into my hand and lovingly sprinkled her there into the creek. Then finding myself overcome by the void of her physical presence, I turned and looked pleadingly at the redwood sentinels surrounding me. At the top of my lungs I shouted into the silence, "Do any of you remember my girl?"

The sound of my voice echoed through the ravine as I sank to the ground crying, my back leaning against sturdy bark. Sometime later, as the heavily filtered light coming through the redwood canopy began to change, I smiled knowing that by now on this hike, Buttons would have had at least three long twigs with pine needles, dragging from her tail. Rising to my feet, I made the climb up, through, and out of the ravine and an hour later was back at Pam's car. Once again, I returned to her place emotionally drained, yet knowing I'd done what ritual I'd needed to do for myself and for my Buttons Girl.

My last full day in Santa Cruz, I awoke to dark, stormy weather. My plan was to return to our beach and spread the rest of the cremains I'd brought. I knew a part of Buttons' spirit would always be a part of that beach and I wanted to honor the fact symbolically. As we sat watching the rain from Pam's kitchen window while we chatted over breakfast, the clouds began to break in places and the rainfall was no longer constant. We decided that on her way to work, Pam would drop me off at the Sea-scape Resort entrance to the beach, the one Buttons and I always took. From there, I would walk a few miles along the beach and then back to Pam's. She was concerned that I'd get caught in the storm, which might easily kick up again, but I had already committed myself to this final ritual, no matter what.

An hour later, the rain had stopped and with a towel in my back-pack and wearing a few layers of clothing, I rode with Pam to the resort. Thanking her, I got out of the car and headed down the winding path to the water. There was no one else in sight, save one bouncy, black canine living in my memory. Walking was an effort as I noted the unusual heavi-ness in my legs. It's funny how emptiness can weigh so much, I thought.

When I reached the sand, a cold, damp wind railed against me and pushing up against it, I made my way to the water's edge. The sky was filled with angry, fast-moving storm clouds that appeared even blacker against the patches of deep blue sky, which had started to show through in places. Every now and then, the sun escaped brilliantly and glittered on the backs of the mighty, rolling waves. I had seen a few people, mostly hard-core joggers, when I first trudged from the path across the sand to the water, but now there was no one.

The wind whipped across my face. I took off my shoes to feel the cold, wet sand squish between my toes. The musky smell of sea kelp mixed with salt air and rain was everywhere. The hot sun warmed my shoulders when I took off my sweatshirt and tied it around my waist. Because I was wearing only a tank top underneath, from the corner of my eye I could see the now-healed tattoo of Buttons' black paw print on the inside of my arm. Looking up I found myself standing in some private, isolated moment in time. Together with the raging sea and the constantly transforming sky, I could feel Someone or Something setting this perfect, dramatic stage for me. I inhaled deeply and with my Buttons jar in hand, I began walking south like we had done together so very many times before.

At the halfway point of what would have been our usual trek, I opened the jar. As I continued walking I poured some of the ashes into my hand, raised it above my head and opened my fist as I spoke out loud the measures of my heart, "God bless your spirit always my sweet, baby girl." The wind carried the ashes in a cloud towards the cliffs where Buttons would have been running to or from had she been there in body. Warm tears streamed down my face and turned cool in the brisk air. A few more steps and I released another handful opened above my head as the wind whisked the ashes away from me and disappeared them permanently into the seascape. "Thank you, Buttons for every moment of joy your life blessed me with." I continued along in this manner until the jar was empty, then I walked a few steps towards the dry sand and filled my jar with it. Now I would always have a little part of that beach with me.

When I returned home to Tucson the following day, there was a message waiting for me from Rev. George of the Community Church For Positive Living. He was planning their Good Friday service and was inviting me to be one of seven guest ministers to speak. It was a definite departure from my limited ministerial experience which up until that point included nothing but weddings: I was intrigued and called him back.

He explained to me that each minister would be given one sentence from Jesus' last words on the cross to interpret and speak on for ten minutes or so. What we said would be entirely up to us. I told him I would be honored to participate and he asked me to be the third minister to speak. My line would be, "Thou shalt be with me this day in Paradise."

Throwing myself entirely into the new project, most of what I would end up saying came to me as I got into bed each night. I invited a few friends to come to the service including Gayle who brought a mini recorder to tape my part. When we arrived, the sanctuary was completely filled with people, softly lit, and quiet. I took a seat in the first row with the other ministers. When the second speaker finished and walked off the stage, I rose, climbed the stairs to the podium, stepped into the spotlight and turned to face the crowd.

First, I'd like to thank Reverend George for inviting me to be a part of the service here today. When my father was thirteen years old, he stopped going to Temple and when my mother was sixteen years old she stopped going to church. Consequently, in my household growing up we ate a lot of ham sandwiches and slept late on Sunday mornings. Then when I reached the age of thirteen or so, all I wanted was to be as much like everyone else as I could, so I started going to Sunday school and church on occasion with my best friend, Cindy Hiller.

I remember the first Easter weekend I went to church with Cindy and heard her minister read the words of Jesus as he responded to the thief on the cross next to him by saying, "Thou shalt be with me this day in Paradise." And I remember thinking to myself, you know, that's really kind of a rotten deal—I mean if ya gotta wait until you're dead to find Paradise.

Well, since then, since becoming an adult, I no longer take things quite so literally. I don't strive to be just like everyone else, and I've come to learn that in our lives we die many, many times before the actual death of our body. We die a little bit every time someone we love leaves us, every time someone abandons us and every time someone betrays us. And the thief that lives inside each one of us: we die a little bit every time we abandon someone, every time we leave someone, and every time we betray someone.

When Reverend George asked me to come up here and speak on the words, "Thou shalt be with me this day in Paradise," I began soliciting the help of several friends. We all went to our bookcases and started pulling out our metaphysical Bible interpretation books and our metaphysical dictionaries and came up with some wonderful New Thought definitions of the term Paradise. But something felt funny to me about that. It didn't feel right. And I realized that Reverend George didn't ask me to be up here to spew out information you all already have in your own brains. He didn't ask me to come up here and explain terms that you could go home and look up in your own metaphysical libraries. He asked me to come up here and share something that was in my heart. 'Cause that's why we gather like this. We gather like this so that we can remind each other what's in our hearts.

I never had the kind of adoring, devoted relationship with Jesus the teacher and Savior the way so many people do, but I <u>have</u> been blessed with a wonderful teacher. Now I think what makes a teacher really good is that they teach by example—by how they live their life. And for the last nineteen years, I have been privileged and honored to watch my teacher live life by embodying all of the qualities that Jesus taught us to strive for, that Buddha taught us to cultivate. I made a list of just some of these qualities: (I picked up a sheet of paper from the podium I stood next to) Goodness, understanding, unconditional love, forgiveness, acceptance, devotion, sincerity, gentleness, strength, happiness, gratitude, trustworthiness, integrity, humility, honesty, loyalty, joyfulness (I set the paper back down). If in my life I demonstrate any of those qualities to even the smallest degree, it is all because of my teacher.

I brought a picture of my teacher to show you. (And then, I held up a framed, color, 8 x 10 studio photo of Buttons, smiling big with one ear up and one slightly cocked. A gentle wave of sweet, surprised laughter rolled through the room.)

This is Buttons. And for the last nineteen years, she has shown me how to love. For the last nineteen years, she has shown me how to live life with an open heart. And so ten weeks ago, when she died in my arms, her soul may have gone to Paradise, but mine was in hell. I didn't care about anything.

Luckily, I have a few wonderful people in my life who care about me. One of them who's here today is my friend, Gayle. Gayle's no stranger to pain. Three years ago her beloved husband, Leroy, with whom she had an incredibly wonderful, joyful marriage for almost thirty years, very suddenly and unexpectedly died.

For the first five weeks after Buttons passed, Gayle checked in on me at least once a day, every day. She didn't check in on me to see how I was 'cause she knew exactly how I was. She didn't try to fix me, she didn't try to change me, she didn't try to make me feel better or tell me that everything would be okay. She checked in on me so I would know I wasn't alone and so that I would know I was still loved. And I will always be grateful to her for that.

One morning when I woke up there was an e-mail waiting for me from her. It brought me great peace and comfort. I'm grateful to have her permission to share it with you all today. She wrote: 'When we "lose" someone we love, we are like little children who want a certain toy. We can't listen to reason, we can't be patient, we don't care about anything but what we want. And we want them back. Loved ones are gifts to us. They're a gift to us while they're here and we can keep company with them. And they are a gift to us when they leave. If they didn't leave, we'd always look to that physical representation for our love and comfort. We'd never go deeper—and that would be a cruel gift. So when they leave us, the gift is that we learn to be still and quiet and experience life and love where it's really happening—not in the physical body, not in the world, not in dramatics or excitement. In silence. They are leading us into the silence. As painful as it is to us as the little children we are, it's a beautiful gift of life and love.'

Now, for those of you who understand the bond (I pointed to Buttons' picture), you know exactly what I'm talking about. For those of you who might be entertaining some version of the thought, "What is she talking about, it's just a dog?" I gotta tell ya... you don't know what you're missing. Jesus claimed that we have much to learn by observing the lilies of the field and the birds of the sky. I suggest he meant that we have much to learn from all creatures.

"Thou shalt be with me <u>this</u> day in Paradise." <u>That</u> is the promise.

I encourage you, the next time you hurt so badly you feel like you're dying... the next time you're in so much pain that if someone were to come along and nail you to the cross, you wouldn't even notice... surrender... go deeper.

Paradise... is right here, right now. It's deep within our pain.

It's deep within the silence.

It is the love.

I'd like to share one more thing with you. In the language born in silence and the beautiful, healing voice of Josh Groban, this song is called, "To Where You Are."

Right on cue, the CD began playing over the sound system. With my entire being, I fell into Josh Groban's voice as my body signed the song, aware of little else other than the music and Buttons' presence filling the room.

Afterwards, as I took my seat in the first row, I noticed that nearly everyone in the room, men included, were wiping tears from their faces. When the service was over, I was not prepared for the line of folks who approached me sharing things like, "I understand that bond completely. Thank you for helping me feel proud instead of guilty." And, "What you said today has changed my life. I mean it, really, you've changed my life."

As I thanked them, I told them that it was indeed Buttons who had touched their life that day and assuaged their guilt. I was aware that my entire performance had her paw prints all over it. As Gayle and I left the church, I was grateful to realize I had taken the opportunity to give my girl's eulogy. I was counting on the good feeling of that experience to carry me through the first Easter in nineteen years without my Funny Little Love Bunny.

In the living room, Buttons' bed now had her collar, leash and camping sweater on it along with the pillow Laurie made for us. The corner of the coffee table still held her ceramic bowl and three candles with her picture on them. To that I had added a precious carved angel holding a small dog on her shoulder, and a silver picture frame with the words, "Mom and Me" etched on it that my cousin had given me. In the frame was a smiling photo of Butts and me in front of the wall of blooming Tombstone Rose bushes in our back yard.

Buttons' stainless steel food and water bowl set was also on the coffee table, filled with soil from the back yard and flower seeds. Every day I wore the Balinese vial around my neck and every night I kissed it as I took it off and strung it over my bedpost. The altar in the bedroom that held my most sacred objects now included several of my favorite, enlarged photos of Butts, the bottle of sand I'd taken when I spread her ashes on the beach and a picture of the redwood tree by the waterfall where I'd also left some of her cremains. The black plastic box containing the rest of her ashes sat in the middle.

My birthday fell on the three-month anniversary of her death. There were friends who tried their best to get me to celebrate in the ways they were comfortable with, and I was able to thank them graciously for their intentions while declining their invitations. On the morning of my birthday, after finishing my meditation and cup of herbal tea, I went into the bedroom and opened the closet door. Pulling down a box from the top shelf, I lifted the lid. Inside were four, fully exposed disposable cameras. Randomly I chose one of them and headed to Walgreens. One hour later, I picked up my precious birthday gift, so alike in many ways and yet so different from the one I'd picked up nineteen years before. I waited until I got back home and was sitting in the rocker before looking at the thirty-six new pictures of my sweet baby girl.

Happy birthday, Mom. I love you.

The day before Mother's Day, the mailman knocked on my door and when I opened it, he handed me two packages. I could see from the return addresses that one was from Turner and Breanne and the other from Pam. Pretty sure of what was in the one from Turner and Breanne, I sat down on the floor and opened it first. It had been months since I'd called Turner and asked him to make a box for Buttons' ashes, and I had begun to think he'd forgotten. Amongst the bubble wrap there was no note, no letter—just the most beautifully crafted, black walnut box. Every corner of box and lid was hand-dovetailed and perfect. Each lovely, grained surface was stained and sanded smooth as silk. Turner had spent many loving hours on it, I could tell.

I picked up the package from Pam and tore it open. The only note was a Post-It which read, "Happy Mother's Day to the Mom of the Century" and with it the most delicate, handmade piece of white, Italian lace tatted with the softest shades of pastel pink, green, yellow and blue. I was blown away by Pam's thoughtfulness, by Turner's creation, by the fact that the lace was the perfect size to fit under the new box on my altar. And it did not for a moment, escape my attention that those two packages had "accidentally" arrived together on the same day at my door.

The black, plastic container holding Buttons' cremains fit perfectly inside the wooden box. After setting it on the lace in the center of the altar, I walked outside, sat down on the back porch and said out loud, "I miss you so much, Buttons, I wish you were here in your yard, happy and healthy."

I heard no answer, only the mourning doves cooing from the fence. Just as I was about to freak out thinking that Buttons was no longer able to communicate with me in my mind, I noticed a movement to my left. I quickly turned my head and there, a few feet away was something I'd never seen before, not only in my back yard, but anywhere. For the next five minutes I sat mesmerized as I watched the small, pitch-black butterfly fluttering about. It was all black... except for one tiny, white spot at the tip of each wing.

You can never lose me, Mom. I am everywhere... a part of every- thing. Please don't be sad.

I felt like I was living in two worlds. One I could see and one I could feel. I knew that as long as I was in my physical body, with eyes and ears and arms, that I would long to see her and hear her and hold her. Somehow, I had to find a way to live my life in the physical world and at the same time not lose touch with the world I couldn't be in physically, but could only feel and sense.

Many people started telling me I should get another dog. They didn't understand. I didn't want to simply blot out my grief with some replacement. I was finding, however, that I felt more love for other dogs now. In the past, I'd always felt some sense of betrayal towards Butts when I'd admire another dog. She had even displayed jealousy when I lent my attention to some other being of the canine persuasion. It was one of her few, less than exemplary qualities, but one I selfishly enjoyed. Still, there was no way to replace her in my life, and I was reminded of something I'd once heard at the ashram.

Someone had asked one of Sri Easwaran's longtime students who lived there, a smart, talented, interesting, and very good-looking man, why he wasn't married. He had chosen to not only dedicate his entire life to meditation and the spiritual teachings, but as is often the tradition for the most devout, he had practiced celibacy for decades. His answer was that instead of having one lover, he had chosen to have the entire world be his beloved. I felt like that now about dogs.

Instead of a new dog, I decided that it would be a good time for me to take up a new musical instrument, something that would require a lot of concentration and attention while at the same time provide the deep healing I knew music could bring. With a rental from the local music store, and an incredible teacher from the Tucson Symphony Orchestra, I began taking weekly violin lessons. I found I liked practicing best at night. Nights were always the hardest for me, the time when I missed

Buttons the most, and it was at those times I'd pick up the violin and start screeching away.

Afterwards, I always felt better, comforted somehow. And then one night it dawned on me: here was this beautiful, vibrating, wooden instrument, cradled between my left shoulder and chin, right where Buttons' head would be cradled every night as she lay on my chest. All the same cells of my body that had felt her loving presence so greatly, were being reactivated as I played. The world I could not see, the realms of feeling and intuition, were fast becoming more prominent in my life, and I knew they were the only places I could find true solace.

For months, I had been turning down social invitations. Even though I was catching up on over a year's worth of lost sleep, my energy was still extremely low, and I used most of it doing massage and weddings. The few times I'd ventured out, I found I wasn't ready to be back in situations with people where I'd have to pretend everything was normal, it just took too much energy. I discovered it was much more healing for me to honor the grief I was in and give it plenty of room to breathe.

Until the end of July, my only outings besides weddings consisted of running errands, going to the walking track, and my weekly violin lessons. Even going to the grocery store could be brutal: every time a cashier would hurl an enthusiastic, "Hello! How are you today?" at me, my gut would wrench. Answering "Fine, thank you," was a lie. Saying anything else felt rude. Finally I began simply answering the question with, "Hello. How are you?" I wished there was some kind of retreat or place apart, geared specifically towards the grieving process, where I could go to work my way through the emotions and memories, anger and sorrow, without having to deal with earning a living, mail, phone calls, or public interactions.

One afternoon as I sat reading the local independent newspaper, an event listing caught my eye. It was an announcement about an upcoming book signing at Border's. I didn't recognize the author's name, Dr. Betty J. Kovács, but the title of her book, *The Miracle of Death* screamed out at me. The blurb explained that Dr. Kovács, with a Ph.D. in comparative literature and theory of symbolic language, had written the book after her mother, twenty-year-old son, and husband had all died in three separate car accidents over the course of three years. I knew I had to hear her speak.

The night of the signing, I arrived well before the lecture was to begin and found a seat in the corner. There were still plenty of moments when my fragile emotional state would sneak up on me, sometimes triggered by merely hearing other people laugh and I wanted the safety I felt a corner seat could provide. I was sitting there reading when two, smiling, petite women approached me and said hello. Not wanting to interact with anyone, I wasn't too friendly, barely mumbling a hello in return. They politely left me alone. Part of me was still resenting the simple happiness of others.

In the next half hour about thirty other people arrived and sat down, and then one of the petite women who'd said hello to me earlier walked to the table at the front and began to speak. She introduced herself as Betty's publicist, Kim, and then she introduced Betty, the other woman who'd greeted me. For the next hour I sat enthralled as this tiny woman opened her joyful heart and eloquently shared her story. She was clearly in touch with all three of her deceased loved ones through both dreams and visions. Everything she had experienced told her that not only was there no death, but that there was nothing <u>but</u> life. At the same time, her demeanor portrayed her vast experience as the seasoned professor and lecturer she was with all her worldly and respected credentials. This was no self-proclaimed psychic or New Age nut. I drank in every word she said like some healing potion. She had lost everything and she had lost nothing: I wanted some of <u>that</u>.

When the lecture ended, there was a short question and answer period. Afterwards, people got up from their chairs and stood in line at the little table Betty sat behind to sign their books. I wasn't ready to move. Part of me was still reeling from all I'd heard, from the validation I felt about my own "beyond the grave" communication: with Buttons, with Dave, with Grandma, and even with my mom. And then I felt someone's hand touch lightly on my shoulder. Turning around I found myself looking into the warm, kind face of Betty's publicist, Kim. "Are you okay?" she asked.

My only answer was the tears starting to run down my cheeks as she took my hand and guided me to a more private corner for us to sit down. There I told her about Buttons and showed her one of our black and white photos that I carried in my purse. Kim's loving energy embraced me as I shared about all the communication I'd had with Buttons, my grieving process, and my experience of the insensitivity of others in relation to it. For twenty minutes, she listened and handed me Kleenex. Every few minutes she'd wipe a tear from her own face. I realized then how for months I had been feeling starved to be truly, deeply, and completely heard. After assuring me she'd be right back, Kim excused herself and went and said something to Betty.

A few moments later she returned to my side and a few minutes after that Betty joined us. I apologized for having been rude to them earlier. They just smiled and shook their heads knowingly. Kim then gave Betty a quick synopsis of all I'd told her and for a very long minute, Betty gazed at the photograph of Buttons and me that I'd handed her. And then Betty spoke.

"You're still adjusting to the new ways of communicating with her. That's okay. You're still in a lot of deep grief, but that will subside as your new way of feeling your connection with her strengthens."

Then, sitting in-between the two of them, I shared the story of my grandmother's garden at Griswold Lake and how Buttons had led me to the lot years later when I couldn't find it. As a professor of Jungian psychology and someone who'd lived through what she had, none of it was surprising to Betty.

"Nadine, can you write at all?" she asked.

"Well... one of the things I do for a living is write wedding ceremonies."

She and Kim exchanged a look.

"You need to write these stories down. There are so many people who have deep relationships like this with animals, and the world is not so supportive. If you can write at all, you need to share your story with them. They need to know that they are not alone. You and Buttons need to let them know."

My entire body was resonating. Buttons' and my mission to help other dogs and their humans wasn't over yet.

That night I had the most vivid dream:

I am hiking with Buttons. I have her on her retractable/extendable leash. We are walking a narrow, well-trodden trail through a bright green, lush forest. She is very happy and excited. She takes off down the trail at full speed. All I can do is hang on. I am holding on with both hands. She is pulling me effortlessly. I can't keep up on my own power, so I stop trying to keep up and the next thing I know I am on my rear end gliding painlessly behind her at enormous speed as I hold on to my end of the leash. We are almost flying as she leads the way from her end of the leash.

That morning I got out of bed, took Buttons' small, soft blanket with the turquoise felt buttons and wrapped it around a long, narrow piece of bumper foam from the bottom of one of the kitchen cabinets. Around that I wrapped her <u>Healing Halter</u>™ so its anti-radiation bead was perfectly centered. Sitting down at the desk, I turned on my laptop and placed the covered foam in front of it so I'd have something comfortable to lean my forearms on. With eyes closed, I took a long, deep breath. As I exhaled slowly, I opened my eyes, looked at the screen and typed:

My cousin Rachel and I were relaxing in the courtyard of my Chicago apartment building, enjoying the first spring-like day of the year, when she suddenly turned to me and said, "You're going to be twenty-nine next month, you've got no kids, no husband, and no prospects. How 'bout I get you a dog for your birthday?"

"Everything is on its way somewhere... everything."

– John Travolta as George Malley

Epilogue...

My perception was keen and acute the first year after Butski's passing. Being ultra-sensitive, I couldn't help but be in touch with an additional reality: the realm of spiritual, nonphysical things. The second year after Buttons discarded her body, I had to really concentrate and focus my attention in order to be in touch with that finer vibration. Daily life produces so much static and is so much denser than what I know to be real and of significant, consequential value. Now, after a few years of practice, I can tune in relatively easily.

I am so grateful to currently be an avid student of the teachings of Abraham-Hicks, Eckhart Tolle, and The Work of Byron Katie, which have brought me a clarity and peace regarding my entire life: past, present, and future. I am now able to take a proactive, conscious role and responsibility in creating my circumstances rather than being tossed around by them.

As far as my physical health goes, it turns out I wasn't suffering from chronic fatigue syndrome at all, but rather, from severe, life-threatening sleep deprivation caused by obstructive sleep apnea. Tissue from my tongue and throat, when fully relaxed, blocks my airway until my brain wakes up enough to signal the muscles to constrict again so I don't suffocate. Tests show this happens seventeen times an hour, meaning my brain wakes up every three and a half minutes throughout the night, though I am not conscious of it as it occurs. So, even when I think I've slept a full eight hours, the reality is, I've only gotten approximately thirty-four minutes of sleep the entire night. Talk about a bad mood! With the doctors' help, we've determined I've had apnea since my early twenties.

It seems the allergies, breathing difficulty, irritability, and other acute symptoms that I began experiencing shortly after moving to Santa Cruz were actually due to my immune system breaking down after decades of minimal restorative sleep. While I continued to struggle and push myself, my body was literally in the process of dying. I can now say I've personally experienced why the Geneva Convention categorizes sleep deprivation as a form of torture. Today I continue to experiment with several alternative fixes for Sleep Apnea, including custom-fitted oral appliances that either hold my lower jaw or tongue positioned at an angle that keeps my airway open. I'm also, much to my neighbors' dismay, learning to play the Didgeridoo, which according to Swiss scientists, comes close to curing the condition altogether.

As of this writing, I do not yet share my home with another dog. But, as a recently certified Holistic Animal Care™ Consultant, I'm busy helping other pet parents understand and practice the methods I used to save Buttons, through one-on-one Holistic Pets/Toxic-free Living consultations. More than anything, I want to see Buttons' story continue to educate and inspire so that our journey might help other doggies and their companions have longer and happier lives together.

As relieved as I am to finally have a handle on the causes of my physical and emotional distress, sometimes I feel a bit guilty that I didn't figure it out sooner; that I was operating from a far less than adequate condition while Buttons and I were in each other's care. It saddens me deeply to think that when I am fully recovered, she won't be here to reap the benefits. At those times, it comforts me to recall some words from one of my favorite films.

It's a scene towards the end of *Cast Away*, after Tom Hanks' character is rescued and temporarily reunited with the love of his life, Kelly Freers, when he faces the fact that he must continue to live on without her for she now has a husband and a child. It was his love for her that had kept him alive and hopeful all the years he was a castaway, and so to a friend he muses,

"I'm so sad that I don't have Kelly… but I'm so grateful that she was with me on that island."

And so in this physical realm of ours, I continue striving to live my life as happily and lovingly as Buttons lived hers. There will probably never be a day that I don't long to see and hold my girl. But always, in the stillness, she is with me still… and here in my open heart, joy is her legacy.

Reference Page

**Now you can learn how to "Clear/Cleanse/Build"
from someone who's done it successfully!**

HOLISTIC/TOXIC-FREE LIVING CONSULTATION: It's all about prevention, pet parents! What our pets are exposed to regularly has a HUGE impact on their health. We are all what we eat, breathe, and absorb through our skin. Our pets' bodies metabolize everything so much faster than ours: what everyday chemicals may take 40 or 50 years of exposure to create disease in our bodies, may only take 3-6 years of exposure to create disease in theirs.

In our one-on-one, personalized consultation, we'll discuss your choice of food, treats, toys, home and personal products- thoroughly examining everything you currently expose your pet to- including insidious things you are not even aware of! After explaining why some of those things may be extremely harmful to your pet, I'll share some simple, easily attainable alternatives that I myself use and help guide you into creating the safest, healthiest environment possible in your home. Let me help you stack the odds against your pets ever developing cancer. ** NOT a veterinary or diagnostic service** Also offering Grief Consultations.

For information on phone consultations with Nadine, please go to:
www.TheHealingArtOfPetParenthood.com.

Reading

Three Simple Steps to Healthy Pets: The Holistic Animal Care
LifeStyle™ by Lisa S. Newman, N.D., Ph.D. ISBN-9781420863833/
authorHOUSE. If you are interested in adding healthy years to
your dog's life, then I would strongly encourage you to make this
the very next book you buy and read. Dr. Lisa Newman, one of
the experts who I worked with personally to help heal Buttons of
cancer, remains on the leading edge of natural healing and holistic
animal care.

Letters To Strongheart by J. Allen Boone: ISBN-0-933062-19-2/Robert H. Sommer, publisher. A must-have for every pet parent. May be a bit difficult to find, but totally worth the search!

Spiritual Notes to Myself by Hugh Prather: ISBN-1-56731-295-0/MJF Books/Conari Press. Actually, every book by Hugh and his wife, Gayle, is a valuable read.

Your Deepest Intent: Letters from the Infinite by Rev. Deborah L. Johnson: ISBN-10: 1591795745/Sounds True

The Miracle of Death by Betty Kovács: ISBN-10: 0972100539/Kamlak Center

The Astonishing Power of Emotions by Esther and Jerry Hicks: ISBN-10: 1401912451/Hay House

Pyramid Energy: The Philosophy of God, The Science of Man by Mary and Dean Hardy ISBN-0-932298-58-7/Cadake Industries & Copple House

Science of Mind by Ernest Holmes: ISBN-0-87477-921-9/Penguin Putnam Inc.

The Power of Now: A Guide to Spiritual Enlightenment by Eckhart Tolle: ISBN-10: 1577314808/ New World Library. Life-changing and empowering beyond belief.

Healing

Azmira Holistic Animal Care: founded by Dr. Lisa S. Newman over 28 years ago, is where you can find many of the products and supplements I used in Buttons' cancer treatment. Their technical support staff is ready to discuss your pet's symptoms and how to best use their products. More information at www.azmira.com or 1-800-497-5665.

Dr. Gloria Dodd, DVM: www.holisticvetpetcare.com. A great resource and the place to purchase the Healing Halter™

Intestinal Cleansing: www.AriseAndShine.com, www.BernardJensen.org.

Fun and Artsy

"Tower bar and Grill" musical CD by Calico: available at
www.cdbaby.com. Calico is Dennis Graf and Dave Van Delinder,
two of my favorite songwriters in the world. Their engaging
melodies and enchanting lyrics have comforted me through the best
and worst of times.

"Not Too Far To See" musical CD by Pamela Hanson: available at
www.cdbaby.com. The angelic voice of Buttons' mother-in-law!

www.BlackSheepVideo.com: Exceptional videography, photo montages
and more, by a devoted pet parent.

Charley Thweatt: www.MusicAngel.com. His songs are inspired,
powerful medicine and I encourage you to give yourself the gift
of attending one of his interactive concerts, or at least, purchasing
some of his CD's to sing along with often.

www.jennea.com: The incredibly sensitive and talented photographer
who did the final photos of Butts and me. This book's cover is one of
those photographs.

www.MyGenChan.com: The GenChan (genetically challenged). Now
mutts have their own breed and can even get their "papers" just like
purebreds!

Personal Growth

The Teachings of Abraham: www.Abraham-Hicks.com. Self-
empowering books, tapes, cd's, dvd's, and workshops. All is well!

Blue Mountain Center of Meditation: www.easwaran.org. Educational
and inspirational books and tapes by Sri Eknath Easwaran.

Inner Light Ministries: www.InnerLightMinistries.com. It is the intent
of ILM to demonstrate the possibility of living together in harmony
through the daily practice of Universal Spiritual Principles.

The Work of Byron Katie: www.TheWork.com "A simple yet powerful
process of inquiry that teaches you to identify and question
thoughts that cause all the suffering in the world. It's a way to
understand what's hurting you, and to address your problems with
clarity."

CPSIA information can be obtained
at www.ICGtesting.com
Printed in the USA
FSOW01n1045250118
43790FS